Seeking Love in Modern Britain

Seeking Love in Modern Britain

Gender, Dating and the Rise of 'the Single'

Zoe Strimpel

BLOOMSBURY ACADEMIC
LONDON • NEW YORK • OXFORD • NEW DELHI • SYDNEY

BLOOMSBURY ACADEMIC
Bloomsbury Publishing Plc
50 Bedford Square, London, WC1B 3DP, UK
1385 Broadway, New York, NY 10018, USA

BLOOMSBURY, BLOOMSBURY ACADEMIC and the Diana logo are trademarks
of Bloomsbury Publishing Plc

First published in Great Britain 2020

Cover design by Tjaša Krivec

Cover image: Rendezvous with actress Linda Thorson at home in London, December 22,
1970. (© Photo by Jean-Claude Deutsch/Paris Match via Getty Images)

A catalogue record for this book is available from the British Library.

A catalog record for this book is available from the Library of Congress.

ISBN:	PB:	978-1-3500-9939-5
	HB:	978-1-3500-9591-5
	ePDF:	978-1-3500-9592-2
	eBook:	978-1-3500-9593-9

Typeset by RefineCatch Limited, Bungay, Suffolk
Printed and bound in Great Britain

To find out more about our authors and books visit www.bloomsbury.com
and sign up for our newsletters.

Contents

Figures

Introduction

In February 1981, Elaine Weeks, a newly trained nurse working at St Mary's Paddington, was still single. She was thirty-one and had tried various means of meeting men – membership at the BFI, a series of subscriptions with a computer dating firm, and even a temporary office job where she knew there would be more male colleagues than there were in nursing. But nobody special enough emerged. So she decided to look at the well-known lonely hearts section of *Time Out*. Among a sea of men 'bigging themselves up', one ad caught her eye.[1] This man didn't boast about his directorship of a company (what those companies were almost always remained vague); instead the ad read: 'NOT a thrusting CEO . . . but rather, a calm, articulate arts graduate.' 'That sounds more like it,' Weeks remembered thinking, and wrote to him.[2] Their first date at a pub in Paddington led to subsequent dates and an eventual happy marriage.

Elaine, born in 1951, was – like many of her contemporaries – a new kind of woman: the first in her family to go to university, the first in generations to leave northern England for London, the first to take the Pill as an unmarried woman, the first to work alongside 'brazen' socialist feminists. Her romantic story has a happier ending than many, but she was also just one of thousands of people that had for the first time moved away, either figuratively or literally, from their social and family networks and turned to mediated matchmaking – defined in this book as the search for dates via a paid-for third party – between 1970 and 2000. Singles like Elaine faced an expanded field of businesses pitching solutions to their romantic status, from singles clubs to lonely hearts adverts to dating agencies. Indeed in the three decades preceding the rise of internet dating in Britain, matchmaking services proliferated sharply, cashing in on a swelling supply of singles resulting from soaring divorce rates and a loosening in attitudes towards sex and marriage, and gaining visibility in print and on broadcast media.[3] Matchmaking services in Britain were centuries old, but had, since the matrimonial adverts of the seventeenth century, been both disparate and ephemeral. Ephemerality remained a defining feature, but it wasn't until the

1970s that commercial solutions to singleness began to form a critical mass. In one article on the subject in 1970, *The Daily Mail* noted that 'the lonely hearts business is booming as never before'.[4] By 1992, one newspaper estimated that 130,000 people were using agencies, most of which had been set up after 1970, with a spike in the 1980s.[5] In 2000, the British dating industry was estimated at a still relatively modest £50 million but was attracting ever more extreme forecasts of growth, in line with rising numbers of single people.[6]

The heterosexual dating industry in Britain in the three decades preceding the normalization of internet dating – 1970–2000 – is the subject of this book. The industry was not an exclusively heterosexual one, and had included a rich queer culture revolving around contact ads since the Edwardian period.[7] Magazines such as *Time Out* (founded 1968) and *City Limits* (1981–93), which were important forums for personal ads, marked out their progressive political ambition by welcoming homosexual and lesbian personals. By the mid-2000s, gay dating innovations, most notably Grindr, would profoundly shape the development of the broader online dating landscape, visible in the worldwide success of Tinder and other location-based dating apps since 2012.[8]

This book, however, charts the emergence of the straight dating industry, and its focus is on the attempts of matchmakers and their clients to locate themselves within prevailing – heteronormative – discourses of romantic and sexual normalcy. It therefore follows Laura Doan's assertion that it is heterosexuality, not queerness, that 'lurks obliquely' because, as queer scholars have argued, heterosexuality has been defined as in constant opposition to homosexuality; negatively determined, it is a 'blank canvas … a category beyond and outside history'.[9] Although heterosexuality is hegemonic, especially in cultural representations of romance, we still know relatively little about how modern heterosexual subjects negotiated new sexual terrains. Homosexuality, like sex and permissiveness, has been a magnet for scholars of late twentieth-century intimacy and, predictably, its attractions have further accentuated the negation of heterosexual courtship, while endowing would-be scholars of the latter with a rich and instructive literature. Drawn to the intellectual challenge posed by the encodedness of desire, historians of homosexuality have worked to uncover the volumes spoken by different types of silence. An expanding body of work tells us ever more about post-war queer life in terms of, to name just a few areas, the intimate topographies of post-war European cities; religious communities; media and literature; and the cultural politics of gay pornography.[10] An irony underpinning the relative scarcity of historical work on twentieth-century heterosexual life (outside of marriage and prostitution) is that the accepted languages of heterosexual romance have taken place in plain view. The challenge, then, is not to excavate the experiences of straight singles below the text, but to find it despite, or amid, the din of the discourse surrounding heteronormative coupling. Once again, Laura Doan's observation that 'the history of straightness is not straightforward because heterosexuality begins life as a social norm' is apt, further hinting at why 'hetero-relations' may have slipped through the net.[11]

This book originated, partly, in a desire to test assumptions about internet dating as a discrete phenomenon, one that has reinvented the norms and practices of searching for a partner. Contemporary digital dating has attracted extreme analyses. To Nancy Jo Sales, an editor and writer at *Vanity Fair*, its web app form constitutes a 'dating apocalypse'.[12] Other commentators, such as Michael Norton, a psychologist at Harvard Business School, call our era 'one of the first times in human history there was some innovation' in one of 'the biggest problems that humans face'.[13] Undoubtedly digital technology has completely changed the appurtenances and affordances of matchmaking via a third party. The lonely hearted no longer need to arrange subscriptions to services by post or phone, or write laborious letters by pen. Now they can instantaneously access a roulette table of geographically convenient options for free on their Facebook-enabled smartphone apps. But as this book demonstrates, the assumption of total rupture on a social level hides how digital matchmaking fits within a longer history of mediated dating, in which the methods of matching have constantly interacted with social dynamics both new and old. Wrenching apart the new from the old conceals important sites of continuity in the transition from older technologies and practices of dating to more recent ones. It is too often assumed that the rise of digital dating signifies year zero in mediated dating. This book is an attempt to place the current period of matchmaking in a spectrum of older technologies, practices and discourse, while also showing what is unique in the preceding period.

Despite its rapid growth both in real terms and visibility in this period, mediated dating remained a relatively uncommon method of finding a partner through the end of the twentieth century. Based on the conservative figure above of 130,000 (not including those who placed or responded to lonely hearts adverts), only about 3 per cent of an unmarried population of around 6 million were using mediated dating. As will be discussed in more detail below, precise or reliable figures for how many people were actually using these services at any given time are not available. Moreover, there are inconsistencies in how 'single' was defined, since actual romantic status could be obscured by terms such as 'single person household', 'cohabitation' and 'unmarried'. However, the general reluctance surrounding the use of mediated dating is key to understanding the constitution of romance at this time. What kept people away from dating services, apart from possibly the price tag, was the lasting stigma associated with the use of paid-for interventions. These deterrents are explored in depth in the analysis of first-person motivations in Chapter 4.

Mediated dating did not have the mass culture following in the period under study that it does today. But it was growing, and the discourse that flowed from its expansion and around (and from) its customers put a magnifying glass to on-the-ground experiences of changing gender dynamics. It also illuminated the challenges of self-articulation and self-presentation amid a romantic terrain that new sexual opportunities had hedged with ambiguity.

The central contention of this book, then, is that by studying mediated courtship, we gain a new window onto the very heart of change in late twentieth-century Britain – namely, the transformation of the gender order. Courtship lets us see how this transformation – normally studied in political, sexual, demographic or cultural terms – was played out in the everyday affective and social lives of individuals. Mediated dating demands the articulation of romantic hopes and self-perceptions that were (and are) heavily invested in the status of gender at any given time. It thus offers a privileged lens onto the question of how developments like Women's Liberation discourse, universal access to contraception and no-fault divorce shaped or reflected choices and experience on the individual level in the high-stakes arena of relational future. Deborah Cohen has suggested that contemporary British history must explore 'how everyday actions ... create new subjectivities as well as new forms of social action'.[14] This book starts from the reverse point of view, asking how the social, political and cultural action that comprised sexual liberalization and the expansion of feminist discourse were interpreted in the 'everyday actions' of individuals for whom these changes had immediate implications.

Cohen also foregrounded the importance of 'charting the often quiet revolutions in attitudes and expectations' that underlie broad historical change.[15] This book probes the textures and perimeters of such a 'revolution' in understandings of gender and relationality in the post-1960s era. In so doing it owes a debt to the methods and concerns of historians interested in unpicking the relationship between gendered self-understanding and the state in wartime and post-war Britain.[16] But it also offers something new by focusing on those outside of the 'centre stage' act of 'the making and securing of... British family life'.[17] As we will see, those who found themselves offstage either by choice or by chance were in the position of observers, with a heightened consciousness of the pressures on them either to pair up or to realize the opportunities that being single provided. The market that evolved to cater to their needs and incite their demand, and first-person experiences of romantic clienthood, represent something of a lightning rod through which the emotional, political and consumerist workings of romantic promise were conducted with peculiar directness.

In mapping fresh terrain in the study of late twentieth-century relational life, this book opens three new fronts in the study of modern British heterosexuality. The first offers a new perspective on the periodization and nature of conservatism and traditionalism in post-1960s British sexual life. The second concerns the emergence of a new type of emotional pragmatism. This was a subtle but significant shift in the affective norms linking self-understanding and romantic performance, one that normalized failure, and reshaped the courting self as a self-fashioned product that would succeed or 'sell' based on the effort – emotional, psychological, physical – put into it. And third, a new front is opened on the reading of romance in late twentieth-century Britain. Cultural scholars, including those interested in the wedding industry, have shown that despite sinking rates of marriage, romance remained a powerful imaginary among people living in 1970s, 1980s and 1990s Britain.[18] This book, however, demonstrates something about the conditions in which romance could thrive – or not thrive – at this time. Mediated dating, in exposing the context of love's production, was not compatible with the retention of romantic idealism, and produced a completely different set of approaches and understandings of the purpose of forming a couple. The following section outlines these three interventions in more detail.

A revolution in attitudes? The persistence of old feelings in new times

The advent, timing and extent of permissiveness has been widely debated. In the late 1960s and early 1970s, numerous books tackled the implications for British life of the 'permissive society' that had arrived at some point since 1959 – a term not limited to, but weighted towards the sexual. Since then, historians have continued to locate a dramatic loosening in norms around sexual culture, or sexual 'revolution' in the 1960s and 70s. Arthur Marwick pinpointed the late 1960s as a time of clear transnational ferment, while Brian Harrison and Avner Offer have extended the chronology of 'revolution' into the 1990s, with Harrison calling the period between 1970 and 1990 as one of 'permanent' sexual overhaul.[19] Yet contradictions abound in understandings of the pace, causes and substance of change in sexual morality and practice in the post-1960s period. Callum Brown locates in the 1960s the century's key decade of sexual change, with single women's sexual choices driving the final conquest of secularization, while Hera Cook persuasively shows how contraceptive provision profoundly altered women's sexual liberty in that decade.[20] But Frank Mort set out to 'profoundly question the idea that the sexual regime of the 1960s was progressive' while others also stress the persistence of conservative sexual morality in the 60s, including contemporaneous chroniclers such as Geoffrey Gorer, Michael Schofield and Alex Comfort.[21] To some, meanwhile, the 1970s is seen as the watershed decade for the transformation in the gender order through new possibilities around women's economic status, sex, sexuality and family structure.[22] Others have seen a *tightening* in sexual morality in the first decade following universal provision of the Pill, abortion and no-fault divorce – Claire Langhamer, for instance, has pointed to a decreasing tolerance towards infidelity in the decade, while Pat Thane and Tanya Evans saw new types of institutionalized stigma directed at lone mothers in the 1980s and 1990s, arguments echoed by Ben Mechen in his assertion of a 1970s sexual regime that was restrictive in new ways.[23]

These accounts are generally presented along strong empirical axes either of drastic change, or of lingering conservatism; of sudden rupture or of a longue durée in the evolution of sexual reform.[24] Both understandings of sexual revolution, each stressing a wide array of evidence, are convincing. Yet this book attempts to get beyond the either/or interpretation of British society as either sexually permissive or surprisingly conservative after 1960. Clearly, one inspiration for this approach is the work of Michel Foucault. In linking greater sexual freedom with greater forms of constraint and control, Foucault prompted scholars to think about sexual liberalization and the history of sexuality in terms of freshly restrictive 'regimes' and codes of normality and power.[25] However, while the problematization of sexual progress frames aspects of this book, the focus here is not on institutional forms of power per se; it is, rather, on the relationship between non-institutional discourse and individual response. In this it fits more within a newer historiography on experience, emotion and the everyday.[26]

In looking beyond the 'either/or' approach to sexual change, this study attempts to integrate the two currents by focusing on the everyday micro-transactions of romance and singles' articulations of amatory intent, placing them in dialogue with bigger patterns of discursive and behavioural change. In prioritizing the micro, the textured and the everyday, the methodology deployed here follows that of historians keen to develop approaches for better understanding the 'the long sexual revolution of the second half of the twentieth century' and the 'global explosion of sexual possibilities' that came with it.[27] As these historians have stressed, we need to know more about the 'everyday emotional lives' and 'day-to-day interactions' buttressing the 'sexual and emotional character' of European nations right up to the millennium.[28]

One persuasive example of how the choices of individuals can be better scrutinized in terms not just of sex but of the social manifestations of sexual or romantic intent is to be found in the literature on Christianity and the sexual revolution. Influenced by Hera Cook's survey of British attitudes towards contraception since 1800, as well as Callum Brown's work on secularization and sex, historians such as Alana Harris, David Geiringer and Carmen Mangion have focused on the experience of Catholics in 1960s Britain to show how individuals struggled to square personal value systems with new sexual possibilities.[29] This work has helped demonstrate the complex relationship between people and wider sexual politics and culture, and mitigated against the tendency among scholars of the 1960s and 1970s to 'downplay the significance of the *popular* sexual revolution' [my italics].[30] Katherine Holden's more isolated study of single people between 1914 and 1960 is another good example of how the desires and choices of individuals can be set off against institutional change.[31] This book is both temporally and thematically distinct from the studies mentioned above. But with its reliance on first-person testimony and its close interest in the workings of a relatively small, cottage-style industry, it too tries to place the micro-interactions of individuals within the context of their 'everyday emotional lives'.[32]

This book contributes another angle on the history of late twentieth-century liberalization in Britain. While sexual behaviour changed in ways that have been well documented by demographers, discussed in Chapter 1, these changes were nonetheless buttressed by attitudes to gender that remained traditional, sometimes angrily so, producing new tensions between men and women that – as the century drew to an end – increasingly surfaced on TV, in manuals, polemics and memoirs.[33] Marcus Collins's prominent history of British intimacy in the twentieth century discussed these tensions in terms of 'sex war', while Jeffrey Weeks, Lesley Hall, Avner Offer and others have acknowledged the persistence both of the monogamous ideal and of sexual inequality on a number of levels.[34] European scholars have thought more structurally, however, about the effects of rapid sexual change, with Beck and Beck-Gernsheim observing a 'paradoxical [result]: the more equal the sexes seem, the more we become aware of persistent and pernicious inequalities between them'.[35] Sociologists and feminist thinkers have looked to love and romance as the theatre in which the dynamics of this paradox are played out, mining terrain that Europeanists including Josie McLellan and Dagmar Herzog have recently begun to explore historically.[36] British historians have much to gain by turning our attention to the particularities and contradictions of gender as it was hitched to love and vice versa in the final stretch of the twentieth century.[37]

In examining love, gender and romance, clarity of definition is important since the terms overlap. Although love now has its own multi-disciplinary literature, scholars often elide it with romance. I do the same here: any more serious engagement with love as distinct from romance must remain on the periphery of a book focusing on the history of romantic aspiration *outside* of an established couple.[38] Importantly, while the idea of finding love inevitably informed the way people articulated their hopes, the terms in which my subjects explained their choice to use matchmaking services were different. The desire for intimacy (another recurring term) – a flexible idea of closeness with a person of the opposite sex – was more dominant.

Joan Scott's famous definition of gender is particularly useful for thinking about changes in dating since 1970, especially if we understand coupledom as a 'social' as well as private relationship.[39] For Scott, gender is 'a constitutive element of social relationships based on perceived differences between the sexes, and ... a primary way of signifying relationships of power'.[40] And if, as Scott argues, power relationships between the sexes must be understood as invested with copious symbolic trappings, then dating – with the centrality of gift-exchange, delayed sexual gratification, chivalrous etiquette and taboos of 'easy' women and unmasculine men – would seem particularly rich in gender clues. More broadly, however, gender is understood here as a dynamic system that provided the framework of meanings in which people pursued relationships, and that shaped people's feelings and desires about what constituted an attractive romantic prospect. (I also use 'sexual' as in 'sexual relationships' or 'sexual antagonism' to do the same work as gender: namely, to indicate interactions or feelings harnessed to the sexual difference, perceived or real, between men and women.)

If gender is one broad category of analysis central to this book, then romance is another cognate term used more specifically in conjunction with courtship and the activities, rituals and feelings that accompanied it. Susan Ostrov Weisser has emphasized the diversity of understandings of late twentieth-century romance, stressing the dominance of cultural, gender-political and commercial accounts.[41] Of particular relevance here is the idea of romance as a form of specialness, with rituals and feelings that take people outside of the everyday and the humdrum.[42] As will be discussed in the next section, the contest between the special and the everyday in mediated dating generated particular friction among my subjects. As Carol Dyhouse and Stephen Brooke have demonstrated, we also need to appreciate the centrality of culturally stimulated imagination and fantasy if we are to historicize twentieth-century romantic sensibilities.[43] These feature narratives that weave between prudence and passion, with love at first sight, finding 'the one', and – sometimes – finding a man of fortune at the same time.[44] And Judy Giles has highlighted the need to think historically about women's attitudes to romance, arguing that social and economic shifts in the interwar period encouraged working-class women to reject romance.[45] The models of romance based on prudence on one hand and serendipity and passion on the other did inform the rhetorics of the matchmakers studied here and sometimes structured the articulations of singles, but they fed through in complex, often muted, ways.

'Romance' and 'romantic' are used here in three additional meanings: in an open-ended sense to refer to the feelings elicited by the courtship process; as a hoped-for future with someone (possibly as yet unknown); and the more transactional trappings of romance – eating out, dancing, drinking. Emotionally, then, romance here indicates a palette of hope, desire, disappointment and expectation (and the repetition of these feelings), while romance as a form of consumption – applied romance – is understood as key to the production of amorous feeling.[46] In sum, the term 'romance' is generally (though far from exclusively) used here to conjure an unstable constellation of actions, hopes, articulations and desires integral to dating in the period under scrutiny rather than as a synonym for a fixed romantic attachment.

By focusing on romance – as a process and set of aspirations – we can elaborate a picture of sexual change more sluggish than the one that emerges from a historiography which, as discussed in more detail below, has tended to focus on sexual practice. We can also see more closely how traditional sexual morality – manifested in the desire for monogamous, committed, male breadwinner model relationships – expressed itself *in relation* to a growing plethora of sexual opportunity and women's equality discourse. The rhetorics of the matchmaking industry and the experiences and memories of daters themselves show that though the trappings of sexual change were fairly ubiquitous, romantically up-to-date impulses did not necessarily follow for men or women. In fact, feelings about intimacy and about the proper role of gender at the heart of intimacy could often move *against* new sexual opportunities. Dagmar Herzog's idea of syncopation in European sexual cultures is useful in thinking through this tension.[47] Herzog uses the term to explain the conflicting moments of liberalization in different European countries at any given time.

Syncopation, or the idea of multiple speeds of change and retrenchment, is also suggestive of the ways in which individuals interpreted the new relational scaffolding of sex and gender in late twentieth-century Britain. A study of romance and courtship takes us beyond the physical encounters that surface in surveys about sex and family, and opens up a wider range of responses to 'sexual liberalization' – including the delays and complexities that characterize the relationship between individual feeling and collective change.

Emotional pragmatism

Dating services represented a phenomenon that applied the practices and language of an increasingly market-oriented world to a domain in which self-worth was constantly being measured. This relationship between self, feeling, romance and the business of finding love requires some teasing apart.[48]

Courtship has long lent itself to market metaphors, tied to the literal values of dowries, 'portions' or other marriage settlements.[49] But in the 1970s, an irony became more pronounced. For the first time for adults, indulging in courtship as a lifestyle or exploratory period rather than a route to marriage had become normal. The economic framework for courtship, while far from dissolved, as we will see, nonetheless became less formalized.[50] At the same time, new discourses from psychology, therapy, management and personal development were encouraging individuals to internalize market logics in new ways: namely to view themselves as work-in-progress products whose desirability (and options) were subject to refinement.[51] The romantic journey was increasingly being experienced as a figurative measure of worth, with worth defined less explicitly in financial, religious or class terms and more in the lexicon of emotional and sexual nouse or 'technique'.[52]

Late twentieth-century romantic relationships have already been identified as a site in which people were expected to take responsibility for their failures and to improve, paying to help the process along with 'psychoanalysts, psychologists, and therapists of all kinds, the publishing industry, television and numerous other media industries'.[53] Yet generally the focus has been on the coupled aspect of love – marriage, relationships and their breakdown. Courtship, however, occupies its own space at the coalface of changes in emotional culture surrounding heterosexual intimacy in the post-1960s period. As singles saw more people, and a singles culture developed through newspapers, magazines, wine bars and singles clubs, rejection became increasingly allied not with the loss of an individual but with a process. And those who used dating agencies and placed personal ads, and who therefore went out on blind dates, were confronted in quite explicit ways with rejection and failure. As this study suggests, these rejections came to signal the need to rethink self-presentation, expectations and attitude. The paradigm of pre-marital intimacy, then, began to echo the patterns assigned to the status of sex in the late twentieth century. The idea that one should work to improve sexual performance for the sake of a relationship was not new.[54] But Stevi Jackson and Sue Scott's more recent meditation on sexual 'antinomies' captures the sense of intensifying pressure to remake and update the sexual self as the century drew to a close: 'Sex can no longer be taken for granted, rather it must be constantly improved upon in the pursuit of perfection ... to be bad at sex is almost to fail as a human being ... both sex and the relationship itself [have] become projects to be worked at and worked upon.'[55]

The only thing potentially worse than dysfunctional sex and relationships was to have neither, and yet those without them have remained marginal to the historical agenda of the period, an omission that will be returned to below. This book observes the way those outside of relationships, and quite often those lacking sexual options, experienced the pressure to remake and rework themselves in order to gain those things. It brings to light the ways in which that work required a new form of emotional pragmatism in the approach to finding intimacy. This rationalism of feelings helped singles navigate the increasingly widespread confrontation between the commodification of the process of mate-seeking, and the fact of themselves as the industry's frontline products. Inevitably there was discomfort with combining the search for love with the profiteering of matchmakers. But market conditions – in terms of both the romantic options open to single British men and women in a demographic sense and demand and supply at work within mediated dating services themselves – meant a growing number of singles were having to get used to this combination. How they did, the focus in Chapter 4, opens up a moment in the history of modern romance that not only reveals the way the emotional culture around intimacy was changing at the time, but also how the affective terrain of contemporary digital dating was developing before the internet was even invented.

Intimacy and the business of romance

The idea of finding 'the one' hovers around the conversations and debates traced in this book, inflected according to who was speaking: journalist, psychologist or matchmaking entrepreneur.[56] Yet the yearning for romance was generally codified rather than explicit in the ever-thickening picture of desired outcomes, taking shape instead in concepts of emotional and physical fulfilment. This opacity around romance – at least in its popular representation as a fast-growing physical and spiritual chemistry sacralized with gifts – is particularly pronounced in the personal testimonies of Chapter 4.[57] While the 'architecture of choice' informing my subjects' relational quest was generally underpinned by monogamous hopes of meeting one lifelong partner, the picture that emerges lacks idealized imaginaries of love at first sight or wealthy knights in shining armour.[58] Singles favoured instead a concern with good manners, personal compatibility and financial accountability.[59] Acknowledging this helps illuminate the relationship between the procedures of romance and romantic sentiment at a juncture in which the two were yoked together in ever more ambiguous and close-knit ways. Rather than fantasy, my subjects stressed the desire to find someone who was honest, decently attired, financially independent, good company and able and willing to commit. Partner specifications were concrete and realistic, with little mention, as alluded to earlier, of 'falling in love'. Crucially, however, the experience of mediated dating – which laid bare the machinations not only of the matchmaking business and its profit model, but also of the minutiae of economically loaded interactions with strangers – pushed uncomfortably against romance understood as a 'dramatized, intense' experience *outside* of everyday life, dominated by feelings rather than rationality.[60]

In his work on the meanings of domestic space (houses) as a site of romantic attachment and fantasy, Joe Moran has argued that the modern British romanticization of home is only possible by denying 'its more quotidian realities'.[61] Moran, echoing Bachelard, noted that the 'mundane everydayness of the house' remained unacknowledged because of its 'ideological' otherness from the dreary public spaces of everyday life.[62] Even if homes were mass produced, or the same as the rest on the street or development, they were seen as refuges from the mass-produced sameness of the public built environment. Yet this otherness was only achieved through fairly heavy 'symbolic work' made possible by the entanglement of domestic space 'with a logic of privatized consumption'.[63]

These relationships are highly suggestive for the way we think more widely about sentimental attachments in late twentieth-century Britain. Regarding perhaps the most sentimental of all – romance – this book suggests that in failing to conceal the 'mundane everydayness' of love in its earliest stages, commercially mediated dating – with its forms, questionnaires, payment and logistics – stacked the odds against clients.[64] Chapter 4 elucidates how this visibility of the context of production in which singles found themselves as both client and product threatened the romantic project as much or more than bad dates. The 'logics of privatized consumption' may have allowed homeowners to forget the context of production in which their private unit was built next to dozens or hundreds more like it, through refurbishment projects and almost silent new appliances concealing the work of cleaning or rubbish disposal. Yet these logics of consumption posed serious problems for those actually trying to be consumers – i.e. paying customers – of romance, demanding of them a perplexing and effortful task. This task was the triangulation of the commoditization of the process, commoditization of themselves (as the industry's products), and the development of amorous feeling. As singles struggled to reconcile these factors, their approach to coupling jettisoned the vocabularies of romantic longing and took on a day-by-day, experimentalist outlook that would come to underpin contemporary digital dating. Much has been written about the marketization of private life and specifically of romantic life, a literature whose relevant aspects will be discussed further on. Yet when we look at romantic intent as it was actually mediated by a market – not a figurative market but an industry – we see in the experience and conceptualization of romance a high degree of resistance to the logics of consumption. Romance – despite becoming increasingly allied to paid-for leisure in an implicit sense – was not, in fact, easily convertible into loving feeling when it was hedged by the explicit workings of cost–benefit analysis.

Research context and dominant narratives

Rather than consider how individuals articulated and pursued romantic visions against the backdrop of sharp sexual change, social historians have focused on the major legislative, demographic and cultural changes surrounding sex and marriage, including the introduction of no-fault divorce, the free universal provision of contraception, the 'unprecedented' rise of cohabitation and single parent households and the withdrawal of censorship laws.[65] The richness of survey material has further boosted the empirical tendency of this work.[66] Meanwhile, a key manifestation of scholarly response to the sexual-political upheaval of the 1960s, 1970s and – with the rise of AIDS – the 1980s, is to be found in the discipline of sociology, which continues to reinforce the link between politics, demography and sexual practice. Indeed, in line with testing assumptions about the rise of permissiveness and sexual liberation, as discussed above, historians have paid closer attention to all aspects of sexual practice than to its chaster social counterpart of courtship.[67] Sex has rightly been placed at the forefront of understandings of change in the period; as Rosalind Brunt reflected (albeit with feminist irony) in a 1982 essay on 'permissive' 1970s sex advice, '"sex" is the new gateway to an exciting life and the final bestower of individual identity and absolute meaning.'[68]

Cultural historians in particular have made use of the growing body of erotic material in print and on screen to explore sex in the period and to test the meaning and timing of permissiveness.[69] Often, responses to such cultural products have been evaluated through the debates of the intelligentsia and in the media rather than in the responses of their audiences.[70] There is little equivalent in the post-1970 era of the efforts of social historians of film and music such as Annette Kuhn, Jeffrey Richards and Adrian Horn, or scholars of popular magazines and romance novels and films such as Carol Dyhouse, to tease out the lived and imaginative responses of ordinary people to 'permissive' artefacts.[71] The same applies in areas of cultural analysis concerned with the interplay between feminist and traditional messages: Janice Winship's important study of women's magazines in the 1970s and 1980s, which now sits among a wide scholarship of such periodicals, focuses squarely on content rather than reception.[72] Work on youth and popular culture, however, has been keener to explore the experience of audience.[73]

This book aims to illuminate the complexity of sexual liberalization – in gender politics as well as attitudes to physical intimacy – as it was interpreted by a heterogeneous group of straight single adults. It is therefore focused on the ways it cropped up in debate among singles themselves, informing their view of the romantic landscape, as well as in the moral articulations of various media. This task seemed particularly pressing in relation to 'ordinary' adults, the very people whose experience generally remains unpublished as memoir or analysis.[74] Unsurprisingly, more is known about how certain feminists, musicians and broadcasters experienced the romantic landscape in the 1960s and 1970s than about how someone like Elaine, the mental health nurse who found her partner through a *Time Out* lonely heart, did.[75] Such memoirs add vivid colour to the period but produce a bias towards London-based experience played out within the worlds of activism, politics, culture and the media. Unsurprisingly, little light is shed in these accounts on the everyday experience of unwanted singleness or on perceptions of the pressure to pair up. By contrast the people whose experience informs this book faced the mundane hardships of singleness, including financial struggle and social isolation.

Moving to the 1980s, a different set of historiographical concerns have emerged around the sexual contradictions of the Thatcher period, ranging across family and sexual policy, the campaigns of the moral right, and the motif of sexual consumerism. Jon Lawrence has argued that Thatcher unleashed a 'radical transformation' throughout all levels of British culture more extreme even than the permissiveness of the 60s or militancy of the 1970s.[76] The focal point was a 'radical individualism' that permeated private as well as public life.[77] Individualism and consumerism were linked with new intensity in this period. As Frank Mort has suggested, a sharp emphasis on market economics promoted slippage of a consumerist ethic into private domains, with sexual identity becoming both a good itself, and dependent on cultures of stylized consumption.[78] Chancellor Nigel Lawson's 1988 budget marked a moment, according to Mort, when 'consumption featured as a whole way of life' and Mort goes on to show, through the construction of topographically rooted London masculinities, the ways in which consumption in 'theory and in practice existed in a complex, but interconnected, relationship'.[79] Sociologists took up the idea of an ethic of panoramic consumption with gusto, seeing in it a picture of general post-industrial Western emotional decline. Zygmunt Bauman, Anthony Giddens and Eva Illouz offered theories of throwaway 'liquid' relationships, cloakroom communities (also disposable), and a new fungibility of interpersonal relationships.[80]

The matchmaking industry

Far from evoking a vanished past, the impressive literature on the Victorian matrimonial business is crucial for understanding several aspects of the matchmaking industry a century later.

The first is medium. Early matchmaking services were rooted in the hectic, multifarious world of print periodicals and were inseparable from their expansion after the repeal of the Stamp Act by 1860.[81] Development of newspaper advertising, which expanded after 1855, shaped the rise of matrimonial personals, which by the late Victorian period had become 'one of the most prominent forms of specialized advertising'.[82] Although matrimonial advertisers were barred from British broadsheets after the mid-century, Harry Cocks cites the appearance of at least twenty-two matrimonial newspapers between 1880 and 1914, while newspaper sales quadrupled in the same period.[83] Matthew Rubery, in his literary study of Victorian newspapers, highlights the fascination and centrality of personal adverts, which occupied the front pages of some broadsheets until

1908.[84] Although not explicitly matrimonial, there were lines by spurned lovers hoping to find their jilters and other 'agony' columns alongside a range of other, often shady interests.[85] The adverts' attraction, based on their anonymous human drama, was intermixed with their potential danger. As Rubery observes, 'unlike other sections of the newspaper, the advertising columns brought readers into potential contact with a variety of criminals'.[86]

Close contact with duplicity and criminality in British newspapers became a growing part of their appeal in the early twentieth century, with editors in the interwar period mining the confessions of the new breed of 'entrepreneurs of experience' – often ex-crooks – for all they could.[87] Unsurprisingly, the criminal possibilities encoded in newspaper personals – and particularly in the matrimonial ads of the specialist press – had a deeply gendered aspect. In particular, the tension between freedom of choice and danger provided a ready vehicle for knitting together anxieties related to the status of women. These revolved around the perception of increasing female romantic autonomy, which was linked to growing female economic independence – if women were driving sales in department stores, what might they do in the 'sales' pages of spouses?[88] As late as the 1970s, personals attracted moral censure, with vice squads intervening in the publishing of contact ads, prosecuting countercultural magazines like *Oz* and *International Times* over 'obscenity' – in reality, the legal meeting of men over twenty-one.[89]

There were more material grounds for concern in the allegations of fraud and sleaze affixed to the industry. WT Stead, the newspaperman credited with inventing the tabloid press, had an enduring interest in the commercial and social possibilities of matrimonial bureaux and had founded a club of his own, the Wedding Ring Circle, in 1898. Having made 'an exhaustive investigation into all the then existing matrimonial agencies' by instructing a member of staff to advertise as both a man and woman, Stead was able to conclude that there was a desperate hole in the market for an honest service and that the existing offering was 'worse than worthless'.[90] Without specifying the gender of the respondents, Stead stated that 'in nine cases out of ten', people wanted either 'a mistress or cash'.[91] The matchmakers themselves were also regarded with suspicion – often depicted as immoral and degenerate.[92] In Cocks's chronology, it wasn't until the 1960s that the 'dubious status of lonely hearts ... ended'.[93] However, rather than concur, it is the enduring inability of matchmaking services to shed their 'dubious' status, well after the 1960s, that provides one key strand of this book. The fraudulent aura surrounding such services remained an integral part of their image, and had constantly to be kept at bay by those who ran them. Instead of dissipating, the duality of a pragmatism and seediness, not to say danger, that attended such methods of mate-seeking would re-emerge with a vengeance in depictions of the lonely hearts business of the 1970s, 1980s and 1990s and has since transferred to the internet.[94]

Respectability was another recurrent motif in matchmaking discourse, arising from the differing agendas of customers, proprietors and commentators, and setting in place a tension that would linger into the late twentieth century and beyond. It hung in the balance between pursuit of romantic choice, social class and gendered danger. It was also at stake in the clash between respectable customer motivation – the desire to achieve a romantically and socially felicitous union – with the questionable milieu in which it was pursued. Often the milieu seemed to eclipse or cast a bad light on the motivation. In a debate in the *Review of Reviews* in 1897 about matrimonial bureaux, Walter Besant drew attention to the 'shameless Register' of such agencies, pointing to the kind of young woman forced to spell out her desire for a 'man who will marry her'.[95] Her sort, he scoffed, wrote that 'she is five feet six in height, that she is considered good-looking, that she has a good temper and is "domesticated"'.[96] But, reasoned Besant in a criticism that would echo up the twentieth century, 'imagine a girl of self-respect proclaiming that she is "domesticated!"' In other words: if a woman is attractive, why advertise? For Fyvie Mayo, another contributor to the debate, 'the very idea of such an institution [was] wholly repugnant'.[97] Mayo ploughed a different corner of the critical field, reasoning that it was precisely the brazenness behind the mere contemplation of a marriage bureau that should have nixed the need for them – 'it is hard to believe that [such people] could not easily get a "suitable partner" (of some sort) soon enough.'[98]

The idea of dating agencies as damaged goods clubs remains part of the conceptual baggage surrounding commercial matchmaking, prompting a central line of questioning here about the extent to which this baggage impacted the industry and its users, and the ways in which it did so. Moreover, the discomfort surrounding both paying money to find a spouse and the necessary articulation of financial standing in print would later move inwards to shape heated sexually antagonistic debates among daters themselves, who took aim at the financial expectations of the opposite sex. Social snobbery, another facet shaping the development of the mediated dating business between 1970 and 2000, was also a clear feature of unease about the respectability of matrimonial advertising, since, as Cocks has illustrated in some detail, the primary customer base came from the 'new' clerk class.[99] However, in the rounds of social commentary, it was pointed out that the upper classes were even more mercenary in their approach to matrimony than the upper-working-class or lower-middle-class *Matrimonial Gazette* advertiser, pursuing the exchange of wealth for title on the grander scale of the Season.[100] It was also clear that marriages of all classes arranged in more traditional ways – especially second marriages – involved a pragmatism that could be seen as encroaching on conjugal sentiment.[101]

Methods and sources

Before internet dating, lonely hearts culture was inherently print-based, dependent on widely read newspapers for both editorial and advertising coverage. Indeed the history of post-war mediated dating has largely been set out in a sporadic but enduring media discourse – particularly in broadsheet newspapers aimed at a professional or middle-class audience: *The Times* and *The Guardian* each ran close to 1,000 articles containing the term 'lonely hearts' between 1970 and 2015; *The Daily Mirror* ran just 312. Newspapers also allow us to see the evolution of a linked editorial and commercial interest in dating, since features and news coverage eventually became linked to the newspapers' revenue in the form of sections such as *Guardian* Soulmates (launched in 1995) and *Times* Encounters (from 2002). This book pursues dating as it was viewed and experienced by a public of both men and women, and is particularly interested in the conversations between the two sexes that were vented in various forms of print media. While women's magazines frequently discussed strategies of pursuit and relations with the opposite sex, their readership was predominantly female. By contrast, newspapers were read by both genders, and the lonely hearts only worked because both sexes read them. Consequently, gender-specific journals play less of a role in this source base than either newspapers or general readership magazines.

The focus here is on four newspapers: two broadsheets and two tabloids, approximating a fair representation of the total British national newspaper offering in this period. These are *The Guardian* and *The Observer*, *The Times*, *The Daily Mail* and *The Express*. Articles using the terms 'lonely hearts', 'computer dating' or 'dating ads' were tracked over the thirty-year period under study. *The Times* and *The Guardian* covered dating services in a wide range of writing, including arts, opinion, first-person and in-depth features as well as news stories. *The Guardian*, unlike *The Times*, analysed the state of dating in such a way as to highlight its progressive politics, paying close attention to foul tactics in the industry and highlighting flare-ups of sexism within it. Its seriousness of reportage about the industry has made it a key source of information. *The Guardian*'s coverage reflected its concern for social issues, while *The Times* stressed class by implication, through its self-consciously breezy, detached tone of reporting. Using dating agencies, it was conveyed in *The Times*'s editorial voice, was probably something other people did, but none the less interesting for that. Despite the tone of detached interest or amusement in much of their reportage on the dating industry, it was the broadsheets, not the tabloids, whose expanding coverage would eventually (in the late 1990s) lead to the launch of national personals sections of their own. As will become clear in Chapter 2, lonely hearts were a cross-class business, with services such as the *London Weekly Advertiser* and *Singles* focusing on the needs of lower-middle or working-class singles. By the late 1990s, singleness discourse (as we will see in Chapter 3) had rendered the solo state a 'lifestyle', one at least partially associated with professionals too busy to find love, or those who were seeking love after a divorce. A market had clearly emerged among single readers of the *Guardian*, *Times* and *Telegraph* who were prepared to try a commercially mediated approach to dating bolstered by the respectability of their go-to broadsheet.

The Daily Mail offered rich coverage as its combination of prurience and conservatism meant a fervent interest in the sexual implications of singles' strategies and of the development of the singles market. In contrast to *The Guardian*, *The Mail* and *The Express* used a conservative, generally anti-feminist lens to chart the ways in which loneliness moved across the romantic landscape, emphasizing sexual deviance, crime, and both male and female menace. All of these newspapers are used to highlight different aspects of mediated dating, but are also to be drawn from as needed to add texture as well as to substantiate points of information and chronology in the absence of more official documentation.

Among the selection of magazines I consulted, two of particular note are *Time Out* and *Singles*. *Time Out* represents the metropolitan scene, and played an important role in the development of London as a lonely hearts centre after 1970. *Singles* magazine (1977–2004) is a particularly unique, rich and voluminous source, and represented the concerns of British singles with generally conservative, if often contradictory, beliefs about gender and family. Produced by Dateline, the computer dating firm, it was the only mixed gender magazine dedicated to singleness and the concerns of daters in Britain in the period. The magazine was at its most editorially dense and diverse between its launch in 1977 and 1983, when the emphasis moved away from the social aspects of singleness towards the commercial in the form of personal ads. In its editorial heyday before 1983, feature articles covered a large range of topics relating to relationships, sex, psychology, intimacy, dating and singles lifestyle, while an intriguing political voice was deployed for a range of news items. *Singles* also carried an expanding section of personal ads, of between eight and twenty-four pages, which operated at a seeming tangent from the Dateline computer service with whom it shared a stable. Apart from the wealth of otherwise obscure information relating to dating and singles, *Singles* is a valuable source of first-person testimony, expressed via a letters section that took missives from a wide range of readers. *Singles* letters pages are valuable for both composition and content. The section was relatively lengthy at two to four pages each month carrying letters of varying lengths, some up to 600 words or more. Letters were divided fairly equally between men and women, allowing the creation of a debating terrain which would become increasingly fractious and antagonistic. The equal gender representation in the letters pages allows for a privileged glimpse into the workings of sexual politics set against intimate aspirations.

The value of this collection of letters accrues in light of the fact that they were knowingly ephemeral, written often out of pique at other letters or indeed at social or political events, rather than for posterity – by contrast those writing diaries for Mass Observation, another key first-person lens onto the period, were often reflexive about their status as contributors to an archive. *Singles* readers were generally situated outside of activist networks, the intelligentsia or the commentariat and, crucially, London. An average letters section contained just two out of eight from London, showing how pressing were many of the issues of romantic isolation – and solutions for remedying it – beyond the capital. Furthermore, many readers had financial or other economic worries, and found the contemporary dater's pressurized cocktail of expense and aspiration somewhat toxic. Their concerns and opinions offer insight into the play of class, income and age across romantic structures and norms.

Interviews include the testimonies of both clients and matchmakers, and these people were reached in a variety of ways, the most successful being through a small notice in *Saga Magazine*: six former mediated daters replied this way. In addition to *Saga*, one interviewee – Elaine – overheard me interviewing another respondent in a café in central London and chimed in. Hilary responded to a mass email to students at Birkbeck, a college for mature students within the University of London. In terms of age, my respondents were between sixty and seventy-six at the time of interview, and had used singles services between the early 1970s and the mid-1990s. Elaine was in her late twenties and early thirties when she began using mediated matchmaking services between 1978 and 1981;

Marsha was the same age at the same period when she answered ads in *Time Out* and *Private Eye*; Michael, Millie and Mary had used agencies when previous marriages ended (Michael and Millie were fifty-six and fifty when they met in 1990; Mary was forty-nine in 1995), Adele had been in her early twenties in the early seventies when she used an agency, and Hilary was in her late twenties and early thirties when she used first an agency and then *City Limits* lonely hearts.

Saga's readership is the largest of all British monthly general lifestyle magazines, at around 421,000 readers.[102] Yet all of the replies came from London or its surrounds, and all but one were from women. While self-proclaimed class varied among respondents, all lived independently and apparently comfortably. The prevalence of responses from women from the South-East echoed the patterns of response of Mass Observation diarists.[103] In the case of dating, it is also likely that women felt more comfortable responding to another woman, and less constrained in discussing the topic. This would be in line with well-explored issues of masculine reticence around intimate or private matters.[104]

For any historian of twentieth-century Britain interested in how changing romantic norms were seen and felt by ordinary people, Mass Observation is a crucial staging post. In particular for those interested in post-war Britain, the Mass Observation Project (MOP), the series of questionnaires or 'directives' established in 1982, is particularly useful.[105] The 'unrepresentativeness' of Mass Observation, through the self-selectivity of respondents and the prevalence of women and people from the South-East, has been folded into nuanced appraisals of the archive's distinct strengths.[106]

While a number of MOP directives relate to intimacy, Courting and Dating is unique in drawing out dating from sex, gender and marriage. The directive provided a sense of historical change in how people navigated a path through social convention and private desire. Respondents reflected on the traditions shaping their experiences of pre-marital friendships and romances, including methods of wooing and location of dates, as well as on dating as a barometer of sexual norms before marriage. Indeed memories of sexual expectations in courtship emerged as one of the strongest markers of historical change, and were particularly strongly rooted to the historical moments they belonged to.

This book also relies on a number of first-person testimonies that fall outside MOP and my own oral histories. One set were gathered by John Cockburn, a self-styled social researcher who undertook an investigation of lonely hearts advertising in the late 1980s. Cockburn 'analysed over 6,000 ads', interviewed over 200 people who had placed or responded to personals, with a roughly even mix between men and women, and transcribed significant passages from these interviews.[107] The under-representation of male respondents to the MOP courting and dating directive, and to my call for interviews is one reason Cockburn's data is valuable. Another is that his own framing of the study underlined the ways in which mediated dating was perceived to be tied up with broader changes in gender politics and particularly women's status. This is not an academic study, and Cockburn's rather heavy-handed categorization of themes and subjects raises questions about his interview methods and the degree to which he steered his respondents' answers. Nonetheless, his methods – which involved advertising for interview subjects in newspapers, writing to people 'direct, via their box number' and even going undercover as a lonely heart himself – resulted in an unparalleled collection of first-person views, many of them transcribed at enough length to assuage fears of interviewer interference.[108]

If the dating industry relied on print media, then dating discourse also emerged in a number of television programmes concerned with matchmaking, which make up a relatively small but revealing section of my source base. While game shows such as *Mr and Mrs* (Border Television, from 1961) and *Blind Date* (ITV, from 1985) testify to the fascination with putting people on the spot in romantic scenarios, I found more sober and informative investigations such as the documentaries *Singles* (Carlton, 1993) and *Man Seeks Woman* (BBC, 1995) valuable in offering a snapshot of a hidden part of social experience, and emphasizing the marginality of its subjects.[109] While the print sources examined here ran a mixture of types of articles about the matchmaking industry, with one dominant theme insisting on the normalization and even glamour of dating services and the single lifestyle, the television documentaries offered close-up textures of dejection and isolation. In addition to offering important material, visual and informative clues about the industry and its perception, it is also a barometer for the status of dating as an entertainment concept, which is an important part of its development in modern Britain. Mediated dating has always occupied a point somewhere on the line between modern pragmatism and a seedy fringe, and its depiction as an object of televisual investigation adds to our understanding of the place of commercial dating on that line.

Structure

Chapter 1 begins by discussing demographic change relating to marriage and introduces the idea of a new kind of 'singleness'. It outlines the new affective-romantic landscape facing singles and daters in the period in terms of a new set of discourses around coupledom and sex. The 1970s, I will suggest, marked the start of a key period in the evolution of singleness from being 'in the shadow' of marriage to being a social status of a different nature.[110] Rather than being seen as a problem because it signified un-marriedness, singleness began to be an area of concern for emotional health on the one hand, and promise on the other, in terms of both 'lifestyle' and sexual freedom. But when figured as a problem, singleness now suggested a concomitant array of solutions, in which mediated dating figured centrally. Solving the problem of singleness, it was increasingly suggested, could be done by taking control, whether through lonely hearts or by joining an agency.

Chapters 2 and 3 examine the contours of the mediated dating industry from different perspectives. Chapter 2 focuses on the composition of the industry over this period, elucidating the range of services and the differences between them. Chapter 3 moves from an examination of the industry itself to its representations and the perceptions these engendered, and charts the emergence of a dating discourse concerned with what it meant for gender, class and safety to meet strangers.

In Chapter 4, having examined the interplay of the relational climate and the industry, I focus on the customer in a range of first-person accounts. These sources are used to explore why and how people deployed singles services, and crucially, how people squared the consumer aspect of romantic clienthood with the pursuit of a romantic connection. The evidence considered in Chapter 4 leads me to reflect in closing on the long-term paradox inherent in dating services: the simultaneous virtuousness of taking control over romantic destiny and the immovability of fate in determining happiness.

In shifting the lens from couples to active daters, this book puts the emphasis on how people with everything to play for romantically negotiated their pursuit of a match. In doing so, it argues for a reformulation of the relationship between sexual change and feelings towards the opposite sex at the end of the twentieth century as one of lag or 'syncopation' rather than either progress or stasis.

1

'Live alone and like it?' Singleness in late twentieth-century Britain[1]

This chapter explores the emergence of 'the single' from the 1970s to the 1990s, uncovering the bigger macro shifts that enabled the growth of the category alongside psychological formations related to broader trends. In drawing the contours of the social, cultural and emotional landscape in which many thousands of singles chose to deploy the services of matchmaking forums, this chapter makes a case for the emergence of a new single subjecthood after 1970. This was a unisex category whose key rubrics seemed to apply to both men and women. But given that romance was highly gendered (along with corollaries like loneliness and need) sexual differentials are key to the picture. Indeed Katherine Holden has underscored the gender polarities inherent in meanings attached to singleness in mid-century Britain, with her analysis resting on the terms 'bachelor' and 'spinster'.[2] She uses 'single' descriptively as a synonym for unmarried; however, it wasn't until the 1960s that the word was increasingly used to signify an identity. The emergence of the 'single' as a distinct phase or lifestyle category aligned with a broader shift in post-war life as a collective or marital framework of duty was increasingly modified by a more inward-looking selfhood.[3] This shift has been a key marker for scholars of post-war British life, and most agree that 'individualism has been a driving force in Western democracies'.[4] The decline in marriage, or 'marriage crisis' of the late twentieth-century West has been attributed to deepening individualism.[5]

For those who could afford it, the single state more than any might appear to offer individual freedom and privilege individual wants.[6] However, the satisfaction of those wants and the enjoyment of those freedoms was not necessarily within reach of people whose economic, cultural and gendered outlook made singleness into a state of anxious uncertainty and self-doubt. This chapter therefore explores a double irony, stemming from the observation that the opportunities entailed in being single and 'free' were always framed by the promise of both sexual felicity and personal growth on one hand and monogamous commitment on the other.

This made being single stressful and sometimes sharpened the sense of loneliness, since the lack of sexual ties was compromised by conflicting feelings about, and opportunities for, actually accessing sexual liberty. Second, if – despite apparent freedoms – the single state could cause misery, the blame for this was attributed not to bad luck or fate but to a lack of emotional robustness and poor self-management on the part of the single herself.[7]

Legal, social and cultural context

There is a plenitude of data on twentieth-century British lifecycle events and sexual habits, norms and desires, interpreted in different ways by scholars from history and the social sciences.[8] Key among these, at the start of the period, were Geoffrey Gorer's *Sex and Marriage in England Today* (1970) and the National Survey of Sexual Attitudes and Lifestyles (NATSAL) 1 (1994) and 2 (2000) at the end.[9] The outbreak of AIDS in the early 1980s prompted a new field of epidemiologically urgent research into sexual habits. Indeed, taking a longer view of the post-war period, Liz Stanley has shown how vigorous the twentieth-century British sex survey tradition was, with Mass Observation forming an unprecedented sexually and methodologically progressive element in a field 'fetishized' in the 1950s and 1960s for its authority in explaining 'what is happening'.[10]

Scholars differ over the causes and their periodization, but there is a consensus based on survey data and historical analysis that British people, like their American and European counterparts, conducted themselves differently in relation to their sexual and romantic lives after the 1960s, with the conceptual and practical detachment of marriage, sex and reproduction at the heart of this change.[11] Demographic, legislative and activist milestones, including the 1970 launch of the British Women's Liberation movement, need to be viewed together in order to appreciate the external and internal landscape faced by heterosexual singles in the period. The relationship between legislative change and behaviour is complicated and not necessarily direct.[12] Nevertheless, the raft of 'permissive' legislation, and ensuing legal modifications, informed the sexual vantage point from which single men and women both clashed with and sought each other out.

The movement towards gender equality was fractured and inevitably for many people – depending on generation, occupational, ethnic and regional community – confusing.[13] One broad shift was represented in a series of acts that formalized the ability to sever sex from its unwanted consequences. First came the Abortion

Act of 1967, which legalized abortion without insisting on its provision by local authorities; with the 1974 NHS Reorganisation Act, family planning services were incorporated into the NHS, evening out provision around the country. The Pill, having become legally dispensable for all women in 1967, enjoyed a rapid uptake too – by 1989, over 80 per cent of women born between 1950 and 1959 had used the Pill.[14] If the consequences of sexual choices had become less punitive (seen also in the decriminalization of homosexuality in 1967), overall progress towards gender equality was uneven. The Equal Pay Act (1970) opened up opportunities for women, while the Sex Discrimination Act (1975) legislated against discrimination at work based on sex or marital status.

Yet if Britain appeared to be liberalizing in important ways for women as well as men, then surveys of domestic and sexual life suggested that women's sexual and economic freedoms were not evenly taken up or distributed. In 1973, Young and Willmott found that men did less than ten hours of housework a week, while wives did between twenty-three and forty-five hours depending on whether they worked or not.[15] Ann Oakley's 1974 study emphasized unequal division of labour between men and women, longer working weeks for housewives than for male workers, and high levels of dissatisfaction.[16] By 1990, Ferri and Smith found that dual-earner households were the norm but that more than twice as many women as men were in part-time work, and that a significant number of women felt that their partners prioritized work over taking an equal share in household duties.[17] Many women continued to face bullying and discrimination privately as well as publicly – in the upper echelons of political culture, Thatcher was elected to a house in which just 27 of 650 female MPs (this rose to 40 in 1990). High rates of domestic violence continued throughout the period.[18]

Singles: an emerging group

Singles were formulating their expectations of the opposite sex in a landscape of gender reconfiguration, but also – apparently – at a moment of particular promise. In the first place, the uncommitted seemed to be a growing group. Single people categorized as neither married, divorced nor widowed, accounted for 21 per cent of the population of England and Wales in 1970, and 30 per cent of it in 2000.[19] This increase was more pronounced for 'not married' women aged 25–59, a group that increased from 18 per cent to 40 per cent of all women over the same period.[20]

The problem with such figures is that the 'single' classification included cohabiting or otherwise romantically entwined couples, while cohabitation figures themselves were marred by the informality of the term.[21] Coleman and Salt estimated that 12 per cent of unmarried men aged between sixteen and fifty-nine and 14 per cent of unmarried women in the same age bracket were cohabiting in the late 1980s, leaving a relatively high proportion of the total number of 'singles' as romantically non-committed.[22] Indeed, singles – defined as single-person households – increased from 17 per cent of the total number of households in 1970, to a quarter of all households in 1989 to around 30 per cent in the decade after 2000, though it is not clear from these figures what proportion of these were career singles who had never found a lasting partner or had children.[23] However, market research firm Mintel subsequently shed some light on this question in a 1992 special report focusing exclusively on single-person households: *Single Person Households 1992: Single Living, Diverse Lifestyles*.[24] Mintel, using figures from the Central Statistics Office and Family Expenditure Survey, put the number of single-person households at 6 million in 1992. Crucially, it differentiated between retired and non-retired singles, and among the non-retired, between pre-family (under forty) and post-family singles, e.g. divorced, separated or widowed. It cited non-retired singles at between 11 and 13 per cent of all households, with single pensioners at 14–15 per cent.[25]

Empirically it is clear that single people – both the technically unmarried and single householders pre- and post-family – were a growing group between 1970 and 2000. But as Coleman and Salt remind us, people were (and are) single for 'very different reasons' across different age, social and income groups.[26] However, following the 1969 Divorce Reform Act, a surge in the number of divorcees changed the profile of the numbers, a factor that contributed to the success of dating agencies.[27] From 50,000 divorces in 1970 to 150,000 roughly a decade later, the rise in divorce and consequent changes in family structure in the 1970s and 1980s has been widely documented.[28] By the 1980s, divorce supplanted death as the main reason for marital termination; indeed it had reached the same rates as death in marriage for those married at the average age in 1820.[29]

The Mintel report underscored the potentially lucrative knowledge of singles' spending patterns, but it was also forced to acknowledge the world of economic difference between the young and old and the rich and poor. Not only was it 'a feature of single person households that they represent widely different lifestages' and also that 'a high proportion of single person households have low incomes (especially retired households on State pensions).[30] The Mintel report did not dwell on the well-chronicled poverty of elderly people living alone but instead developed the idea of a consumption-led model for thinking about singleness as a lifestyle.[31] The firm found that 'those who are comfortably off are particularly worth targeting as they generally have fewer responsibilities than others' and spent more on 'frivolous items' such as luxury pre-packaged foods, alcohol and tobacco and cinema trips.[32] But the most significant finding of the report, and the most widely reported, was that single people appeared to feel highly positive about solo living. The never-married were the most positive, 'emphasizing the freedom and sense of achievement in coping alone more than the loneliness'.[33] The media embraced the opportunity to debate whether singleness was liberating or lonely, situating the debate within a longer-term social trend towards greater flexibility, individualization and atomization – a trend represented in part by the growing dating industry.[34] Moreover, it was evident that the Mintel report formed part of a broader shift in market research towards a qualitative concept of 'lifestyle' that increasingly focused on affluent singles. Notably, marketing 'segmentation tool' ACORN (1977), built by marketing firm CACI, launched a Lifestyle List that classified every UK household according to a list of eighty-one 'lifestyle segmentations', including 'affluent single metropolitan dwellers'.[35] SAGACITY and TGI pursued similar classification strategies, streamlining the way marketers thought about singles, and helping to cultivate and differentiate the category of 'the single' as a status of economic interest, foreshadowing the contemporary marketing forecasts of companies like LSN: Global and JWT Intelligence.[36]

New opportunities and traditional desires

Daters – whether divorced, separated or first-timers – faced more than simply apparent strength in numbers. They seemed to be perfectly poised to take advantage of new options and experimentation in sexual and relational terms, as singles themselves sometimes vocally asserted. 'Women are now the hunters as much as men', observed a reader of *Singles* magazine, in 1977.[37] By 1980, 'getting girls into bed' was 'not to be confused with love and romance just in case you were misguided enough to think they had anything in common'.[38] Statistical indicators of new norms included the lowering age of first intercourse and a softening in attitudes towards pre-marital sex.[39] A 'genuine' generational shift among those born in the 1960s and 1970s emerged in NATSAL (1994) data showing that significantly more women between the ages of twenty and thirty-four had had 5–9 sexual partners compared with the 72 per cent having had just one among their elders aged fifty to fifty-nine.[40] This supports Geoffrey Gorer's findings

among young people in 1969, of which 63 per cent of women reported themselves
to be virgins at marriage.[41] Jane Lewis neatly describes a picture of sweeping
change in the generation growing up in the 1970s and 1980s: 'the numbers
marrying have halved, the numbers divorcing have trebled and the proportion
of children born outside marriage has quadrupled.'[42] However, there are two
generations here, both of whom contributed to the overall sense of change
between 1970 and 2000: Gorer's young adults and Lewis's. The first were born
between the 1920s and the early 1950s, and were sixteen or older before the start
of the sexual upheaval of the 1970s, while those discussed by Lewis were born
later, becoming the first generation to begin their pre-marital sex lives with the
Pill. This generational divergence in experiences of singleness and sexuality in
this period highlights the need to consider age and romantic history together to
some extent, as the analysis in Chapter 4 will demonstrate.

The overall sense at the start of the 1970s that singles faced options like never
before was enhanced by popular and high culture, with reams of investigations
of 'permissiveness' among journalists and sociologists and successful cultural
phenomena celebrating its ideals of sexual liberty, personal discovery and
pleasure.[43] Alex Comfort's *The Joy Of Sex* (1972), though directed at couples, is
still a prime example of the genre in which more sexual experimentation rather
than less was the watchword. But the relationship between broad sexual change
and individual attitudes and feelings about the gender order in the decades after
1970 requires closer analysis. Empirical evidence suggests that a complicated
relationship existed between changing relational norms and romantic attitudes.[44]
As we have seen, the period between the 1960s and the 2000s saw the parameters
of sexual behaviour completely change.[45] New forms of intimacy replaced the
old marriage-only model, with sex becoming, in Avner Offer's brusque terms,
'part of the non-committal and casual practice of serial mating'.[46] But the ideal
of what John Gillis called 'conjugality' – in which 'the couple ... is the standard
for all intimate relationships, the unmarried and the married' – was not in
fact considerably weakened either by greater sexual freedom or the heightened
ethic of individualism linked to it in the late twentieth century.[47] Couples took
seriously their moral obligations, especially when children were involved, and
preferred monogamy, even when they weren't married.[48]

The increasing popularity of cohabitation throughout the 1970s, 1980s and
1990s, as a precursor and an alternative to marriage, is routinely stressed as a
sign of liberalization as well as growing individualism.[49] But the popularity of
cohabitation hardly signals a radical or even a significant rejection of monogamous
commitment among heterosexuals.[50] In NATSAL-2 undertaken 1999–2001, the

majority of cohabiting people stated that their 'ideal relationship in five years time' was marriage, with no other sex partners (57.9 per cent of cohabiting men; 60 per cent of cohabiting women).[51] Among singles at the time, 34 per cent of men and 31.3 per cent of women desired monogamous cohabitation with a live-in partner five years down the line and 39.7 per cent of single men and 45.7 per cent of single women wanted to be monogamously married. Only 1.6 per cent of single men and 0.8 per cent of single women wanted 'no regular partners but casual partners when I feel like it'; 2.4 per cent of single men and 0.3 per cent of married men wanted a few regular partners; these were 0.2 and 1.6 per cent for women, respectively. Overall, non-monogamous relationships were cited as ideal by one in eight men and one in twenty women.[52] These figures varied by age, class and region, with class representing the most suggestive differences. Both men and women in 'social class I' – the professional elite – preferred relational monogamy, and particularly marriage, to those in class V, who also substantially preferred the idea of living apart from the partner in five years. This may be to do with the greater strain of shared financial life among those with low incomes or potentially unstable employment.[53] So while the sexual options available to the unmarried had undoubtedly expanded, and were being utilized (in the lower age of first intercourse, for instance), these figures suggest that sexual opportunity in this period was overlaid with the expectation of the monogamy of a traditional marriage.

Meanwhile, despite rates falling, marriage retained an enthusiastic, large-scale following. In 1982, an inquiry carried out by the Study Commission on the

Table 8.8 Ideal relationship in five years' time, by marital status*
Base'all

	Men				Women			
	Marital Status				Marital Status			
	Married	Cohabiting: opposite sex partner	Divorced, separated, widowed	Single	Married	Cohabiting: opposite sex partner	Divorced, separated, widowed	Single
	%	%	%	%	%	%	%	%
Prefer to have no sex activity	0.5	0.3	0.8	0.7	0.5	0.4	1.6	1.2
No regular partners but casual partners when I feel like it	0.4	0.4	3	1.6	0.2	0.3	1.3	0.8
A few regular partners	0.3	0.7	1.4	2.4	0.2	0.1	0.7	1.6
One regular partner but not living together	1	1.5	16.6	13.8	1.7	1.6	25.3	1.6
Not married but living with a partner and some sex activity outside the partnership	0.6	4.3	2.5	5.4	0.3	2.3	1	2.9
Not married but living with a partner and no other sex partners	0.7	32.9	29.8	34	0.7	33.7	27.8	31.3
Married with some sex activity outside the marriage	7.2	2	3.4	2.3	2.6	1.4	0.9	1.7
Married with no other sex partners	89.4	87.9	42.5	39.7	93.9	60	41.6	45.7
Bases (weighted)	222.5	871	232	2165	2381	966	404	1594
Bases (unweighted)	1540	608	302	2124	2455	974	685	2089

*Due to small base, respondents with a same-sex cohabiting partner are excluded from the table.

Figure 1 Ideal relationship in five years' time by marital status, NATSAL-2, Table 8.8, p. 82. Republished by kind permission on behalf of NATSAL.

Seeking Love in Modern Britain

Table 8.10 Ideal relationship in five years' time, by social class

Base: All (except those who had no job in the last 10 years)

Social Class						
	I	II	IIINM	IIIM	IV	V
Men	%	%	%	%	%	%
Prefer to have no sex activity	-	0.3	0.5	0.5	0.9	0.9
No regular partners but casual partners when I feel like it	-	0.1	0.8	1.9	1.6	0.5
A few regular partners	0.1	0.9	1	0	1.3	2.2
One regular partner but not living together	4.1	3.5	6.9	5.1	8.3	6.2
Not married but living with a partner and some sex activity outside the partnership	2.6	2.6	4.1	2.7	3.2	4.5
Not married but living with a partner and no other sex partners	15.4	16.5	23.7	19.5	23.0	20.3
Married with some sex activity outside the marriage	4.2	4.5	3.6	4.3	6.2	4.8
Married with no other sex partners	73.5	71.7	59.3	65.1	55.5	60.6
Women						
Prefer to have no sex activity	0.4	0.4	0.7	1.0	0.7	1.0
No regular partners but casual partners when I feel like it	-	0.3	0.2	0.8	0.5	0.9
A few regular partners	-	0.3	0.2	0.1	0.3	0.2
One regular partner but not living together	3.2	4.6	5.0	8.1	8.2	10.0
Not married but living with a partner and some sex activity outside the partnership	0.9	1.2	1.2	1.6	1.5	2.5
Not married but living with a partner and no other sex partners	12.3	15.0	16.9	17.1	21.0	15.7
Married with some sex activity outside the marriage	3.0	3.0	1.9	2.9	1.6	1.8
Married with no other sex partners	80.3	76.3	73.9	68.4	56.1	68.0
Bases (weighted)						
Men	*381*	*1469*	*652*	*1517*	*721*	*240*
Women	*153*	*1254*	*1745*	*387*	*838*	*212*
Bases (unweighted)						
Men	*322*	*1268*	*565*	*1188*	*601*	*204*
Women	*200*	*1546*	*1996*	*443*	*952*	*246*

Figure 2 Ideal relationship in five years' time by social class, NATSAL-2, Table 8.10, p. 83. Republished by kind permission on behalf of NATSAL.

Family found that 90 per cent of young people expected to marry.[54] Scholars such as Sharon Boden, Chrys Ingraham and Celia Lury have analysed the attachment to marriage as a growing consumer obsession with the wedding as a collection of symbols asserting heteronormative romance.[55] Certainly, the public response to Princess Diana's wedding – watched by 750 million people globally – implied if anything an intensifying conception of marriage as a fairy-tale, whose universality and widespread problems did nothing to dent its popular appeal and perhaps even enhanced it.[56] Weddings, which decreased throughout the 1980s and 1990s, became more expensive, reaching £16,000–£17,000 on average in the UK in 2005.[57] Feminist scholars Jackie Stacey and Lynne Pearce, who organized a British conference on romance in 1993, recalled a media frenzy stemming from the 'combined fascination and anxiety with romantic love … against all the odds (social, political, intellectual)'.[58] Susan Faludi argued that the heightened discourse on the benefits of coupledom and marriage in the 1980s and 1990s particularly targeted single women.[59]

So far this chapter has attempted to explore some of the empirical evidence of the change in heterosexual relationality in the 1970s, 1980s and 1990s, focusing on single-person households, divorce and attitudes to cohabitation. It now turns to the psychological and cultural context surrounding singles to investigate first the emergence of new theories of self and relationship; second, trends in thinking about couples and coupling, and third, perceptions of singleness. I argue that increased romantic choice combined with greater pressure to exploit its potential produced a paradox which shaped the development not just of marital disharmony as has been widely argued, but of the modern British single. Echoing a Foucauldian idea of sexual liberalization, I suggest that for many singles in this period, the appearance of greater freedom actually meant new forms of constraint. Singles experienced self-inflicted pressure to take control over romantic destiny, the fear of ending up alone, genuine loneliness and the sense of being socially abnormal. These factors informed singles' turn to mediated dating and helped the industry grow.

'The age of the meaningful relationship': self and other

Romantic relationships have been widely historicized through a shift from the 'self-overcoming' marriage-oriented model to a model of 'inward-looking authenticity', in which people sought more in terms of personal development and happiness from their relationships.[60] Such self-ward facing developments tally with recent historical work positing multifarious new forms of individualism from the 1970s. For Robinson et al., these emerged not in the Thatcherite years but in the previous decade's leftist liberation projects, with feminism the best example of a movement at once concerned with the collective and rooted in the centrality of individual experience.[61] And in his major study of community and class in modern Britain, Jon Lawrence has rejected a collectivist view of working-class life in the post-war decades, arguing that the desire for community and belonging among the working class has long been in dynamic tension with 'individualism and concern for the self'.[62]

In terms of romance, Claire Langhamer has most recently and thoroughly made the case for the mid-century period as the moment in which love and marriage became burdened with greater expectations for self-realization.[63] The quest for authenticity in feeling and experience, however, has longer roots.[64] Scholars have differed over the timing of the shift towards individualism and the self, with some rooting it in the pre-Freudian period and some directly as a result of Freud.[65] Twentieth-century critics such as Adorno mocked what he saw as the obsession with the authentic in Germany, particularly in relation to emotion; Queenie Leavis had also despaired at modern readers' critical metric of the 'touching' and 'the true'.[66] Yet if the older discourse was principally concerned with either shallow sentimentality or the labelling of abnormality and the assignment of pathologies, the 'individual' gradually took on new resonances throughout the twentieth century, extending into the vernacular, the personal and the everyday.[67] Langhamer has suggested some of the ways in which ideas of individual psychic well-being shaped the vocabularies surrounding love in the 1940s and 1950s. Her map of evolving models of selfhood and self-actualization in mid-century Britain concerns the desire to find betterment in an emotional, not a clinical sense: 'love promised an emotional connectivity which would improve those involved by creating something more than the sum of its parts: the co-actualizing heterosexual couple.'[68]

Langhamer's framework feeds into a broader chronology of psychology suggested by Mathew Thomson, who has argued that the discourse of the knowable, treatable self changed significantly in the 1960s and 1970s, although never uniformly.[69] Critics in this period took aim at the expanding remit of the self. In 1971, AE Dyson attacked contemporary education, born of the requirements of the welfare state, for its 'labyrinthine . . . self-analysis': 'the modern "self" is at once too sacred and too shattered to be pulled together in old-fashioned ways'.[70] The push to 'self-actualize' in the 1970s and 1980s was also widely linked to the spread of the 'the therapeutic attitude', manifested in a wealth of new publications, wide-ranging discussion of psychological factors in social, political, personal and medical spheres, and a quadrupling of mental health professionals between 1970 and 1995 in both the US and Britain.[71] If the connection with therapy per se is overstated given how few could either contemplate or afford private therapy, then the pressure on individuals to 'be and use all one's essence' in 'mobilizing' themselves was more diffuse.[72] Although self-actualization did not necessarily implicate sexual union, the two concepts overlapped, with romantic success seen as a fulfilling, equal partnership as well as a sexually meaningful, compatible one. As the more countercultural 'personal growth' movement developed in Britain in the early 1970s following the proliferation of American centres like Esalen in Big Sur, the greater stress on getting in touch with the true self involved increasing focus on physical and more specifically sexual experience.[73] This went far beyond fringe movements. *Company* magazine's first 'book of the month', in its inaugural October 1978 issue, was *Self Creation* by Dr George Weinberg with a lengthy section on 'How To Get More Out of Sex', which ran alongside a piece called 'How To Love and Succeed'.[74] Other featured books included *Getting Together: A Guide To Sexual Enrichment for Couples.*[75] Marje Proops, the *Daily Mirror's* agony aunt and activist, while noting that 'the importance of good sex in marriage cannot, of course, be minimized', was 'disturbed by the modern tendency to overestimate its importance and what I regard as the wrong emphasis all too often placed on it by psychologists and counsellors'.[76]

In such light, David Shumway's designation of the 1970s and 1980s as the age of 'the meaningful relationship' seems apt; the prevalence of the word 'meaningful', alongside 'sincere', 'lasting', 'caring' in lonely hearts ads even irked some onlookers.[77] Certainly there was overlap between the politicized 'self-actualization' of the countercultural humanistic movement and more mainstream attitudes to coupling up: reflecting on his trade in the 1980s, the lonely hearts ad manager at the *New Statesman* believed that advertisers, 'at least in the serious magazines', were using the pages 'as part of the self-awareness movement' and to 'explore their selfhoods'.

> Some advertisers are regular users of the Heartsearch columns and come back with several ads a year. They experiment with image and 'stage' a new one every time. They've turned ad design into a kind of art form and try out different wordings, styles and designs; it's part of self-exploration. The same people also answer ads in abundance because they enjoy writing about themselves . . . each letter is a voyage of discovery. Some people write ten letters of reply over the weekend about themselves. They arrive here on Tuesdays and we send them on.[78]

The framing of the modern self in relation to romantic relationality was to change in other ways too. The magazine *Psychology*, which tellingly became *Psychology and Successful Living* in the mid-1960s, increasingly turned away from the traditional question of the self's inherently political and ethical relation to society, and towards the body and sexual success. As Thomson has observed, vegetarianism and clothing reform were replaced by lifestyle guides to looking and feeling good.[79] Another trend, represented by the launch of *Psychology Today* in Britain in 1975, saw the normative aims of social and spiritual healing through psychological insight replaced by a focus on digestible updates in new science and research. Nonetheless, one of *Psychology Today*'s central aims was, according to Thomson, providing 'insights for self-development'.[80] By the mid-1980s, a series of new women's magazines were targeting a readership that was 'vulnerable', 'self-critical' and 'insecure inside'.[81] *Cosmopolitan* expanded its 'Zest' section for the woman focused on 'herself' and 'relationships', as well as 'maintenance of body, soul and appearance' and therefore desirous for the insights of popular psychology.[82]

But when it came to romantic love, some commentators asserted that the desire to explore the self through love and sex was unlikely to end in happy relationships.[83] American sociologist Robert Bellah argued that love between 'self-actualized persons' was incompatible with compromise.[84] Indeed the idea that late twentieth-century people had become more selfish – wanting more materially and spiritually out of life – has been a magnet for scholars of love and intimacy from Anthony Giddens to Zygmunt Bauman.[85] Marilyn Strathern's concept of 'hyper-individualism', arising from the politics of Thatcherism, made the pursuit of an inherently compromising formation – coupledom – seem even more paradoxical in the 1980s and afterwards. Those outside academia could be even more damning about perceived selfishness.[86] As Jane Lewis has pointed out, late twentieth-century people had not morphed from self-denying to selfish, but changing patterns of selfhood accompanying numerous cultural, institutional and normative shifts had re-calibrated the meanings, stresses and desires associated with partner-hunting.[87]

Pleasure and fulfilment: the pressure to pair up

Single people in the 1970s and afterwards were under great pressure to remedy their situation for a variety of reasons. From the middle of the century, a variety of discourses – from agony columns to marriage council materials – increasingly urged heterosexual commitment to heed the ethic of authentic, true love. Yet by the 1970s, fresh importance was being assigned to 'conjugality'.[88] Following Katherine Holden's insistence that singleness is defined in relation to coupledom, these new ideas inevitably had implications for the self-perceptions of those outside relationships. Emotional connection would bring important personal development, while spiritual balm was to be attained through suitably liberated coitus – Alex Comfort's *Joy of Sex* offered not simply a how-to but an 'ethic' of sex for 'people who knew something about sex but wanted to know it all', for a deeper experience of life's pleasures.[89]

The sex-as-self media discourse seemed excessive to some. The sociologist Maurice North felt that the idea of self-fulfilment through sex had been developing for nearly seventy years, identifying DH Lawrence as 'the high priest of the religion of fulfilment by sex'.[90] Yet the 1970s, when North was writing, marked a culmination of a century of evolving professional, quasi-professional, creative, social-scientific and everyday interest in the experience of heterosexual union. At the close of the decade, literary and film scholar Stephen Heath wrote: 'I've suffered and suffer and I think others must too – it's difficult not to in our society – from "sexuality", the whole sexual fix. To the point of nausea.'[91] The emphasis on sexuality as a key platform in the relatively new field of identity politics may have been particularly felt among the academic avant-garde such as Heath.[92] But over-emphasis on sex and sexuality fatigued and dismayed more down-to-earth figures. In her reflections on its ubiquity, Proops, writing in 1976, would be unexpectedly echoed by Germaine Greer's preface to the Paladin twenty-first-anniversary edition of *The Female Eunuch* (2006) in which Greer called for 'freedom from the duty of sexual stimulation'.[93] Proops wrote:

> People have been encouraged to expect such perfection, such expertise that those who fail to achieve it can only feel a powerful and damaging sense of failure. The modern approach to sex has made it seem one of achievement. It has become a technology, a test, a performance, a kind of contest instead of a demonstration and culmination of tenderness and emotion.[94]

As Marcus Collins has shown, erotic material also proliferated in the decade, while according to Maurice North, 'the legitimating of sexual freedom' resulted in a 'public pornography' in which sex pervaded 'advertising, dancing and pop music, in the theatre, television and publishing' in ways never before so obvious and untrammelled.[95] The 'public legitimation of almost all varieties of sexual experimentation' was, according to the American sociologist Joseph Bensman, evident even in coarser language.[96]

Women and singleness

The pressure on women to pair up was particularly visible, conveyed explicitly through popular periodicals of the period and more indirectly in a variety of media promoting ways of being attractive, from makeup to diets.[97] The most notable of the women's magazines was *Cosmopolitan*, which was unique in directly targeting relationships and sex under an explicitly liberatory banner, although *Woman's Own*, an older publication and a weekly, was also concerned 'that as women we should be "our own woman"'.[98] Launched in 1972 in Britain, *Cosmopolitan* reached a circulation of 440,000 by the middle of the decade and, although circulation fell at the end of the 1970s, it remained the monthly women's magazine market leader into the 1980s.[99] *Cosmo*'s messages were various and often contradictory, but the idea that 'there is no life without a man' was persistent throughout the 1970s, and was later affixed to the magazine's ailing health in the following, 'post-feminist' decade.[100] The magazine's substructure revolved around material both sexually explicit and forthright, threaded through with stories whose moral was that both staying single and pairing with the wrong person could damage physical as well as mental health.

The uneasy attitude to female singleness was more pronounced in *Woman's Own*. In perhaps its 'one' attempt at celebrating 'the growing number of single people', the magazine set up the consensus view that 'we used to be slightly sorry for single people.[101] Of course, all they really wanted was a husband or wife to cosset and care for'.[102] Tentatively following up on 'research' showing that 'singles today are happier, healthier and more fulfilled than their married friends' – happiness, health and fulfilment being the cornerstones of coupling up correctly – the magazine notes with clear detachment, suggested by the quote marks, that 'women aren't "required" to marry any longer'.[103] Yet the argument that it might be better point blank to stay single was eclipsed by the argument that some marriages were just as lonely too. Marriage was no guarantee of happiness, but the idea that even a good marriage may not be as rewarding as single life was firmly shut out. 'There are obvious problems about being unattached,' said a quoted expert, psychologist Mike Gossop. 'Having someone else to confide in and lean on when necessary is a very important psychological support. But it would be naïve to imagine you always get that in a marriage.'[104]

Contradictions in the way women were encouraged to think about romantic status reflected the wider confusion over what opportunities could or should be accessed by singles. These contradictions came through in the debates that revolved around gender. Embracing the changes in gender politics to emerge from feminism was portrayed as a key means for women to access emotional modernity – but feminism also always threatened to undermine sexual difference and therefore ruin romance and happiness. An example of the contradictory treatment of feminism in relation to romance was in coverage of marriage and wifedom, in which the idea that giving up 'everything for one man' was not only unwise but unmodern too. 'Now I've learned to love myself,' wrote a *Company* reader in 1982, 'I am confident, and know that I can and will cope. In my opinion, self-respect is the most worthy ally any woman can have'.[105] In a 'going out alone guide', the journalist noted that 'unfortunately, some of us still have difficulty thinking of ourselves as independent. We've got stuck with the notion that it's only OK to be seen at somebody else's side'.[106] *Company* often seemed to take female liberation as a fait accompli, and was more genuine in its support for women choosing to be single for other reasons: cover stories such as 'Ways to meet men now you are liberated', 'Why it's ok *now* to be a femme fatale' and 'How to be lonely in London', if optimistic, were often more sincere than those in *Cosmopolitan*.[107] Singleness, as Janice Winship has argued, was glamorized in *Cosmopolitan*, but as a platform from which carefully modulated 'permissive' behaviour and certain types of consumption (cigarettes, holidays, fashion) could be best enjoyed.[108]

Sexually, too, singleness was both opportunity and danger, and needed careful management. Women could be vixens for a time, but to a purpose of pairing up.[109] While *Cosmopolitan* endorsed sexual exploration, the promotion of promiscuity was curtailed, with the emphasis often on pleasing 'your' man rather than pleasing many men.[110] When the man-eater model was condoned, it was done so under the banner of celebrity glamour. Actress Sarah Miles, for instance, was billed as 'the cool man-eater', in an article written, typically, by a man.[111] More often, worrying confessional stories of nymphomania – as both psychological and physical compulsion – were printed.[112] Messages were persistently mixed, with back-to-back articles promoting sexual qualities for ambient application, and marriage. Readers were offered a quiz, 'How sexy are you?', and an avowal of their sexual power ('Girls, you and your body are driving me mad'), followed by 'What I want in a wife' – according to 'forty trappable bachelors'.[113] Above all, the woman of 1972 was responsible for developing her sex life and the pressure to do so became as strong as the pressure to look attractive. However, weeklies such as *Love Affair*, 'The New Weekly of Real-Life Romances!', launched in 1971, more straightforwardly capitalized on the idea that every woman dreams of romance and desires marriage. *Love Affair*, unlike *Cosmo* and *Woman's Weekly*, was uninterested in what feminism might offer, harking back to the interests of teen magazines such as *Jackie, Honey, Marilyn, Roxy, Valentine* and *Boyfriend* and to the narrative genre of Harlequin romances, gothic novels and other forms of 'mass produced fantasies for women'.[114]

Experts

Lifestyle magazines alert us to the ways in which heterosexual pairing figured in the tug of war between normative and contested discourses of gender directed at women, and how those discourses were shaped through the quasi-expertise of journalist, fashion editor, agony aunt and first-person confessor. Yet the evolution of post-1960s relationship wisdom promoting the benefits (rather than the propriety) of monogamous pairings extended beyond women's literature, especially via the amateur expert.[115] A measure of the burgeoning involvement of both experts as well as ordinary people in the drama of relationship formation and maintenance, as well as failure on both counts, was in the surprisingly vigorous trajectory of the agony column. Marje Proops noted that despite the proliferation of family services and sexually educative information in the 1970s, she and her colleagues were filling a 'vast need' left unanswered by both church and state.[116]

Agony aunts of the 1970s reflected but also influenced the views and experiences of a substantial number of Britons. Their increasingly liberal attitudes to sex, marriage and singleness, particularly where women were concerned, were therefore a social force extending well beyond newsprint, and a key part of the relational context in which singles of the 1970s, 1980s and 1990s set about their search for love. Their own reflections, some of which are considered here, point to the urgency with which people were trying to make sense of themselves and their situations in relation to a prevailing belief that getting sex right was vital to happiness.

The trajectory of the agony aunts themselves point to the growing emphasis on having more sex and better sex. Adrian Bingham has identified several phases in the popularity of agony columns, with a wide-ranging popularity by the 1930s and 1940s for columns that, nonetheless, kept to strict moral discipline. The 1960s saw more earnest emphasis on open-mindedness and female sexuality.[117] Proops declared of sexual union: 'Without it (or without the best of it) life is arid, boring, wearying, unenticing, uneventful, uninspiring. With it (or the best of it) life is rewarding, exciting, moving, amusing, exhilarating and splendid. Those who maintain the myth that sex isn't everything have my profound pity.'[118] By 1974, the *News of the World* had assembled 'a team of 100 experts' and the section cost £100,000 a year to run, while Proops had a team of 'eight dedicated girls'.[119] In 1974, Claire Rayner at *The Sun* estimated that she received between 700 and 1,500 letters per week.[120] In 1976 Proops reflected that 'close to a million people have written to me'.[121] Proops avoided a purely cultural analysis of the huge demand for her services, stressing neither the ubiquity of eroticized cultural artefacts nor the pervasiveness of institutional sex discourse. Rather, in her reading, a genuine anxiety drove letter writers, people of all ages who had fallen between the very wide gaps between popular romance narratives, reticent parental birds-and-bees chats, scanty institutional sex education and scantier psychological guidance. 'Many people with personal problems are afraid to face doctors, scared of anyone who might seem to be authoritarian. They fear the pointing moralizing finger of blame. Or they are too inarticulate to express themselves.'[122] To those who thought her profession merited a 'nudge nudge', Proops wished she could 'invite them to read just one day's distressing mail.'[123]

The expert interest in romantic status was further accentuated by an emerging 'science of relationships' which – quite distinct from the much older field of sexology – saw a new raft of publications focusing on partner choice and the management of love. Many of these originated in the US but were published in Britain too; for example, *A New Look at Love: A Revealing Report on the Most Elusive Of All Emotions* (1978) by academic duo Elaine Hatfield and G. William Walster, who themselves were the perfect embodiment of progressive sexual union (Hatfield is credited as a founding mother of 'relationship science').[124] 'You may remember reading about Elaine Hatfield and William Walster in the newspapers or in *People* magazine', the introduction prompted (American) readers. 'They are the beautiful, hard-working pair of professors who were photographed in bed.'[125] To George Harris, erstwhile editor of *Psychology Today*, and author of the introduction, 'the underlying crisis of our time ... has to do with those problems of trust and intimacy that we discover in passionate love, and in the aftermath, if we are lucky, that is – true companionship.'[126] The ensuing 'revealing report' broke love into categories of human development, from mate selection theories at the ethological end of the spectrum to the need for validation at the psychoanalytical end. While it offered tips for successful dating and relationships, the book fell into the post-Kinsey line of regarding humans as evolutionary, not cultural products – this, in step with the language of computer dating and eventually internet dating matchmakers, was a treatment of 'the latest scientific findings', as the back cover informed readers.

A particularly revealing example of this genre was *Man & Woman*, the Marshall Cavendish Encyclopaedia of 'adult relationships', first published in 1970 and consisting of ninety-eight weekly instalments of a densely packed thirty pages. In 1972, a digest was published, called the *Encyclopaedia of Love and Sex*, which summarized key themes in terms of 'The Physiology of Sex', 'The Art of Loving' and 'The Psychology of Love'.[127] None other than Dr Alex Comfort headed up the *Man & Woman* editorial board, along with an obstetrician from Charing Cross Hospital and the National Marriage Guidance Council, which lent its 'help and support': such a board firmly demonstrated an insistence on the intermeshed nature of physiological pragmatism, sexual technique and romantic feeling. Circulation figures for the 'encyclopaedia' are unavailable, so its analytic strength lies in the ambition and scope of the encyclopaedia itself. Billing itself as 'a new kind of publication', *Man & Woman* placed the accrual of sexuo-relational knowledge at its core in almost pedagogical terms. As with Comfort's observation that his readers were those who wanted to know 'all' there was to know, *Man & Woman* encouraged readers to carefully collect each issue by placing a regular order: 'when you have completed the series, you will find you have a magnificently bound, permanent reference work' – detailed instructions followed (and were repeated severally) about how to bind the issues together.[128]

Foreshadowing many of the reader debates in *Singles* seven years later, John Wilson, editor of *Man & Woman*, fixed on 1970 as a watershed moment for sexual and romantic heterosexual relations. 'What we are witnessing … is not simply a change. It is also an enlargement, an expansion of the area of social and personal living about which questions may be asked.'[129] Articles followed including those such as 'The playground of marriage', which asserted that 'for a man and a woman love-making can be a beautiful and satisfying experience' only if 'they … understand and care for each other's needs': a world of bliss could be had for those lucky enough to have a partner (and a self) with sufficient emotional dexterity.[130] But sexual heat was the ubiquitous visual code of *Man & Woman*: the marriage article, one among many, was paired with a picture of a man kissing a woman's naked breast. The next article considered whether men can get away with loving (and having) two women, before the lens zooms outward to consider the broad question, 'How permissive is the permissive society?' – accompanied with (another) picture of a slim, naked woman atop a man's shoulders at a festival.[131] Subsequent issues continued this relentless formula of the reflective, the coaxing, the smoothly liberatory, the visually titillating, the empirical and the diagrammatic (genitalia was repetitively depicted in textbook style).

But while promoting all the possibilities of 'cordon bleu' sex, the monogamous model still underpinned analysis, with lifelong single people seen as troubled outsiders; even possibly pathological. In 'The men who won't get married', bachelors were diagnosed with 'emotional alienation' that 'may stem subconsciously from childhood fears and inhibitions' – their unsmiling photos, ranged mugshot-style down the side of the page, enhanced the optics of marginality.[132] Sex was always best enjoyed in marriage, and marriage best enjoyed in sex: it not only 'provides a good basis for marriage as a whole' but it is 'the fullest expression of two people's love for each other'.[133]

Moreover, a growing emphasis on partner 'compatibility' stemming from psychological research and presented as the science of experts fed hopes of finding 'the one', and added importance to the notion of correct selection both sexually and emotionally. The idea that some people were right and some irrevocably wrong for one further turned up the heat on singles, who not only had to contend with the fear of emotional and physical withering without sexual love, but of making the wrong choice should they meet someone. In an article called 'Sexual incompatibilities', the *Encyclopaedia of Love and Sex* warned that 'sexual incompatibilities can irrevocably undermine and disrupt a marriage', and could stem from such helpless factors as 'social conditioning'.[134] Such assertions coincided with the extension of both personality and compatibility testing among psychology researchers; by 1964, a large swathe of books on family research focused on questions of mate choice and in 1970, the American researchers Bernard Murstein and Zick Rubin wrote their 'taxonomy of love' and 'The measurement of romantic love', respectively.[135] These took an ongoing, American-led interest in attraction and dating behaviours into a realm of more depth, seeking a range of more primal factors in determining emotional and sexual response.

The interest in compatibility in mate choice and its central role in creating long-term romantic harmony extended beyond the social sciences. Astrologers were particularly interested in this line of research in conjunction with the softer-edged type of psychological 'humanism' discussed above. Straddling the resurgent school of 'parapsychology' – with its emphatic emphasis on telepathy and out of body experiences – along with New Age wisdom and the more pragmatic strand of behaviourism emerging from institutionalized psychology, astrologists defended their craft as a 'basis for understanding' how a potential partner ticked.[136] Decoding their 'program[ming]' could 'show what each individual is looking for in a relationship and in a partner and what each one needs'.[137] Notably, the email address of one successful matchmaker contained an astrological term, while Brian Snellgrove, founder of The London Village dating and social club in the 1970s, was an entrepreneur and 'psychic' and to this day coaches therapists in Kirlian energy photography.[138] In the 1970s, women's magazines such as *She* began promoting computerized horoscope services; by 2000, between 25 and 70 per cent of the adult population read one (the width of this range testifies to the unreliability of the measurement).[139] And if the idea of partner compatibility captured a wide range of imaginations, the belief in the romantic applicability of star signs was also widespread beyond committed spiritualists, forming part of a wider 1970s interest in psychic powers extending beyond the fringe into the readership of, for example, *The Times* newspaper.[140] Astrological dating agencies were advertised, alongside credulous articles exploring the validity of star signs.[141] *Singles* magazine made much of star signs too: one reader wrote a letter encouraging the magazine to stipulate that personal advertisers state their sign: 'a very reliable method of finding a compatible partner'.[142]

Across a variety of discourses, single people felt the pressure to pair, often expressing frustration and alienation in terms of 'discrimination' in a society dominated by 'the couples' philosophy'.[143] This was a society still wed to traditional notions of coupling up rather than a more liberal or simply more just world in which singles were treated with 'equal' rights and respect. One reader, writing into *Singles* magazine suggesting a range of measures the magazine might adopt to remedy the punitive social position of singles, advocated countering couples' hegemony with 'articles on singles [in] other countries so that singles in Britain recognize the normality of their existence'.[144] The problem, however, was wider than the persistence of a 'norm' structured around the romantic ideal of long-term partnerships and marriage. Not only was the couple still a normative fixture, but sex – in being extricated from marriage – had become instrumentalized through agony aunts and authors like Comfort as a conduit for a fulfilling type of pleasure. If it was cultivated, that pleasure could be integral to personal development. Singles were often reminded that they were not only missing out on love, but on the promise and pleasure of sex too. For some, the struggle to carve out a fulfilling identity under these circumstances was deeply vexed, made worse by the very real problems of isolation and loneliness.

The problem of loneliness

Commercial matchmaking, singleness and urban alienation have been linked since the nineteenth century. As stated in the Introduction to this book, London had long been known as a lonely place; what W T Stead called 'the city of dreadful solitude'.[145] In 1890, General Booth, advocate of marriage bureaux, decried the impossibility of provincial courtship rituals in London, where 'many hundreds, nay thousands, of young men and young women, who are living in lodgings are practically without any opportunity of making the acquaintance of each other, or of any one of the other sex!'[146] But in the late twentieth century loneliness, a 'disease' seen to face singles above all, extended far beyond the capital, sometimes even reaching a national platform. In the Crosby by-election of 1981, from an eclectic party mix, Donald Potter – the founder of a Young Conservatives lonely hearts group called Close Encounters – wanted to install a phone line for lonely people for The Humanitarian Party.[147] This was clearly facetious, but it was another example of the way in which loneliness had taken its place in the roll-call of symptoms of modern malaise.

The full range of the experience of social isolation in Britain is beyond the scope of this study. Moreover the majority of my subjects, and the targets of the growing dating industry, fell within the ages of twenty to seventy and were generally within an actively aspirational framework of personal and economic striving rather than of elderly poverty and social neglect. I therefore sketch here aspects of the cultural more than the social context of loneliness, first as a problem, then transmogrified into opportunity.

Whereas loneliness is often figured as a universal, atemporal component of the human condition, alienation – marked by the tenor of the relationship between individuals and social structures – is a sociological term usually linked to a notion of 'modernity'.[148] The two clearly intersect, but unlike loneliness, alienation in Western societies has been an explicit, wide-running motif in twentieth-century art and sociology, and its thematic territory is useful in considering the context of a predominantly metropolitan singles industry. The proliferation of urban dating services served growing numbers of people without the community or other social or personal bonds to meet a partner. As Lonely Hearts, the 1977 documentary for Thames TV made clear, some of the most lonely were also signed up to numerous services; one young man it featured belonged to three dating agencies and also placed personals in the London Weekly Advertiser and Time Out. Such admissions were valuable, and – as my own research experience showed – not readily available, due to a heavy layer of reticence surrounding romantic loneliness, perceived as a deep-seated vulnerability. One Lonely Hearts subject insisted nobody (until then) knew about her ad in Time Out: 'it's all very hush hush; people think there's something wrong with you, and perhaps there is.' The influx of young adults into the metropolis in the 1970s who had left behind home comforts and community relationships, of which this young woman was one, could suffer greatly. Catering to them were several new services whose focus was not simply on courtship but also simply providing human contact to people who in some cases were near suicidal with loneliness; these included Nexus and The London Village, with 2,500 members in 1977, aimed at 'anchoring' people by 'breaking down' the metropolis into a series of local events.[149]

Frank Furedi argues forcefully in *Therapy Culture* that 'the most significant feature of therapeutic culture is not so much the promotion but the distancing of the self from others', a process of fragmenting informal dependencies that 'both reflects and promotes the trend towards … alienation'.[150] Durkheim's concept of 'anomie' described what happened when norms were violently disrupted by rapid social or economic change. Bereft of the limits and rules required for psychological integration, a catastrophic disjunct between internal desires and external structures opened up, leaving people floating dangerously outside a meaningful framework. According to Durkheim, writing on the cusp of the twentieth century, the fatal effects of living a life untethered by embedded historical structures hit the romantically separated particularly hard, since the institution of marriage provided an essential horizon in which the potentially endless itch of (male) desire could be contained. Bachelors, experiencing unbounded freedom, would be more likely to succumb to severe depression.[151] Georg Simmel, also working at the turn of the twentieth century, pioneered the concept of alienation as a by-product of 'modern' urban life, a seam that has continued to be richly ploughed by sociologists.[152]

The sociology of alienation in cities had reached saturation for some by the 1970s: in his classic *Soft City*, Jonathan Raban's opening description of a pleasant feeling of dislocation is accompanied by the weary thought that: 'A sociologist, I suppose, would see [being "adrift" and disoriented] as classic symptoms of alienation, more evidence to add to the already fat dossier on the evils of urban life'.[153] All the same, the imaginative terrain of Raban's London revolves around estrangement, down to the deepest psychic level: 'If a city can estrange you from yourself, how much more powerfully can it detach you from the lives of other people, and how deeply immersed you may become in the inaccessibly private community in your own head'.[154] For Raban, the proliferation of dating services was a central image of the isolating experience of 1970s urban life. He noted that

> coming out of the fog, making oneself visible and available, is prickly and difficult' but that 'one can, if one is sufficiently bold or desperate, advertise one's loneliness in the newspaper … in the Personal Column, you can reach into fog by proxy, then see who comes to you through the mailbox: Here loneliness has a solidarity, even a kind of respectability; fellow isolates are stacked neatly in columns of fine type.[155]

Raban was damning about the practice, however, viewing personals as meaningless 'overworked' missives delivered 'in the language of bruisedness, of feeling too exposed'.[156] Advertising for a partner, then, was 'one of the darker freedoms of the city [in which] the individual [is] at liberty to barely exist . . . [the personals] bear witness to the stunted conception of character which the city permits as its worst'.[157] Indeed, in Raban's brand of urban lyricism, those singles who advertise have been 'consumed' by the 'latent discontinuity, emptiness and helpless solipsism' that is always threatened in the city.[158] Considering that in 'the last two or three years the computer-dating industry has mushroomed spectacularly', he noted the way it 'boldly exploits the shame of loneliness, and answers to the peculiarly big-city condition of sexual isolation'.[159] The city and the computer had much in common, since both were 'mysterious and impersonal'.[160] The imagery of lonely singles suffering urban alienation, set against the whirring of impersonal machinery, shaped popular depictions too: *Lonely Hearts* repeatedly panned across desolate nocturnal scenes of London, from lonely traffic lights changing from red to green on isolated roads, to a chaotic constellation of bright lights illuminating an otherwise incomprehensible black terrain. Unlike the makers of *Lonely Hearts*, however, Raban was content to limit his observations to Dateline slogans and thumbnail sketches of harried lonely commuters. Yearning singletons have long lent themselves to pastiche, and the work of this book in excavating the experience of daters beyond such pastiche remains clear.

The problem of loneliness was not, of course, new in the 1970s, but its outlines had changed along with lengthening lifespans, norms around autonomy, privacy and communal living, and changes in access to the housing stock, for instance with the end of rent control (Rent Act of 1957). Amy Froide has shone a light on early modern single women, 'imagined as isolated and lonely individuals, bereft . . .' in contemporary perceptions.[161] She shows, however, that the prevalence of widowhood helped normalize the never-married, estimated at up to 27 per cent of the population in the seventeenth century, and that a close network of same-sex relationships characterized their lives in ways that would disappear in the centuries following.[162] Katherine Holden has drawn attention to the high numbers of unmarried men and women in Britain in the forty years leading up to 1931: only one-half of adults over fifteen were married at any one time, while over a third never married.[163] But in the post-war years higher marriage rates added stigma to those who remained solo – in 1961, only one in five women had never been married.[164] Holden has explored the ways in which single women in particular suffered from isolation in the post-war years, caught between poor pay, high rents and the stigma created by record high marriage rates. The spreading popularity of the playboy image left men 'less isolated', while bachelors were more likely than spinsters to be taken in by families because of their perceived need for domestic services.[165] Even so, as the sociologist Peter Townsend found in his study of old age in Bethnal Green, 'these kinds of relationships had their boundaries' – one such 'surrogate son' felt that his 'age and single status made him reluctant to get too close to them'.[166] Studies of mid-century loneliness centred on the elderly: Townsend found that the ten most isolated people of a survey of 203 over-sixties were single or childless.[167] In 1961, the unmarried were also found to be over-represented in NHS hospitals, homes for the elderly and psychiatric hospitals.[168]

Yet in some ways, the picture for unmarried people was less lonely than it would become in the following decades. American observers were particularly convinced that contemporary life had birthed an acute form of widespread loneliness: 'Life … has exploded, and loneliness is one main ingredient in the fallout', wrote the social researcher Suzanne Gordon in 1976.[169] Concern about the social disconnectedness of life caused by the disintegration of American community resurfaced in Robert Putnam's global best-seller *Bowling Alone* in 2000.[170] In Britain, many, particularly single and childless older women, lived in boarding houses or hotels; of 20,000 people living in such places in 1952, there was more than twice as many women.[171] By the late 1970s, large boarding houses, with their modicum of daily human contact, had faded away, while the 1980s saw the construction of more self-contained social housing, including tower blocks and suburban single occupancy retirement units with porters rather than co-lodgers and landladies. Private as well as public house-building firms responded to forecasts about the rise of single-person households, offering 'starter homes' and 'studio flats' for the younger that accompanied an increase in the number of one-bedroom homes being built: Barratt Homes launched The Mayfair house for the growing number of single householders, in 1977.[172] *Singles* magazine reported in 1980 on a 'one room living' stand at the Design Centre Exhibition at Haymarket. 'Two room constructions in particular will be of interest to readers – the bachelor pad (no cooking area here) and the student's bedsit.'[173] However, while 'bedsitter land' had become a reality for many renting converted and carved up flats in London, the fresh construction of single-person residences was contained, growing only 3.5 per cent in both public and private sector housing completions between 1987 and 1990.[174] Nevertheless, single people were a significant force in the transitory rental market; those aged sixteen and fifty-nine made up 41 per cent of all privately rented furnished homes, according to Mintel and the General Household Survey.[175]

Certainly, amid the steady increase in private, self-supported living, often with financial worries (shaped but not caused, necessarily, by recession), many

Britons in the late 1970s and 1980s articulated strong feelings of isolation, loneliness and repression. The dating documentaries *Lonely Hearts* (Thames TV, 1977) and *The Love Tapes* (New Decade Films, 1979) zoomed in on struggling singles in the big city. Both focused, though not exclusively, on young people who had left provincial England, or youths spent in commonwealth countries, for London. One 28-year-old divorcee found her Asian newsagent the only source of comfort in her bedsit existence, noting: 'people gaily assume that you'll meet people [in London] and . . . but I really don't see how' while a young man who had grown up in 'Malaya' spoke of the withering loneliness of retreating in the 'evenings into our own little boxes'. An Irish driving instructor in his twenties, who ate dinner daily at a local diner before going home to watch *Match of the Day*, told the camera: 'they say loneliness is a foretaste of death; if that's the case, I've had a feast.' In *The Love Tapes*, a kind of subtle infomercial for Dateline, the main character was Barbara, who lived all alone in a flat in South Kensington, and was bowed down by the dreariness of nightly dinners for one. And single parents' loneliness was exacerbated by acute anxiety and poverty alongside their loneliness. Of an estimated 700,000 lone parents in Britain by 1976 (83 per cent of whom were women) nearly half the total were living on supplementary benefit.[176]

Singles also took advantage of agony aunts and the 'problems' pages in the expanding magazine offering, leading to several aunts – including Irma Kurtz and Marje Proops – devoting whole books, or sections therein, to the problem.[177] The issue was broached in a number of ways by the experts, from the alarmist to the pro-active. Irma Kurtz universalized and de-historicized loneliness, seeing it as a subjective feature of the human condition, but she also saw it as serving 'contemporary unhappiness and neurosis', noting that 'there are characteristics of our society which exacerbate loneliness, and because we cannot hold loneliness or see it but only feel it, loneliness has become the carthorse of our misery, dragging behind it weights as disparate as stymied lust and the despair of genius.'[178] Kurtz saw that sex was once more at the centre of many people's perception of loneliness, but wished to re-categorize 'sexual frustration' as 'irritation or misery' instead.[179]

Deborah Cohen's narrative of the nineteenth-century reverence for family privacy morphing into a widespread fear of secrecy in the post-psychoanalytic twentieth century serves as a useful reminder of the historically particular experience of marginality.[180] Spinsters and bachelors – themselves diverse groups – may have become less open to institutional and social policing as the twentieth century wore on, but Cohen's analysis reminds us that their social and emotional baggage became tethered in new, stressful ways to the axis of normal/good vs. abnormal/shameful/secret. Even the consciousness-raising movements of the 1970s sexual liberation front contributed to the pressure on people to open up all inner doors in front of others.[181] Indeed, Irma Kurtz perceptively saw the coding of abnormal/shameful in the seemingly progressive sex literature of the 1960s and 1970s: commenting on the treatment of masturbation in David Reuben's *Everything You Always Wanted to Know About Sex* (1969), in which the reader was told 'masturbation is fun . . . certainly, not as much fun as fully-fledged sexual intercourse, but the next thing to it'. Kurtz noted: 'In other words, masturbation is a private confession that no partner has volunteered or been seduced into the better game. Masturbation is the "next thing" to fully-fledged sex and therefore only a notch above nothing at all. . . Is it not shameful to exist alone in a sexual desert while everybody else is splashing around naked in the swim?'[182] Margaret Adams, author of the classic study, *Single Blessedness* (1976) also pinpointed the way shame attached to fear of being socially abnormal when single.[183] The pervasiveness of the idea that 'sociability' is 'what constitutes normal and proper behaviour', with 'solitude' its opposite, meant single people were frequently made to feel worse about being alone than they should. 'Modern society,' claimed Adams, presaging Kurtz, 'gives a very low rating to solitude'.[184] Overlapping with Cohen's later analysis, Adams blamed the destruction of privacy for the denigration of the solitary, pinpointing new mass entertainment and media, 'mega-assemblies' such as Woodstock, as pushing a 'social ideal of corporate mass involvement'. Those who eschew collective social life, Adams' study found, faced 'the fear of being categorized as odd and out of step'.[185]

Coverage of loneliness in *Singles*, Britain's only magazine for single people, helps sketch the dimensions of the issue as it was perceived in the late 1970s, since the problems of – as well as solutions to – being romantically alone were the magazine's focal point. The first five issues of *Singles* magazine saw a multi-part, in-depth feature on British loneliness as studied by the magazine's consultant psychologist Tony Lake in 1977. In it, Lake identified singles most affected by loneliness, concluding they were in their thirties and forties, not their fifties and sixties, and that 60 per cent lived alone, 17 per cent with their parents and 16 per cent with their children. Marriage had reached an all-time high in 1972, but the contemporaneous rearrangement of relational norms would soon mean that more types of people were living alone: the divorced as well as never-married women and men. Fewer people lived in lodgings with their landladies and landlords providing communal dining arrangements, and more sought privacy in bedsits.[186] Singleness in Britain was being refigured in multiple new ways in this period, from a state ripe with consumerist promise to one of sexual emancipation. It was also seen as a problem resulting in a particularly grave symptom: loneliness, often viewed as an illness which might be cured by use of dating agencies and other heterosocial activities. Singles themselves often described harrowing states of emotional and social solitude. One reader wrote in suggesting a phone-in service for singles, during 'lonely peoples' time of lowest ebb [when] you're back from the office and everyone has closed their doors and gone into the snug, the kids are in bed or out, you've broached a bottle of wine, mooned around the house, cried all over the carpet.'[187] One of the magazine's favoured first-person accounts of the single life was billed as that 'of a middle aged divorcee who is desperately lonely', while the lonely hearts ads printed at the back frequently contained the self-description 'lonely', as did those in *Time Out*.[188] *Singles* contributors were aware of being on the sharp end of contemporary freedoms, noting that 'Life is more informal these days [than in the nineteenth century], and there's no doubt we have much more freedom. Trouble is, we are free to be lonely, free to make mistakes.'[189]

As suggested by the women's magazine coverage discussed earlier, the idea that single people were necessarily to be pitied, for loneliness and for sexual frustration, was regularly contested, but the idea that they suffered, mainly from unnatural isolation, was persistent from within and without the singles community. Pierre Bourdieu's idea of pleasure as a duty for citizens of modern consumer society is suggestive here for recreating the position of singles in the 1970s and afterwards. With 'fun' – often experienced through skilful or otherwise boastable sex – a 'duty', those outside the mating matrix could suffer the injurious fate of 'individuality and self-hood' becoming misshapen.[190] Singles often expressed the uncomfortable double sense of being part of a society that for the first time encouraged its inhabitants to explore their sexuality, but which – when those people were unable to or choosing not to do so – infused them with a sense of failure. This aspect rose to the surface frequently in *Singles*. Although it was dedicated to offering ways of relieving loneliness and – if possible – enjoying the single state, the magazine nonetheless emphasized the extremities of isolation. The conception of loneliness was one peculiar to contemporary life, or 'modern' life, and was heavily pathologized: 'Whoever we are, whatever we do, we all have our occupational hazards... If you are single, then there can be little doubt that your occupational hazard is loneliness.'[191] As the introduction to the series of five articles based on Tony Lake's survey put it: 'Loneliness, in its extreme form is a killer. The feeling that nobody cares whether you live or die, whether you scream or stay silent ... can [drain from your body] every last drop of the will to live.'[192]

Sufferers abstain from suicide only by 'the total lack of feeling' wrought by the condition. 'They slump into apathy, sometimes so severe as to resemble a schizophrenic state of withdrawal and detachment.'[193]

Singles employed an eclectic mixture of experts and amateurs, including the psychiatrist Colin Brewer, struck off in 2006 for assisting suicide, of which Lake was one of those respected beyond the magazine.[194] His professional interests fit firmly within the matrix of psychologically and emotionally oriented studies of human happiness and potential discussed above. His specialism was 'communication, love and acquaintance', and he would develop his psychological career around loneliness and its corollaries, including depression. Following his short employment at *Singles*, he went on to write books including (with Ann Hills) *Affairs: The Anatomy of Extra-Marital Relationships* (1979), *Loneliness* (1980), *Relationships* (1981), *How To Cope With Your Nerves* (1983), *Living With Grief* (1984) and *Defeating Depression* (1987). Thus Lake's concern for the singles' affliction was earnest and in-depth, with a methodology more plausible than many used in *Singles* articles, although his commercially expedient links to Dateline framed the study. 'Much to [Dateline's] credit, they were also interested in the other side of the coin' – not simply in 'their business' of 'friendship, happiness'.[195] Lake conducted a pilot with 'thirty single people' from a Dateline 'Breakaway' holiday, 28 per cent of whom said they were 'very lonely people'.[196] Those who had never been married were more lonely than those who had, but the majority rejected the notion that loneliness crept up like a disease, instead blaming themselves for the tendency 'to expect too much from the people they meet'.[197] But Lake acknowledged that the sample of thirty was too small, and that drawing from Dateline customers would produce bias, so he next designed a questionnaire suitable for larger groups. He advertised in the *Evening Standard*, the *Sunday Times* and on LBC radio: ultimately 1,500 people returned the questionnaires. Lake's final sample were spread evenly throughout the British Isles and covered the age range between sixteen and seventy-six, and although they came from 'all social classes' they were 'predominantly white, and white-collar'. More than a third had experienced 'real loneliness' in the month before filling in the questionnaire. Although 50 per cent said they did not consider themselves lonely people, Lake was concerned, advising that 'Pain and misery on this scale must not be ignored', and that 'the reality of loneliness is that an estimated one and a half million single people in Britain are desperately lonely at this very moment'.[198] Although Lake was interested in personality types, loneliness was not overly individually pathologized in his report; instead, it was seen as a social ill, 'accepted as normal' just as was 'scurvy once, and pelegra,

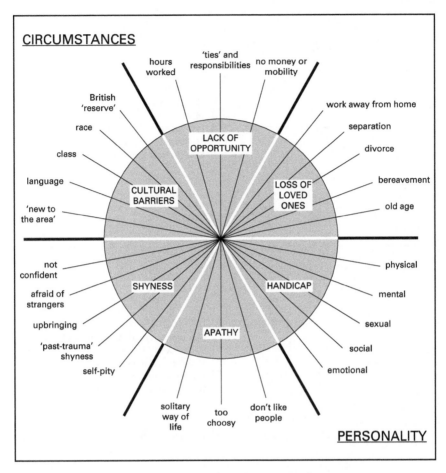

Figure 3 Causes of loneliness chart, *Singles*, 3 (August 1977), p. 34.

rickets and diabetes – all diseases which result from deficiencies which modern medicine can understand. Health should not be a lottery in this way. Loneliness is the sort of progressive disease we would all be better without.'[199]

If Lake's concern stemmed from a clinical tradition favouring facts over judgements, the main node of his research on loneliness concerned social skills, not mental health. Focusing on a more mainstream application of the skills practised in personal growth and encounter groups, Lake firmly located loneliness within a nation lacking 'social skills'. Inspired by the British social psychologist Michael Argyle's 1972 modifications to 'communication cycle' theory, which analysed the patterns of successful one-to-one conversations, Lake identified much of the problem in terms of 'communication disabilities'. Particular attention

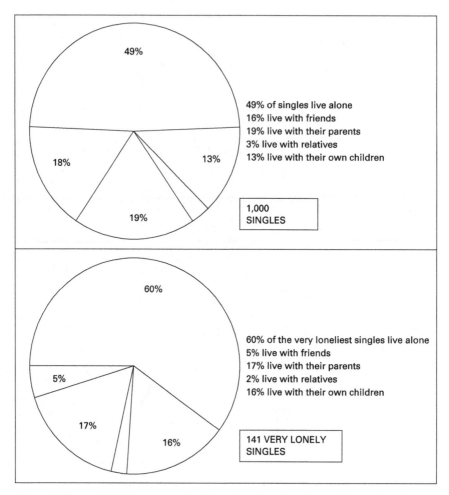

Figure 4 'How singles live': 1,000 singles and 141 'very lonely singles', *Singles*, 2 (June 1977), p. 10.

was paid to body language and facial expression, which was read to exemplify the severing of self from other, rooted in painful personal history. Case study 'Bernard', for instance, who was trying to meet a wife through computer dating, lonely hearts and dating agencies, could immediately be identified as shy, damaged and unhappy in his own skin. 'One only has to look at Bernard to see the disturbed nature of his body movements during communication to realize how deeply damaged he has been by [past] experiences. He takes no pride in his face.' Bernard's body could be read even more closely:

> Only the mouth moves when he talks. The muscles at the side of his mouth are still and short of exercise. By the side of his eyes are equally unused muscles...

He tends to avoid eye contact, and keeps his head still while he talks. He does not gesture . . . His tone of voice is monotonous.[200]

However, 'in no other way than by watching his eyes, is it possible to tell that Bernard has ever been loved ... he wants to be married, but seems to be an entirely sexless person.'[201] Lake is clear that social isolation was bad, but romantic isolation could be even worse:

> the deprivation of intimacy has long-term and short-term consequences. In the chronic cases sexuality can become so badly damaged by ill-use or lack of use that it is permanently destroyed, and the person has no will left to live socially.[202]

The role for dating agencies in all this was clear: 20 per cent of the sample had used computer dating (presumably including Dateline's competitors – there is also the possibility that this number was massaged to please the *Singles* editor, Dateline's director John Patterson), 16 per cent lonely hearts ads and nine per cent dating agencies, still referred to as 'marriage bureaux'.[203]

While *Singles* magazine had a clear vested interest in deploying resources on the horrors of loneliness, the spectre of loneliness seemed to be haunting Britain beyond the magazine's pages. Marje Proops devoted a chapter in her spare *Dear Marje* to 'the anguish of loneliness', which she found afflicted people of all ages, but particularly the old and the shy. Proops diagnosed the problem in two ways specific to the period, both demographic and epidemiological. These were women's longer lives and 'soaring' divorce. Testifying to the topicality of rising numbers of divorced women and single mothers, she noted the proliferation of singles clubs, which sorely lacked male members.[204]

But in other sectors, singleness was being recast as an opportunity to be briskly managed by individuals and maximized by marketers – succumbing to loneliness could and should be avoided. Thus the increasing emphasis on 'lifestyle' marketing, directed towards a more affluent population of young and middle-aged professionals provided a dissonant counterpoint to Lake's brand of honest, even shocking appraisal of real single experience – a proliferation of (sporadically) celebratory depictions of single life in marketing and publishing suggested a world of luxurious steaks for one and sunny group holidays. The can-do attitude towards personal happiness – with or without a partner – also came through explicitly in *Singles*, too. In addition to the 'successful single' column promoting a pro-active and entrepreneurial model for singleness, *Singles* more directly addressed the lonely. In September 1977, *Singles*' editor John Patterson wrote a telling comment in relation to the ongoing study of loneliness in the magazine:

To pity the lonely is to patronise them... To argue that loneliness is not the fault of the lonely is equally unhelpful because it suggests that the individual can do nothing about it... Our policy for the problem of loneliness should be tough and practical. We should increase self-sufficiency of the lonely and help them to help themselves.[205]

Solutions: romantic self management

The 1980s and 1990s were boom decades for magazines, and market research commissioned to shape magazine content repeatedly looked to the young, single and middle class as an influential market, leading to the launch of magazines such as *Esquire* (1991), *Frank* (1997–2000) and *Minx* (1996–2000).[206] If marketers were paying increasing attention to the growing single population, then marketing language grew more prevalent in the ways in which singles were addressed in other spheres. The attractions and prospects of date-hunters were increasingly packaged in a brusque vocabulary borrowed from the commercial world of management and sales, also integrating threads from feminist discourse.

Both men and women across the broad middle of the class spectrum encountered a changing portfolio of terms and concepts encouraging them to approach their single state in the spirit of management and enterprise or – as Eva Illouz has suggested – of 'emotional intelligence' whereby 'emotional management and emotional success' are 'explicitly' connected.[207] This message came from the media, a small crop of dating manuals and from matchmakers themselves. 'Emotional identification with our working environment has led us to apply goal-oriented office skills to finding a mate. If you're looking for a job, you go to an employment agency; if you want a holiday, you call a travel agent; if you want a partner, why not try a dating agency?' wrote a *Guardian* journalist in an article about the high numbers of single women signing up at dating agencies.[208] Karen Mooney, of the Sarah Eden agency agreed: 'People don't want to waste time... It's better to put your cards on the table at the start. That way, you're fishing where the fish are.'[209]

The final section of this chapter focuses on two examples of this genre, which – written as tailored, well-intentioned guidance for ordinary singles – are more telling than the faster-flowing cascade of media representation around singleness in the 1990s.[210] They provide the final piece of the contextual landscape out of which grew the dense and motley crop of commercial matchmaking ventures between 1970 and 2000, and which were instrumental in the development of 'the single'.

For singles lacking Helen Fielding's 1996 creation Bridget Jones's charmed way with chardonnay, lecherous colleagues and close-knit friends, not to mention a family with eligible connections like Mr Darcy, it was necessary to take control. Across the period from 1970 to 2000, but with increasing intensity in the 1980s and 1990s, intense efforts were made by matchmakers not only to normalize but to render mediated dating as sensible and even aspirational. The status of mediated dating remained volatile, but the sometimes intense stigma that remained was set aside a solidifying lingo of pragmatic life management, aligned in ways it hadn't been in the 1970s to the concept of professional busyness. Two figures emerged: the upmarket, time-poor professional keen to outsource the quest for romantic felicity and the more middle of the road provincial single suffering loneliness but – thanks to ever greater numbers of dating experts – endowed with more options. John Cockburn, like Tony Lake, was a teacher-turned-psychologist who in the 1980s joined the ranks of experts and amateurs in the psychological and social sciences who were turning their attention to psycho-sexual dilemmas. Like Lake, Cockburn focused on those predominantly facing the provincial rather than the prosperous urban professional single. His book *Lonely Hearts: Love Among the Small Ads* (1988) proposed to delve into the hidden meaning of the lonely hearts ad in the 1980s, interviewing users and ad managers, and analysing content. Cockburn felt that – whatever the reasons for the popularity of the method – 'what is sure' was an increase in loneliness 'in modern-day society'.[211] For Cockburn, as for the commentators discussed above, loneliness was considered in psycho-epidemiological terms as 'one of the great unrecognized epidemics'.[212] Nonetheless he provided a nuanced analysis of the gendered pressures facing the uncoupled, remarking that ubiquitous marketing and entertainment imagery depicted traditional heteronormative pairings, and that even if the 'same old stereotypes' had not yet caught up with reality, they left singles feeling 'short changed and displaced'.[213]

So Cockburn was admiring and encouraging of those who took steps to change those feelings, noting that advertising took 'guts and enterprise'.[214] He set about helping readers, glossing hundreds of ads to reveal what worked and what didn't – self-deprecating worked better than 'company director with yacht and second house in Paris'.[215] Above all, Cockburn commended the ads that displayed 'considerable self-knowledge' – though like one taking up a whole paragraph long in *Time Out*, they could cost dear. In this context, mentioning shortcomings could be a bonus, showing 'how balanced, self-aware and sincere' the advertiser is.[216]

In itemizing the pluses and minuses of mediated dating through the personals, Cockburn himself deployed a language of economics, using an extended metaphor to explain the demand for 'single girls', intensely courted for providing 'payoffs wrapped in sexual, emotional and financial terms – the ones that count … they are in a buyer's market compared to many other groups, but especially when they're trading relationships'.[217] In some ways, 'advertising' was a zone of business rather than sentiment, though hardly necessarily the mark of the 'bruisedness' Raban saw.

This book suggests that the context of romantic production problematized or cancelled out the production of romantic feeling among mediated daters and I will return to this in more depth in Chapter 4. Certainly, in these accounts of the business of dating, couched explicitly in economic terms, a non-romantic vocabulary was clearly being used. Those embracing business metaphors for their mediated dating were doing so to signify approach, rather than the feeling or even a strong desire for a specific outcome. Adrian, a diamond merchant, said: "'I hope that I might meet a girl by accident but I haven't done that for a long time. That's exactly why I started advertising.'"[218] Others, like 'Susan', adopted the same systematic approach to dating as they might to problems at work. Cockburn's language and Susan's merged in their common vision of heart management:

> Susan is a highly experienced lonelyheart user and consequently has developed skills and insights into the "management" of lonelyheart activity. She keeps a folder by the phone containing all the details and has a quick reference system. Susan can locate an ad or letter within moments while on the phone to a caller.[219]

Susan's system was indeed professional-seeming and she seemed proud of that aspect: conceiving of the process of whittling down candidates as a 'job', she told Cockburn: "'What I do is put an asterisk by all the ads I think are possible… I answer about six a week, just working my way through the men's section from beginning to end.'[220] Concluding his analysis of the tactics of personal columns scourers, Cockburn reflected: 'We are also shown that certain skills or techniques are involved and these improve with practice. Their use can greatly enhance the efficiency of lonely heart dating.'[221]

The skills emphasized by Cockburn revolved around efficient processing of information about the self. But they also included developing the ability to read others, and speed and confidence of assessment among daters was another key aspect of a more seasoned crop of lonely hearts. After selecting his date from two piles ordered according to calligraphic prowess and pictorial attractiveness, the diamond merchant was amused but not convinced. With easy certainty, and showing command in the last clause of relationally intelligent lingo, he recalled that it was '"successful and pleasant [but] I wasn't that keen ... her emphasis on travel was alien to me and we didn't really gel"'.[222] His date was hardly likely to be heartbroken, having offered a casual excuse for meeting him: '"she answered my ad because her group of friends had become claustrophobic."'[223] Themes of efficiency and privacy that would come to underpin the use of internet dating were also part of the professionalized approach to dating. One dater enjoyed the fact that lonely hearts meant: '"I could be selective in the privacy of my own home,"' where '"I picked out those ones that complied with what I was asking for. You have to use some sort of yardstick to whittle down the field."'[224] Compliance, processes of elimination; this was the ossifying language of a self-controlled, platform-based approach to increasing chances that would find full realization in the algorithms of the internet age.

Linda Sonntag, a sex writer, used a different but still professional set of tropes in her useful map of dating services as she found them in 1988.[225] If Cockburn used management metaphors, Sonntag tuned in to electronics: 'I hope this book will encourage you to plug into the network of single people and see who lights up.'[226] Sonntag shared Cockburn's admiration for those who took enterprise culture into their love lives, and her book was designed to help clear up misconceptions about this 'enterprising way of getting together'. It also demonstrated a keen attention to precision of wording in the advert, advising on syntax to help clumsy advertisers accidentally repelling readers who increasingly placed value judgements in demonstrations of emotional intelligence and taste rather than in vital statistics such as income and profession. Being 'natural' and keen on the idea of romantic chemistry – thereby overriding the materialism of the method – was important. Sonntag enlisted Frances Pyne, Dateline's press officer, to advise. Good words were, in order of preference: 'Sense of humour', then 'caring', then 'attractive'. 'Slim' and 'graduate' were also good, while 'fat', 'smoking', 'sexy', 'handsome', 'funloving', 'hunk', 'gent', 'cultured', 'refined', and 'loves cuddles' sent people running.[227]

As demand for dating services grew, and strategies were refined to reflect wider shifts in occupational culture, matchmakers were keen to capitalize on the new figure of the busy Thatcherite professional. Financial deregulation in 1986, the promotion of entrepreneurs and the demarcation of enterprise zones created waves of discourse about wealth increase and professional ambition as hallmarks of the decade. Matchmakers portrayed themselves as a new kind of expert: the bosom friend able to help the busy career person outsource his or her most intimate needs. Hedi Fisher was one matchmaker who adapted swiftly to boom-time sales rhetoric, avoiding any question of stigma or the complex emotional needs of her clients. 'We enrol people in the professional and business world, with high standards, often with busy and demanding lives. We do our best to ensure that our members are attractive, reliable and well-adjusted,' she told Sonntag.[228] Meanwhile, the Picture Dating Agency offered another fin de siècle professional's service: it was a 'modern, intelligent and civilised way of meeting people – it's the 80s and 90s way'.[229]

The workplace, entrepreneurial and management tropes that increasingly infused the rhetoric of matchmakers, daters and their observers spread out with rapidity in the 1990s to bolster a new breed of experts. These were the sexperts, flirt coaches and makeover specialists who – long a staple in the US – began appearing on British television. The sexpert was different from the agony aunt because she was usually young, highly groomed and made for TV. By 2001, the BBC was ready to participate. In 2001's *Would Like To Meet*, Tracey Cox was introduced as Flirt Queen, 'psychologist, author and body language coach', and Jeremy Milnes, 'confidence coach'. Both were to put romantic no-hoper Debbie on 'a six-week assault course to romance'. These two were highly paid experts in reading and recoding humans to make them sexier. Jeremy Milnes said of Debbie: 'We've seen two different people – I want to take the one we saw [earlier] and bring her out, and the one we've seen tonight ... get rid of it'. And Tracey tried to teach Debbie by example of another woman in a bar how to flirt: 'this girl's winning the prize,' she said. 'She's doing rapid blinking, an eyebrow flash, which is what people do when they really fancy each other'. Their comments are particularly pointed in being directed at a woman, but men were not excluded from such treatment either, and could also face withering attacks on their slouching postures or poor grooming.

By the 2000s, intensification of dating expertise, dating culture and dating discourse – apparent in escalating coverage in newspaper articles across tabloids and broadsheets of statistics, crimes and services relating to singles – had entrenched dating as a potentially expensive, difficult, laborious but important pursuit.

In this chapter I have set out to discuss the principal themes in the cultural, emotional and social context surrounding the growth of the British dating industry between 1970 and 2000. Key to this is the emergence of the 'single', an identity carved out of new emphases on the importance and purpose of love, sex and coupling, as well as the acute problems that came with this framing.

Was it possible for people to fully realize themselves as single? On one hand, singles were encouraged to embrace their independence – economically and sexually. But the reality was that most people felt a longing to change their status, their desires shaped by a tangle of internal and external pressures. Psychologists, agony aunts and other experts – however compassionately they addressed their subjects – promoted a similar double-edged vision to marketers, magazines and romance scripts in films and novels. Being single was fine so long as people loved and knew themselves (in the case of fiction and film, it had to also be a temporary state). Self-knowledge and love would also make it easier to meet someone. Yet it was those people at the lowest ebb of self-confidence, the ones whose loneliness and low self-regard caused such concern for Irma Kurtz, Tony Lake and John Cockburn, who most badly wanted a partner. Thus singleness was a respectable romantic status if it reflected rigorous emotional hygiene; for others it ran a high risk of being deeply problematic, and of leaving people feeling socially and emotionally marooned. For marketers, singleness was a boon, but only concerning the well to do or upwardly mobile; once more, the people most in need of attention, the elderly, poor and utterly alone, were of the least interest to both magazine editors and the makers of dating discourse. Without youth, glamour, cash, a social life and resilient emotional health, singleness marked a troubling sort of person indeed. However the numbers of people left out of the young, beautiful, popular and rich categories was very large. The desperate wish of many of them to meet a partner or simply to find some friends was a major factor driving the development of the British dating industry in this period, whose anatomy will be drawn in the next chapter.

2

The matchmaking industry, 1970–2000

This chapter sets out the commercial terrain facing those seeking partners. The mediated dating market in pre-internet Britain was composed mainly of newspaper personals, introduction agencies and computer dating, and these are therefore the focus here. But the options facing singles also included events networks, or 'friendship clubs', such as Singles Society, whose organ was *Singles* from 1977 and the £10 a year London Village, first advertised in *Time Out* in the early 1970s.[1] While computer dating was the best-known technological approach to singleness throughout the period, sporadic publicity around other, generally short-lived electronic matchmaking solutions pointed to a sustained interest in trying to pair machines with the love quest.[2] Throughout the 1980s and 1990s in particular, the market expanded to include gadgets such as pocket 'vibe' bleepers and 'shuddering' devices, alongside TV text advertising such as the service provided by Prestel.[3] The first-ever British dating game show on TV was cited by the *Daily Mail* in 1975,[4] while in 1978, video dating, in the form of Videomatch, was launched.[5] In 1981 'radio's first dial-a-date marriage bureau' was said to have appeared.[6]

Context: the growth of the industry

Numbers of matchmaking and personals clients appeared to notably increase in real terms in the 1970s. Strict numbers are impossible to pin down, due to the unregulated status of the industry, its overblown marketing traditions hinging on unverifiable success rates, the excuse of privacy concerns in withholding data, and the fact that the people who found their matches didn't necessarily inform the agency.[7] But there are several facts that suggest a rise. One is the proliferation of businesses, from computer dating services led by Dateline (founded in 1966) to new personals sections in new magazines, to a range of new regional and London matchmaking clubs.[8]

In 1970 a *Newsnight* investigation revealed an 'estimated . . . 400 marriage bureaux in Britain' – of which only twenty-four were 'long-established', with most run out of people's homes, suggesting a recent swell in have-a-go agencies.[9] The *Daily Mail* even ran an entrepreneurial article on how to set up your own dating bureau.[10] The most solid indicator of demand – rather than supply – for singles services came from the rise in divorce rates, which tripled between 1970 and 1980 from 50,000 to 150,000 divorces.[11] In Britain, the percentage of adults married at any one time fell from sixty-five in the mid-1960s to fifty-three in 2006, with the 1970s the decade of fastest decline (after a marriage rate peak in 1972).[12] John Cockburn, the psychologist author of the scrupulous, interview-led study *Lonely Hearts: Love Among the Small Ads* (1988), observed: 'The agencies are thriving on the burgeoning divorce statistics. We know that at current rates one in three marriages will end in divorce.'[13] Divorcees were folded into the wider pool of daters rather than generating their own agencies. Lone parents, however, eventually attracted a range of specialized services particularly in travel, with help arranging holidays available through the National Council for One Parent Families, single parents charity Gingerbread and more commercial businesses such as Holiday Endeavour for Lone Parents, One Parent Family Holidays and Single Parent Travel Club.[14] Any romantic benefits to such trips were left unspecified, however. There were other regional organizations geared towards helping the lonely and struggling divorced and widows.[15]

Growing interest in an expanding offering of dating services was also evident in newspaper coverage, though the focus was more on the industry, the personalities behind it, and the bachelor/'bachelor girl' population rather than the tribulations and pain of divorcees.[16] A search of digital newspaper archives using dating terms such as 'lonely hearts' points to a notable rise in interest in the 1970s compared to the late 1960s (the impact of 'Sergeant Pepper's Lonely Hearts Club Band' by the Beatles, released in 1967, explains the rise to some extent but not entirely, as a survey of the articles makes clear).[17] In 1970, as noted in the introduction, *The Daily Mail* recorded that 'The lonely hearts business is booming as never before', and mentioned a sharp rise in personal ads placed by agencies.[18] Television programmes and other forms of entertainment appeared that for the first time explored singleness in conjunction with singles services, including *Lonely Hearts* (1977), *The Love Tapes* (1979), *Singles* (Carlton, 1993), and *Man Seeks Woman* (BBC 1996).

Personal ads

The market for personal ads expanded throughout the period mostly in London magazines and broadsheet newspapers (from the 1990s) but also in some regional newspapers and in publications like the *Jewish Chronicle*.[19] More than introduction agencies, personals gained the attention of a wider readership, since they were entertaining, looked-for sections in broader interest publications such as *The New Statesman* and *Private Eye*. In the 1980s, their spread was noticeable enough to begin attracting attention from social scientists and psychological researchers such as Robin Dunbar, the results of whose investigations of mating strategies in lonely hearts adverts were later widely publicized.[20] Dunbar, who normally worked on primates, changed tack in the 1980s 'because [lonely hearts] were so common in newspapers, every newspaper had them at that point, it struck me as a really nice little vignette'.[21]

Of the most prominent national services, *Guardian* Soulmates launched in 1995 (going online in 2002). *The Telegraph*'s Kindred Spirits personals section also launched in 1995 (and went online in 2005). *The Times* only added its print (plus voice messaging service) lonely hearts section, Encounters, in 2002. While *The Times*'s decision to offer print instead of online dating was probably influenced by a readership that preferred traditional media, the late addition of Encounters testifies to the fact that print ads retained genuine usage value and popularity. Their centuries-long precedent came from being the cheapest option and from being read by many more people than just advertisers. The A3-sized *London Weekly Advertiser* – dedicated to classified ads of all types – provided the biggest space devoted to personals in the country and was a good barometer of their growing reach. In 1970 the 'personal' or 'friends' section commanded as many or sometimes more pages than other sections (such as property or motors) and in 1971, the personal column got its own section, formatted separately.

In 1977, *Singles* publisher John Patterson also drew attention to fresh demand among solos. 'The Classified section is growing and reflects the need which many readers have of expanding their social circle', describing *Singles* as 'unique in publishing today – a special interest magazine with a potential 7½ million readers'.[22] The growth in personals after 1970 was marked: in 1987, *Time Out* ran an estimated 13,000 ads, worth £175,000 per year, up from £20,400 per year in 1974, while *Singles* had grown from around 200 ads in 1977 to 700 per issue in 1987.[23] Together, *Time Out*, *Singles* and *Private Eye* were said to have forwarded half a million replies to 30,000 ads in 1987.[24] In 1985, the *Daily Mail* declared 'from the refined souls of *The Tatler* and the ex-lecturers of *New Statesman*, to the Virgo vegan seeking playful Piscean of *Time Out* and *City Limits*, Britain is currently the world's leading market in the "heart-search" column business'.[25]

The London Weekly Advertiser

While the growing personals market attracted analyses rooted in contemporary conditions of social alienation and new freedoms, a portion of the personals landscape retained its links with an older paradigm of courtship, offering something of the self-conscious respectability forged in the 1940s heyday of the marriage bureaux, and foregrounding traditional, less flexible models of gender and class. This aspect of the post-1970 personals landscape took shape in a practice echoing the nineteenth-century matrimonial business model, in which matchmakers placed adverts of behalf of clients. *The London Weekly Advertiser* (1939–82) was the biggest forum for these ads, with A3-sized pages.[26] The agencies that used this tactic represented themselves with a headshot of a smiling, well-dressed woman in middle age, such as Judy Joseph (Prestige), Elizabeth Merry, Kathleen Kent and a female representative of the Mayfair Introduction Service. With or without headshots, however, agencies that advertised on behalf of their clients were keen to promote the image of a company run by a maternal but shrewd, desexualized older woman committed to forging happy marriages while also holding a non-judgemental awareness of the diversity of human need. The Ivy Gibson agency, for instance, was initially run by a man, and then by one Rita Barker, and didn't include a headshot with its adverts. But the name was chosen to sound respectable and reassuring. Meanwhile some dating agencies fabricated names to sound reassuringly exclusive, such as Gray & Farrar. 'I didn't want a cheesy name for the company,' said Virginia Sweetingham, its founder. So she 'scoured surnames listed in the phone book, picking Gray and Farrar as the most suitable'.[27] Sweetingham was no stranger to such tactics; her first agency was called Virginia Charles.

Sexuality was never explicitly referred to in these pages, even while another mainstream publication, *Time Out*, was showcasing new sexually liberal vocabularies of self-definition and romantic longing in the personals. But as in *Blind Date*, Frances Fyfield's evocative 1998 novel about a criminal matchmaker, marriage bureau heads were no doubt aware of the importance of sex in driving business.[28] Indeed an in-depth report in 1981 by *Observer* journalist Liz Jobey drew attention to the shrewd 'crystal ball aura' of Ida Reynolds, one of the most prominent advertisers in the *LWA* on behalf of clients.[29]

Prolific matchmakers such as 'Mrs' Reynolds (founded in the early 1960s), the Ivy Gibson agency (founded in 1946, by Mr and Mrs AJ Masterson, and run by Rita Barker – Ivy Gibson was a name chosen at random) and Kathleen Kent agency were adept at putting a respectable spin on a range of relational needs and backgrounds, from severe loneliness to divorce to broken engagements and, boldly, across a range of classes.[30] Thus one lonely older working-class widow became in Ivy Gibson's words a woman of:

> 51, tall, good figure, fair hair who never pretends to be anything but what she is, and ordinary, honest to goodness working class woman who freely admits she sorely misses the love and companionship of a good husband. Very nice looking, smartly dressed, a neat and tidy council flat where she is most content to be after a hard day's work, but finds the long lonely evenings almost unbearable.[31]

This was a strikingly bold claim to both emotional authenticity and class identity that 'freely' admitted to span extremes from 'unbearable' evenings to a smart outward appearance to an uncompromising work ethic. Looking back to the mid-century, Langhamer has explored the ways in which class underpinned romantic choice but in some cases was considered subservient to love.[32] However, the power of love to trump class was downplayed by Moya Woodside in 1946, who noted that 'husbands and wives resemble each other closely in respect of background, social standing, outlook, interests, even degree of intelligence'.[33] This version of the relationship between class and romance – in which the chances of a successful cross-class romance were in Woodside's terms 'negligible' – seemed to inform the value system of those using the marriage bureaux pages, even as the categories formerly governing romance (class, and the intention to marry and have a family) were clearly loosening in other forums.[34]

Need, loneliness, gender and class were foregrounded in intriguing combinations. One female client of Kathleen Kent 'helped her husband run an extremely flourishing and prosperous business. One day after a tiff, he left never to return...'[35] Although, as the advert implies, it takes two to tiff, Kent presented her as the victim of hard luck wrongfully deprived of her marriage.[36] Meanwhile, the girlfriend of one young man 'broke off their engagement after two years. Now at 25 he finds he does not want to move among his former circle of friends but would prefer to meet fresh people'.[37] Class was emphasized in a variety of contexts, often combined with gender. Women were frequently described in terms of the profession – and class signification of that profession – of their former spouses. Thus in the 'ladies over forty' section, clients included an 'engineer's widow', a 'working man's widow', and an 'executive's widow'.[38] Class informed the search for a partner with an explicitness not seen in other publications, partly because in other lonely hearts forums the reputation of the publication itself – such as that of the middle-class political magazines *New*

Statesman and *Private Eye* – rendered class bearings more implicit. By contrast, adverts like the following were presented by the hundreds each week in the *London Weekly Advertiser* throughout the 1970s: 'Single lady (nr Croydon) in domestic work, seeks intro to bachelor, widower or div. working class, 40/50, view friendship and marriage', 'Widow, 56 ... factory worker, seeks intro. to working class gentleman ... view ult. Marriage' and 'Working class man, 40, wants to meet lady friend. Sincere, Brighton'.[39]

As these adverts suggest, admitting explicitly to bad luck, need and loneliness in the personals was not only acceptable; it also anchored the decision to advertise. Pleas for company that foregrounded severe loneliness and emotional pain were also to be found in *Time Out* in the 1970s. But in contrast to *Time Out*, the *London Weekly Advertiser* personal columns operated within a framework in which singleness and matchmaking were presented as a failure in the romantic marriage market, whose solutions could only be sought within a set of gendered and classed requirements that moved along the axes of traditional femininity and masculinity (the desire for a complementary spouse) and of class homiphily. Co-existing with more 'permissive' explorations of singleness such as those offered in *Time Out*, *Man & Woman* and even *Singles*, the language and assumptions of the matchmakers advertising on behalf of clients here alerts us to the 'syncopation' of sexual frameworks as outlined in the introduction, and reminds us of the limits of interpreting post-1960 sexual life in Britain through a lens of either of mass liberalization or continuing conservatism. In the case of the matchmaking press, the two co-existed at close quarters.

Ida Reynolds, Ivy Gibson and Elizabeth Merry took aim at permissiveness. They explicitly stressed relationships for marriage, reinforcing ideas about proper marriageable age, the urgency of avoiding being on the shelf over the age of thirty, and the fairness and prudence of seeking a good male breadwinner. They addressed 'young ladies' worried about falling behind. The Ivy Gibson Bureau was most direct, asking women in 1973: 'Are you under 30? Are the years ticking off, NEVER to come back!; Are you Tired of the daily grind? Bad travel conditions? Insecurity? The TOO permissive society...?'[40] The desperate search for young women reflected the fact that many bureaux customers belonged to the wartime or pre-war generation, with many divorcees and widows, such that personals were divided into those for women and men 'under thirty-nine' and those 'over forty'.

The traditional emphasis of these adverts appeared successful: according to one 1976 promotion, the Ivy Gibson Bureau boasted an impressive 50,000 marriages since 1946, with an all-time high of 3,125 in 1970 alone – though as contemporaries were aware, such claims were impossible to verify, and there was a clear echo of the hyperbole that marked the adverts of Edwardian matrimonial press.[41] However, the high volume of the ads placed by the bureaux on behalf of marriage-seeking clients drew to an end with the closure of the *London Weekly Advertiser* in 1982, after which self-advertising forums continued to expand. In fact, the growth of self-advertising was already in train from the early 1970s, with the launch of *Time Out*'s lonely hearts section in 1972, followed by that of *Singles* magazine in 1977, which grew from four pages in 1977 to a peak of twenty-eight pages in 1983. A range of tools were proffered to help singles get it right when going it alone.[42] But while the fading of the voluminous personals world of the *London Weekly Advertiser* drew an end to the explicitly marriage-oriented framework in print-based matchmaking forums, some of its more traditional threads surfaced in the marketing materials of the more self-consciously modern 'introduction agencies'.

Certainly, when chroniclers of the 1980s dating landscape John Cockburn and Linda Sonntag focused on personals as the site of expanding demand they were thinking not about the continuation of mid-century marriage bureaux but about a 'modern' paradigm of self-representation and pro-activity in which singles sued for a range of romantic or social ends – not just marriage. These singles, according to Cockburn and Sonntag, were responding appropriately to distinctly contemporary conditions of both greater loneliness and liberty. Yet despite the fact that new forums such as *Time Out* and *Singles* shunned the normative vocabularies around marriage favoured by some of the bureaux, with *Time Out* being the first to accept gay ads, they nonetheless operated within clear moral guidelines. Even *Time Out* 'had to put a note to lonely hearts saying we can't run married lonely hearts' while in the 1970s, according to *Time Out* classifieds ad manager Suzie Marwood, 'there were restrictions on what you could say … we had to be clear to people who were confusing free expression with porn'.[43] The challenge of the mediated matchmaking business had, since the late Victorian period, been to keep itself firmly in the respectable camp of romance rather than in the far more problematic arena of sexual services. Although some parts of the lonely hearts industry took on a self-consciously flexible attitude towards sexual morality in the 1970s, the threat of a sexual underbelly being revealed continued to shadow the business, and agencies and lonely hearts adverts had to insist they were not in fact providing platforms for escorts, prostitutes or porn rings.[44]

Time Out

Time Out launched in 1968 printed on A2 and folded to A5, with a weekly circulation of 5,000.[45] In 1972, with a circulation of 30,000, *Time Out* launched its Lonely Hearts section, setting a new tone within the mediated matchmaking world, and becoming the best-known and most widely used personals service in London.[46] A decade later, *Time Out* was printing 85,000 copies a week to a readership of 350,000, 'mostly' in London.[47] As well as raising the profile of the personals industry, it offered the first service that – woven together with the magazine's reputation for urban, cultural and subcultural insider knowledge – could be seen as socially adventurous rather than shrouded in the stigma of loneliness. From its inception, the section was closely associated with a new type of reader-singleton that was particularly invested in the metropolis's alternative culture. With its audience of students, young people and those who were 'coming to London and being lonely', *Time Out* offered both a vital social network and the first socially acceptable, culturally inflected forum for lonely hearts.[48] Its suspension during prolonged strikes in 1981 showed the extent of the magazine's cultural impact. 'Lost revenue now tops £250,000 [in fifth week of absence]', reported *The Guardian*, 'but even bigger losses are the city's fringe theatres, dance and music venues and independent cinemas which report a catastrophic drop in audiences after the disappearance of their main source of publicity.' The report also drew attention to the 'plight of hundreds of lonely hearts currently deprived of their means of communicating with each other'.

With its prominent affiliation with metropolitan cultural nouse, *Time Out*'s lonely hearts service invites consideration of Bourdieu's theory of taste as a 'matchmaker' seeking out 'affinity' with other like-minded agents.[49] *Time Out* offered a 'field' in which taste as matchmaker led the way, and in which 'the socially innocent language of likes and dislikes' was enacted to promote the 'astonishing harmony' Bourdieu saw in 'ordinary couples'.[50] However we should be wary of assuming that taste – for Bourdieu a key means by which class hierarchies are reproduced and protected – functioned primarily in relation to class reproduction here. *Time Out* readers shared their London location, but came from a wide variety of backgrounds, and the cultural economy of taste at work in their ads reflected the status of artistic and subcultural knowledge that was at least partly rooted in post-war music culture and its evolution through archetypes such as 'spivs and teds'.[51] Moreover, an irony emerges if we consider *Time Out*'s lonely hearts service in conjunction with Bourdieu's theory of taste and class reproduction as set out in *Distinction*: one of the key means of displaying 'cultural capital' in the section was in fact to disparage elitism, formal or restrictive social categories such as class and traditional gender roles. Thus popular descriptors for attractive people consciously evaded, to quote one advertiser, 'all familiar status symbols'.[52] A sample of terms of desirability from a May 1973 lonely hearts section of *Time Out* included 'long-haired', 'sensitive', 'creative' and for women, 'warm chick', 'uninhibited', 'warm', 'affectionate' and 'sweet girlfriend'.[53]

As a listings magazine with special access to metropolitan culture, it is perhaps little surprise that the lonely hearts section developed the reputation of showing how 'cool, liberal you were' – not how middle class or professionally successful you were.[54] According to Suzie Marwood, a *Time Out* ad manager, the typical male advertiser would be 'renting a flat in somewhere trendy like Highbury, or you'd be a cinema/South Bank type'.[55] Meanwhile, the 'home-loving girlie who loves jam and knitting [was] not going to be a huge hit' whereas the 'sophisticated lady who adored Schopenhauer' would get more responses.[56] The personals in *City Limits*, set up by former *Time Out* employees in 1981, and intended to embody the original egalitarian radicalism of the early *Time Out*, featured even more pronounced versions of these permissive cultural codes. Thus a 36-year-old sociology graduate was 'solvent, leftish, anarchistic ... artistic ambitions, particularly sculpture, into creative gardening, decorating ...' while a 29-year-old male sought a woman for 'country life, walks, cinema, theatre, individualist life-style'.[57] Clearly, another dimension of taste in these sections related to a particular metropolitan cultural and social outlook. Performing the same signalling or 'matchmaking' function as a love of the natural life or art-house films was a lexicon of the self that supported anti-traditional sexual culture and psychological self-awareness. A 1973 issue of *Time Out* saw male self-representation such as this: 'together freak, domestic slob, money head ... Feels no need for a brood of children', while a 'female, attractive, well-bred, sensual' sought an 'unemotional relationship ... with completely uninhibited male ...'.[58] On the same page were a 'buxom introvert'; 'two emancipated women', a 'tall chauvinist pig' seeking a 'lady friend' with 'no irritating hangups', along with a woman who 'wants so much to be turned on'.

The section's popularity was evident in its bulging mail sacks. When two of *Time Out*'s Classified managers, Irene Campbell and Jane Rackham, found themselves so stretched with lonely hearts administration they formed a business, Sidekicks (1977–1982), dedicated to handling *Time Out*'s personals. 'When we say we had sackloads of post for the lonely hearts we are not kidding you – we employed someone full-time five days a week to help', Campbell recalled.[59] *Time Out* was also the most important forum for advertising for dating agencies: Mary Balfour, founder and head of the Drawing Down the Moon agency, said that 'most of our business' came from the magazine.[60]

Once more, while taste as matchmaker is a suggestive motif for understanding the success of *Time Out*'s lonely hearts, these services were always used by people for whom simply increasing the chances of meeting someone far outweighed the image or political orientation of the service. A class-inflected sense of an appropriate match may have informed most mediated dating searches, but loneliness could trump the specificities of a desired partner, for instance with the man for whom, simply, 'bad Sundays must end'.[61] Thus echoing agony aunt Marje Proops' analysis in *Dear Marje* of the need in the 1970s for additional sexual and emotional support (as well as information), many advertisers simply expressed pure, precarious need, such as the 'Schizoid, solitary male student [seeking] sympathetic ... woman ... for help, friendship and love' and the man who was 'losing the battle with life. I'm 21, male, is there a genuine girl who can help?'[62] In other words, keen romantic loneliness as well as the realities of social dislocation meant that all lonely hearts sections – including *Time Out*'s – attracted a heterogeneous client base. Simon Garfield, who joined *Time Out* in 1983 and served as editor between 1988 and 1989, recalled that: 'People forget London was like New York; if you were from backwards America and didn't want to work on Dad's farm, you would gravitate towards New York, LA or San Francisco. London's the same; but then, you would come to London with hardly any connections at all. Outside of work, that was how you met people. Lonely Hearts friendship.'[63]

Crucially, the magazine helped stoke broader interest in the lonely hearts genre. Tony Elliott noted that: 'Throughout my life I'd go to dinner parties and people would always ask the same question – are [the lonely hearts] real? And I'd say, of course they're real.'[64] Simon Garfield insisted: 'There were two real reasons to buy *Time Out* at any point in history: it told you what was on at the Odeon, and the lonely hearts.'[65] By the 1980s, it was plain to John Cockburn, the psychologist author of *Lonely Hearts: Love Among the Small Ads*, that personals had become such a classic hallmark of the magazine that they added value far beyond the monetary. 'These columns are playing a pivotal role in the social, emotional and sexual lives of large numbers of Londoners, and they are worth far more to *Time Out* than the revenue they bring in (approx. £175,000 per year).'[66] Newspapers kept tabs on *Time Out*'s lonely hearts section, too.[67]

In addition, *Time Out*'s progressive politics helped open up lonely hearts practice and etiquette to feminist questions.[68] The mid-1970s saw internal rows about the sexual appropriateness of the magazine's adverts, including its personals, which were subsequently monitored for excessive objectification of women.[69] This move in 1974 sparked outrage and confusion among some lonely hearts advertisers, resulting in a 'spate of letters – the largest number the magazine has ever received on any subject – splitting roughly fifty-fifty in their support'.[70] One advertiser who had their advert toned down wrote in furiously, evidently confused about the difference between leftism and raw sexism:

> Is this [advertising manager] McCabe's own priggish personal view? And that she should have the impertinence to be a self-appointed moral adviser to the public! *Time Out* appears to represent a Leftish view of society, so how can it justify such a conservative attitude that McCabe has adopted?[71]

Another threatened to abandon the left entirely over the feminist conspiracy he felt was evident in the editing of his advert: 'Your fearlessly radical image is boring ... Lust is a must and a biological inevitabilitude (and fun). It becomes increasingly obvious that feminists are involved with tyranny and puritanism.'[72] Questions around the sexual tenor of ads were important because of the gender dynamics at play. Female advertisers, particularly young ones, were 'inundated' with messages, while men received far less attention.[73] 'Most men got about one or two letters, but if it was a busty blond with a great sense of humour, she'd get a whole stack,' according to Marwood. Full-up post-bags for women were also a recurrent image in the documentaries *Lonely Hearts* and *Singles*, which showed first-time female advertisers sitting on the floor amid piles of post.

Despite its growing presence and popularity, mediated dating remained on the fringes of relational and courtship norms. Thus even advertising in *Time Out* was 'not something you talked about' even though demand was growing.[74] *Singles*, founded in 1977, would become the main solution for the lonely who lived outside of London. But by the 1980s, as lonely hearts advertisers would learn, the expression of bald need visible in the previous decade's personals was not the best way to sell yourself.

Singles

If *Time Out* offered a romantic platform that knitted together the left-leaning politics and left-associated cultural sensibilities of the metropolis with the psychological language of permissiveness, then *Singles* offered a more conservative and regional lonely hearts rival platform catering to 'respectable pleasant polite people' the country over who were, in the majority, 'to the centre right' of the political spectrum.[75] A high proportion of *Time Out*'s clientele were graduates while just 25 per cent of *Singles* advertisers were.[76] Only a fraction of its readers were from London (about a quarter of letters came from the capital), and *Singles'* choice of topics suggested a readership battling financial stress and unemployment who lived apart from the metropolitan pleasures advertised by *Time Out*. Articles included guides on how to navigate council housing, cost comparison of different types of home heating, and how to be a summer 'char' in Saint Tropez.[77] In our interview, *Time Out*'s founder, owner and former editor Tony Elliott responded to a mention of *Singles* with: 'Oh, yes, God it was *awful*, wasn't it' and a face of displeasure, suggesting that *Time Out*'s superior cultural capital rendered *Singles*, by comparison, almost invisible to a metropolitan taste-maker like Elliott.[78]

Nevertheless, *Singles'* monthly personals section sat within the only national magazine dedicated to single life between 1977 and 2004, sold in 'all good newsagents' and by subscription.[79] From the mid-1980s onward, the magazine was more of a catalogue for dating services than an editorial publication, but it remained a significant national presence through the 1990s since its multi-page lonely hearts section was the only Britain-wide offering on the market. Just as *Time Out*'s image and content more broadly attracted lonely hearts advertisers, *Singles'* position as the only national magazine catering to singles made it a go-to for a wide variety of personal advertisers.[80] Unlike its rivals, *Singles* ads worked within the context of a magazine that uniquely paired its intention to 'represent' singles with a solution to their state, and fostered an intriguing mixture of solidarity and encounter. 'Our proposition that being single is rather like second-class citizenship has evidently been felt long enough by many people – it just needed saying, loud and clear', wrote Patterson, the editor (as well as Dateline's head).[81]

Sex was treated differently than in *Time Out* or *City Limits*, reflecting the tabloid aesthetic that surrounded pin-up culture and, from 1970, *The Sun*'s Page Three Girl.[82] A near-naked or lollipop-sucking woman was featured on the front of every issue in 1977 and 1978. Nonetheless, Patterson hit on changing social mores filtered down from feminism, aligning the brave new world of the lonely hearts 'life style' with engagement (albeit often snide) with the new sexual politics.

> The women's liberation movement has not particularly concerned itself with trivial matters like the next drink, but I think it has managed to get the message across to the least militant of girls that they have the right to do what they want. At least, I hope that that is a factor in events.

And further on: 'The wine-bar girl seems today to be able to handle the situation; to know how to say no without offence, or indeed to say yes when she fancies it.'[83]

Just as *Time Out*'s advertisers were a mixture of the culturally motivated and the plainly, desperately lonely, *Singles* ultimately testified just as much to the demand for national personals forums as to the desire for a politicized, singles-aware magazine. Cockburn called its 'truly national' advertisers 'mostly ordinary people spanning the length and breadth of the land'.[84] Sonntag's manual characterized *Singles* as somewhat downmarket, but stressed that it was a useful tool with a wide readership, and the use of it by the socially and culturally aspirational Colette Sinclair – who also advertised in *The Tatler* – showed just how instrumentally daters approached personal advertising forums. Once again, while the distinctions of taste may have structured some singles' decisions about where to advertise, the personals were primarily about maximizing romantic opportunity and exploratory potential. *Singles* facilitated this on a conveniently large scale. But, as I have explored elsewhere, *Singles* also provided a unique frame for its lonely hearts service, with an editorial package that sought to create singles solidarity, scorned 'women's lib', and promoted a sexual libertinism.[85] Ultimately, Patterson's businessman's mentality meant that the commercial, rather than the singles solidarity aspect of *Singles* was increasingly promoted, and the gender politics that had been aired in the magazine's letters pages between 1977 and 1983 were, by the mid-eighties, suppressed by the imperatives of the more lucrative personals section.

Despite their potential for facilitating dangerous encounters, and the anonymity of the sea of strangers they supported, personals roused less friction in the period than dating agencies. They were longer established, more familiar and more self-contained, and their codes – sexual and cultural – were usually legible. By contrast, as the following sections show, introduction and computer agencies hit the market with higher prices, ambitious advertising and an energetic press strategy. But they were less transparent than personals, leaving the door open for doubts about fair dealing and value for money. Agencies left greater room for customer disappointment, and allegations of bad value, while the veracity of their claims to respectability as helpmeets to the well-intentioned lonely were seen to be fragile, and revealed the persistence and depth of the faultline dividing sexual from respectable, 'conjugal' aims in the mediated dating landscape.[86] Crucially, the visibility of the matchmaker herself, her advertising materials, and the paperwork and money involved in signing up put heavy strain on the romantic process. In laying bare the context of romantic production, dating agencies revealed late twentieth-century concepts of romance to be resistant to commodification, even as more people sought a commodified solution to their loneliness.

Introduction agencies

The British dating agency's origins lay in nineteenth-century 'matrimonial bureaux', which placed adverts on behalf of clients.[87] A new wave of such 'bureaux' emerged between the 1940s and the 1960s, and continued into the 1970s, with agencies such as those discussed above in relation to the *London Weekly Advertiser*.[88] The best-known names, however, were marriage makers Heather Jenner (established 1939) and Katharine Allen (established 1960), both of whom avoided print, instead offering hour-long interviews to every client. In 1981, this cost £5 for an interview and £45 for an introductory fee for Katharine Allen, and a registration fee of £50 plus £450 on marriage at Heather Jenner.[89] With their focus on courtships leading to marriage, Heather Jenner and Katharine Allen held out against loosening relational norms, even insisting that 'permissiveness' had sharpened demand for their services.[90]

In the early 1970s, the numbers of dating agencies began to rise noticeably. If in 1970, *The Daily Mail* estimated that there were 400 agencies in Britain, it also found that only a small fraction of these were long-established, signalling what appeared to be a new rush into the singles market.[91] By the mid-1980s, hundreds of new agencies had joined older, more established matchmakers, including dozens of regional businesses.[92] By the early 1990s, it had become a journalistic platitude to note variety in the dating industry: for instance: 'Whether you are green, glamorous, Asian, vegetarian, handicapped, a farmer, rich, poor, shy or confident, there is an agency for you somewhere.'[93] Agencies with the widest name recognition – not only through widespread advertising across the print press but also through recurrent coverage in feature articles – included The County Register (est. 1984), Drawing Down the Moon (est. 1984), Picture Dating Agency (est. by 1990), Helena International, Hedi Fisher (est. 1968), English Rose (est. 1982), Sara Eden (est. 1988), and Penrose Halson of Katharine Allen (Halson took over in 1986).[94] London in particular was the centre of new attempts to match business with matchmaking, and it was home to successful singles 'friendship clubs' such as The London Village, which attracted a young crowd of newcomers to the city, as well as a new crop of 'wine bars' seen to cater to the unattached and to provide a welcoming atmosphere to women.[95]

If the older marriage bureaux shaped their offerings around the appearance of conventional morality rather than type of client, the new agencies had switched to a focus on occupational status. Their proposed client was too busy to meet someone because she or he was so successful at, or any rate involved in, work. This new emphasis picked up on but perhaps over-emphasized themes in British occupational culture in the 1970s and 1980s. Rather than being a nation of overtime full-time workers, Britain's rates of part-time paid work rose six-fold between the 1950s and 1990s, so that by 1990 a quarter of the workforce were part-time (compared to 4 per cent in the 1950s).[96] However, rising job turnover, the increasing emphasis on entrepreneurialism and the rise of flexitime 'blurred the edges of the nine-to-five day at its start to finish'.[97] Meanwhile, increasing affluence and the expansion of the recreational sector meant more employees had to serve the 'continuous' demand for leisure services, including on weekends.[98]

For agencies, professional busyness was portrayed as highly gendered. For instance, career absorption was a central theme in Penrose Halson's account of the success of her headship at Katharine Allen. Choosing career over personal life was a source of misery for women, while for men professional commitment was an attractive trait that was emphasized.[99] Yet the reality was that the fastest growth in female workforce participation in the 1970s and 1980s was in part-time work, enabling women to serve a domestic role at the same time. By 1981, women made up 84 per cent of part-time workers.[100] In over-emphasizing the degree of change in women's working lives, and stressing the un-natural strain this placed on romantic fulfilment ('Are the years ticking off, NEVER to come back!') agencies appeared to promote a patriarchal model of work and domesticity while also benefiting from women's affluence.[101]

The demands of an increasingly mobile, fluid labour market seemed to be mirrored in the logics of commodified modern matchmaking as, following the already well-established American market, British matchmakers now styled their companies as 'introduction' agencies. The findings of a *Which?* report in 1983 reflected this switch: 'Marriage bureaux are in the minority', it noted. 'Most agencies [now] cater to people who might be thinking no further than a few dates.'[102] But busyness and romantic short-termism did not foreclose a preoccupation with 'exclusivity'. Exclusivity was a key sorting mechanism, along with size of customer base and location, which agencies used to attract clients. Unlike the marriage bureaux advertisements in the *London Weekly Advertiser*, which promoted class homophily among 'working class' men and women, the new introduction agencies directed their marketing towards those who saw themselves as middle or upper middle class, or were aspiring to be so. Mary Balfour's £1,900 per year agency Drawing Down The Moon helped set a tone in which class played matchmaker. 'The whole thing about background, social, educational ... a lot of agencies don't understand how important that is. We find that people from different classes just don't mix.'[103] Balfour admitted that in order to attract 'writers, musicians' some reduction in price could be offered, since these types of customer were essential to the 'media people'-friendly brand. 'BBC White City should have had a sub office of Drawing Down The Moon: you know what it's like as a TV director; no time for love.'[104] Elsewhere she noted that 'because of the nature of their jobs, [my clients] find it difficult to find the right person of the opposite sex.'[105]

Drawing Down the Moon was among those agencies using new vocabularies to align themselves with a new type of busy professional single. The County Register called itself a service for 'bespoke introductions', and claimed to serve 'town and country' people.[106] The English Rose, which put English women together with generally American men, also stressed its upper-class branding: Colette Sinclair, whose memoir *Manhunt* (1989) provided an exhaustive account of her mediated matchmaking career, was described to prospective suitors as 'privately educated' and 'with a charming, well-spoken, cultured English accent'.[107] The early 1990s saw the advertising sections of newspapers and magazines increasingly fill with adverts for 'successful' partnerships. Encounters Dating Agency offered 'A Summer Romance? Personally Selected Introductions For Discerning Professionals Requiring An Excellent And Successful Way To Meet Potential Partners'.[108] For those with ambition but with less money, there was an 'Affordable, selective and discreet' service, claiming to be an 'excellent and successful way to meet your kind of people...'[109] Dinnermates made its own gender-economic calculus clear with 'Exclusive Singles Dinner Parties/Social Occasions in Kent and Sussex' and 'Professional, gregarious men (35+) attractive, thirty something ladies'.[110]

Once again, Bourdieu's analysis of taste can help us to understand how agencies positioned their services in terms of social and cultural capital, and why they so often failed to successfully match customers.[111] In Bourdieu's account, decoding class through taste is an instinctive, immediate and implicit process. Consumption, the sphere in which cultural capital is displayed and read, is 'a stage in a process of communication, that is, an act of deciphering, decoding, which presupposes practical or explicit mastery of a cipher or code'.[112] In the cultural capital-rich domain of art or classical music, for instance, the 'conscious or unconscious ... explicit or implicit schemes of perception ... is the hidden condition' for grasping and making sense of the art.[113] Connecting this idea with taste as a 'matchmaker', then, we would expect singles looking for people like them to seek out cultural codes which both could decipher. Mutual deciphering or the sense of 'affinity' produces the 'sense of the miraculous' that is central to successful courtship in Bourdieu's terms.[114] The common approach of agencies, however, disrupted this process whereas the relatively less mediated lonely hearts ads facilitated it. Matchmakers claimed to offer premium services for introducing people to '*your* kind of person' – a flexible term partly for someone of the same class but also for someone of commensurate socially and professionally aspiring outlook.[115] Such terminology left little chance to demonstrate shared decoding skills, and homogenized useful cultural hierarchies of knowledge into a fairly unitary social ambitiousness inflected with – so the inky adverts with their capital letters suggested – an underlying pressure of desperation. If anything, then, agencies' expansive, non-specific courting of generally ambitious customers made those daters who did want to meet their 'kind of person' work harder by concealing the nuances of the 'field' of play. Thus, the mechanism intended to make singles' mission easier – the supposedly expert deciphering of potential matches by the agencies – actually deprived customers of work they needed to do themselves and that was integral to finding 'your kind of person'. In doing so, agencies created in the dating process something akin to the 'chaos of sounds and rhythms, colours and lines, without rhyme or reason' Bourdieu described of those without the background facing a connoisseur's analysis of Titian.[116] The result was, as we will see in Chapter 4, a high degree of mismanaged expectations, confusion and disappointment: the sense of having been 'mismatched to such an extent that it appeared that no attention had been paid to a client's desire to meet someone of similar interests'.[117]

One of the key themes of this book is the fact that, for many, the reality of dating agency use did not always match branding. As I have suggested, this disappointment may have been exacerbated by the business model of the new agencies, which performed insufficient – because too general – 'sorting' work on behalf of clients, and therefore concealed the particularities and, to use Bourdieu's term, 'distinction' of taste integral to the selection of the desirable matches they posited. The mismatch between promises of retrieving 'your type' of person and the often random-seeming or undesirable dates procured will be explored more in Chapter 4 from the point of view of the customer. From the industry's perspective, however, several formal interventions by the consumer watchdog shed undesirable light on agency practices, making transparent the insalubrious caveats that had dogged the business since the nineteenth century.

The spread of interest in dating agencies and an increase in their number meant that in 1977, Gordon Borrie, the director general of the Office of Fair Trading (OFT), had concluded a year's investigation into industry practices.[118] More than 600 complaints filed around the country led him to conclude there was 'a very sorry picture of substantial amounts of money being paid by lonely and vulnerable people for little or no service'.[119] Following a debate in Parliament in November 1980 in which John Carlisle, MP for Luton, drew impassioned attention to the 'those institutions and marriage bureaux which are unashamedly exploiting the public', a further investigation by the OFT was launched in 1981, resulting in the body urging the dating industry to write (and adhere to) a code of practice.[120] Stories were highlighted such as that of one Mr Peter Simper, thirty-four, who had paid £150, and 'received no dates'.[121] And while it drew a distinction between the 'top and bottom end', nonetheless complaints related to 'every type of bureau'.[122] The most expensive agencies claimed to provide a greater degree of safety than those that offered introductions without personally interviewing each prospective client and the promise of safety was important to singles, as the next chapter shows.[123] But following the OFT complaints, they attempted to formalize their standards with the creation of the Association of British Introduction Agencies (ABIA) in 1981, which appeared a more successful project than the stymied attempt to self-regulate that Patterson complained about in *Singles* a few years earlier, following the first report.[124] Nonetheless, while the OFT discussed introducing a licensing system, formal recognition of the ABIA was rejected and ultimately the dating industry remained unregulated and its practices continued to attract close attention, particularly in the press. A 1982 report by *The Guardian* displayed the unease already in place after a decade of growth, and spoke to the unstable status of the industry in the public eye.[125] It emphasized the shiftiness and unaccountability of certain dating entrepreneurs, such as Michael Oren of video dating service Mastermatch. Oren was the bankrupt director of a clutch of companies including Mastermatch, which had been taken to court three times in eighteen months, liquidated in March 1982, and revamped as Masterview shortly afterwards. The article also pointed to the closure of Prestige Partners' newly refurbished premises since January 1982 and to its dodgy maths. The report was meticulous, noting that Prestige's membership of 6,000 had been 'later revised to 1,800'. It further transpired that Prestige had moved office to the home of its head, Judi Joseph, who had also resigned from the ABIA. (Prestige survived at least until 1983, when it was sued for stealing Dateline's questionnaire and banned from using it in its 'Prestige Connections' brochure.) Dateline's John Patterson, who was often in the press discussing the need for his product, also lacked respectability: only four out of the thirteen companies he'd set up in the past sixteen years were still active.

Moreover, customers who had paid sizeable fees for 'exclusivity' continued to be disappointed – and for good reason. The agency practices behind the claims were slapdash and structured around the pursuit of short-term profit.[126] In 1996, Julia, the head of 'sales' at an American-owned, London-based agency that 'certainly did claim to be exclusive', described a cynical business in which anything was promised to the client in order to 'make the sale': the fee was £1,500 for four introductions.[127] The agency priced and packaged its exclusivity in three classes of membership: gold, silver and platinum. From Julia's perspective, the same problem recurred regardless: a shortage of serious male prospects and a glut of 'really super' women.[128] Julia insisted that the primary goal was selling memberships, and that lack of suitable partners was not a deterrent. Did the agency ever manage expectations or decline a sale on that basis? 'Very rarely. We had to get the credit card, and get it double quick quite a lot of the time, so we would just tell them, "life's not the same without someone else" and get it done if we could.'[129]

When prospective customers sat down for a consultation, they were given a short written 'psychometric test' that evaluated their level of self-esteem on a scale from one to ten. A client's relationship to self-esteem rather than their 'interests', then, yielded more useful information to an agency prioritizing each 'sale'. To 'make the sale', the matchmaker adapted the sales pitch according to the client's pressure point. 'We could sell it on a love basis – if that was the kind of person. Or if people come in talking about their money and property, you sell it on that basis, and say "we've got lots of people like that." You sell people what they want when they come in by listening carefully. I remember one guy in particular who said, "will she have a telly?" And I thought, "she will mate, but you won't."' According to Julia, 'it was really easy to sell to a high self-esteem person, if you had a nine you had an easy sale, if it was a three it was harder'. But there were some people that were turned away from agencies. According to Julia, these were the 'Nigerian men' who would appear every evening – 'my job was literally removing Nigerian men for a while'.[130] And Hedi Fisher remembered 'one awful occasion a tramp came to the bureau' and – although he had the required fee with him – he was sent away, told there 'was nobody suitable for him just now'.[131] Nonetheless, as the concern of the OFT made clear, the advertising worked, and expensive matchmaking firms found that business was brisk. According to Julia, the agency she worked for had seven people every evening in reception interested in signing up, with a pool of over 500 at any given time. It sustained 'expensive offices and an expensive staff'.[132]

By using the language of exclusivity and promising a 'bespoke' service for people 'too busy to find love', introduction agencies opened a new front in the construction of the modern single. Instead of the personal misfortune emphasized by the marriage bureaux in the *London Weekly Advertiser*, singleness was portrayed as a by-product of professional ambition. Assuming that such careerism conferred income, singles were increasingly in a position to spend money on a 'lifestyle' that, as we saw in the previous chapter, would attract the attention of marketers such as Mintel. But the reality was different: not only were agencies unable to produce 'bespoke' matches, the singles they attracted were not necessarily well-paid or absorbed in their careers: some were 'lonely and vulnerable' and the willingness to pay the high fees reflected not wealth but need.[133]

Computer dating

Poised between the exclusivity rhetoric of the new agencies and the take-your-chances world of personals was a third major way to meet a partner commercially. If agencies emphasized the luxury of human wisdom, then computer dating shunned that very wisdom, instead offering the answers of 'science' – in this case of computers and of psychology – to help match singles. Agencies stressed an end result: the retrieval of the right 'type of person' through matchmakers' insights and time, while computer dating pioneered a dating-by-questionnaire approach to 'compatibility' that would enable a high turnover of matches. Thus computer dating marketed itself as a novel technology that promised quantity *and* quality, through a scientific paradigm that made:

> a messy and imperfect emotional process into a clean, scientific, and rational one – one in which both parties could find their perfect complement and shift with ease into a long-term relationship, secure in the knowledge their match had been electronically vetted.[134]

And while the introduction agencies of the 1980s tried to appeal to a new kind of careerist – female and male – who was 'too busy to find love', computer dating also claimed to serve the 'modern' single. The computer dater's modernity was not necessarily defined through a commitment to a non-stop job, but rather to an outlook that embraced adaptability and pragmatism, and to a desire to enjoy social variety. Dateline, as we will see, elaborated more than any other on what it meant to be a modern, single person – and its role in the nurturing of this identity.

The development of computer dating coincided with the expansion of commercial computing in the 1960s, and the ability of smaller firms to buy and operate machines designed for their use, such as the basic IBM System 3. There were a handful of computer dating firms in operation in the late 1960s, including Dolphin, Compat, Operation Match (an outpost of an American service owned by Compatibility Research) and Dateline, the majority of whose customers were in London and the South-East.[135] Computer dating firms were classified as budget-friendly agencies, costing around £1 per match at the start; in 1979, Dateline charged £35 for a year's introductions.[136] Costs were kept down partly because the customer had to do the work by filling in 'a complicated form', while the computer could handle the insertion of hundreds of forms at once, spitting out the paid-for six matches per person.[137]

By the early 1970s, Dateline, founded in 1966, had left its rivals behind with a widespread print advertising campaign that helped bring it as close to a household name as any dating agency of the period.[138] Its relative success as a brand was partly to do with its owner's entrepreneurial zeal: Dateline was part of an umbrella business, Singles Scene Ltd., that included singles holidays and a Kensington singles' wine bar called Tiles. But its success also reflected a savvy branding strategy: unlike its rivals, Dateline's marketing material told an origin story that gave it a cohesive role. Patterson, Dateline's owner, claimed to have been inspired by the original Operation Match, launched at Harvard University in 1965, and used this to stress Dateline's US-style entrepreneurship and ingenuity throughout promotional features and adverts in *Singles*.[139]

The unifying theme, however, in the story of Dateline, concerned its 'modernity', by which it meant its unique appropriateness for contemporary British singles. In a dense, full-page advert from 1980, it explained what it meant by this, putting its case in terms of the categories: 'The Age We Live in'; 'The Shifting Society'; 'What the Friendly Computer Does'; 'Is Dateline Etiquette?'; and 'What Sort of People Join Dateline?'.[140] The first two set out a vision of a social landscape in which the rituals of an older Britain had disappeared to be replaced by 'the new life-style', evoked by such features as a 'social life . . . changing more rapidly than ever before'; entry into the 'the space age', and a mobility unheard of to the previous generation who 'spent their lives more or less in one place'.[141] Computer dating was a salve for those who no longer lived in Edwardian times, when 'the art of introducing people reached its highest expression'.[142]

The 'friendly computer' was introduced as a romantic helpmeet of prodigious 'power' – bringing together the force of technology and the human sciences to allow the company to 'provide you with the world's fastest, most accurate' service.[143] The computer embodied the excitement of the modern, and was imbued with a mythic quality typical of computer discourse in the 1960s and 1970s, such that rather than running counter to it, computers advanced the cause of romantic love: they were a superlative way of creating the conditions for people to meet and mate.[144] But the computer possessed a disturbing inscrutability as well, which added an extra layer inflected with both dystopian and awesome elements. Despite their sinister dimension, these aspects were stressed in *The Love Tapes*, Dateline's 1977 promotional video. Shots of the computer's whirring reels filled the screen and provided punctuation suggestive of electronic power but also of the anonymity and aridity of its industry.

The other dimension of the 'scientific' method Dateline claimed to harness was psychology. The link between computational power and psychological assessment had been in train since the 1950s, when computers started to be used for scoring data. This usage built on the 'punchcard machines' that had begun to be used for organizing data – including the sexological – as early as 1940.[145] By the time Patterson founded Dateline, computers were being used to help interpret the data too.[146] Moreover, researchers found computers a particularly useful tool in collecting sex-related psychological data, since 'respondents may [have been] more willing to reveal sensitive information to an impersonal computer'.[147] Dateline's portrayal of the 'friendly' computer picked up on the invitingly non-judgemental nature of the machine, which would merely process questionnaire data, not judge it. Thus customers were not only offered the computer's 'flash of electronic brilliance' – the rational fruits of its programming – but the fine calibration of a psychologically expert matching questionnaire.[148] Psychological profiling was a centrepiece of the marketing for computer dating, reflecting the growing interest in personality matching in the psychological and social sciences, and foreshadowing the emphasis of global internet dating firms such as eHarmony thirty years later.[149]

While traditional matchmakers claimed psychological expertise based on life experience and wisdom, the computer dating companies laid claim to the empirical insights of psychometric testing. Frequently referred to by Dateline simply as 'science', psychology was deployed for its ability to truly decode the human self and its desires through questionnaire data. To help design its questionnaire, Dateline employed 'a group of young psychology graduates' and vowed that their work tallied with the 'most up to date research' from Anglo-

American universities.[150] Dateline's questionnaire was indeed extensive, with numerous questions not only about appearance, background, education, moral concerns and partner preferences but also about 'personality'. In this – as we have seen – it was mirroring themes in relational discourse more widely, in which the pursuit (or attainment) of a partner was seen as a reflection of the self and its potential.

While computer dating firms' claims to be modern and scientific suggested an improvement on older forms of matchmaking business, they nonetheless raised long-standing questions about respectability and fears about sordidness and fraud. In her study of the intersections between early computer dating and the advancement of a heteronormative model of courtship, Marie Hicks has discussed the idea that emerged from computer dating that 'women and men might meet casually, for sex, instead of within a social context that positioned marriage as the objective' and that this 'hindered computer dating'.[151] Indeed, the proliferation of dating services tested the limits of permissiveness and particularly piqued the older generation, while concerns about sexual morality and respectability were voiced across the social register. When airline BOAC proposed a travel package to Americans involving holidays in London and introductions to British girls using computer dating, the gimmick reached national news because two MPs considered the suggestion 'immoral'.[152] In response, BOAC's spokesman said 'in the United States computer dating was considered as in no way improper', though his wording suggested he understood the MPs' response.[153] Dateline's owner, John Patterson, was caught up in two sexual morality scandals that meant the business continued to have a 'veneer of sleaze'.[154] In 1969, he was arrested and fined £300 for offering to sell several men 'a list of 200 beautiful, sophisticated girls who would act as escorts and provide a night out "never to be forgotten"'.[155] And in 1983, Neville Glick, the owner of a small Harrogate marriage bureau accused him of advertising 'in almost every pornographic magazine in the country' and of being known in London as 'Patterson the porn master'.[156] Glick was responding to a letter that had appeared in *Singles* magazine alleging that his agency had introduced the letter-writer to a non-member – which Glick claimed had been sent to newspapers in the North – and went for Dateline's Achilles heel in retaliation. There were other individual crusaders, such as Lieutenant-Colonel Norman Pannell, who in 1970 made a complaint to the Home Office after posing as a teenage girl to better gauge the respectability of computer dating firms. Pannell's complaint came from the fact that one of the computer dating firms he approached asked his views on 'pre-marital sex and communism'.[157]

Distrust of computer dating agencies took on more formal dimensions, with the OFT investigations of 1977 and 1981 concluding that computer matching firms were contributing to the industry's mis-selling practices. Concerns over decency and legitimacy also meant that it wasn't until 1989 that Dateline was allowed for the first time to advertise on TV, buying a thirty-second spot on Sky. Chris Quinlan, controller of advertising at the Cable Authority (CA), verbalized a telling train of thought regarding the decision to allow Dateline to advertise on TV: 'We needed to know that it was a bona fide introduction agency, which genuinely offered friendship... It must not exploit loneliness, nor be suggestive, such as using large-chested ladies.'[158] *The Guardian* continued the report with its own revealing observation that the CA would 'still not allow escort agencies to advertise because of fears that some may be fronts for prostitution.'[159] Sanctioning Dateline adverts on family TV had come dangerously close to opening far darker floodgates. Indeed exactly what was acceptable on family TV was being rapidly renegotiated – it wasn't until 1987 that adverts for tampons and condoms were allowed, with the latter allowed primarily in response to the AIDS crisis.[160]

Moreover, with its no-frills, relatively cheap service, computer dating was also seen to cultivate a young customer base with unfamiliar courting aims: men were driven by 'a mixture of curiosity and sexual expectation' while women were keen to meet people 'outside their social class'.[161] *The Times* linked the rise of firms such as Compat to a new informal advertising register that made such services seem young and progressive rather than dowdy. It noted shrewdly that 'the breakthrough for Com-Pat came with the pop pirates', citing the 'opportunity they afforded for vigorous and matey advertising'.[162] But while they positioned themselves at the vanguard of modern society, computer dating services were also keen to toe the moral line, measuring success first in terms of marriages and only second in terms of 'friendships'. Thus Dateline was sure to tell the press that it had (unverifiably) produced its 'thousandth' marriage while in 1978 it devoted a feature in *Singles* to its '10,000th' marriage.[163]

Computer dating firms offered singles a means that was explicitly 'modern' in technology and potential. In generating a higher volume of matches, they shaped a new idea of the 'match' that was defined through the impartial and extensive abilities of the machine to crunch data. Yet while Dateline in particular tried to market itself as both socially modern (suiting the 'mobile' populace of the 'space age') and respectable, it too continued to struggle against a 'veneer of sleaze'.

As the 1980s drew to a close with an expanded offering of dating services, users of mediated matchmaking platforms were still accustomed to a level of personal attention unimaginable to internet daters. In particular, people placing ads in publications from *The Times* to *Time Out* to *Private Eye* took for granted that a human or humans, not an algorithm, was taking their cash and aiding their bid for love. Hand-delivering an ad to a magazine was a fairly common mode of delivery, and many ads were placed through the phone.[164] David Jones, ad manager of the Heartsearch column at the *New Statesman* in 1988, noted:

> On the phone they tell us all sorts of intimate details about their relationships and sometimes they get very upset. We inevitably get into a fair bit of counselling when this happens. I've spent over an hour on the phone with people in the past, and have even subsequently received letters of appreciation.

Jones added the *New Statesman* sometimes helps with wording. 'We always advise humour as we know from experience that this works well.'[165] And the ad managers were themselves drawn into personal stories of their customers: 'One interesting point,' said Jones, 'is that sometimes the advertisers flirt! I've been asked away for the weekend on more than one occasion…'[166] Meanwhile, Celia Bogget, ad manager of *Private Eye*, was personally responsible for each ad: 'I wouldn't print something that said sexual encounter wanted or that sort of thing because it is a love column, it's called Eyelove remember.'[167]

Even Dateline – whose matchmaker was a computer – had a well-known face at the helm in John Patterson. With the launch of *Singles*, Dateline had provided numerous pages of space for readers to write in about its services, in addition to the opportunities provided by the hundreds of its affiliated Singles Societies around the country. Whatever organ of self-publicity daters chose, from agencies to computers, there were faces and names helping (or hindering) them along the way. Seen from the vantage of Celia Bogget or David Jones, the depersonalization of the dating process was still decades away. Nonetheless, as this chapter has shown, the expanded range of mediated dating services struck observers as a fundamentally modern sign of a widening compass of freedoms, as well as of the uncertainties, anxieties and feelings of alienation that accompanied them.

This chapter has charted the development of the matchmaking industry after 1970 through its three main categories: print ads, introduction agencies presided over by a matchmaker, and computer dating. Thanks to a buoyant publishing landscape, new ideas about modern relationality and computer technology, the 1970s were a key decade in the growth of the industry and marked the start of the contemporary period of mediated matchmaking. Lonely hearts ads and computer dating services were at the vanguard of the expansion of the singles industry in the 1970s, and catered to a variety of tastes and classes. The emergence of the 'introduction agencies' of the 1980s saw efforts to rebrand singleness as a by-product of success and the hallmark of the professionally busy person. Despite these efforts, concerns about the respectability of dating services continued to linger, and as more and more people used them, the more they caught the attention of authorities. This signalled both a movement towards the mainstream – dating services were increasingly seen as a consumer affair, requiring monitoring as such – and the endurance of unease about what such services were really offering.

Bourdieu's theory of distinction helps illuminate the multiple levels on which different dating services worked: *Time Out*, with its metropolitan, progressive branding offered users the clearest matchmaking opportunities along lines of taste, while introduction agencies, in attempting to do the 'sorting' work for daters, actually occluded important facets of the process, and, in promising 'exclusivity', in fact revealed the limits of such promises by singles businesses.

Overall, the marketing strategies of lonely hearts platforms, introduction agencies and computer dating firms all tapped into discourse about what it meant to be a modern single. All three self-consciously served a population it claimed suffered from an underdeveloped or unstable social network, and provided choice and control to busy professionals, an advantage stressed in particular by dating agencies. If dating agencies were geared towards those who were (mostly) serious about love, and had the means to pay for it, then the less expensive business of computer dating targeted young people, with new tastes and romantic aspirations. Whatever their strategies, however, respectability issues dogged all forms of mediated dating – whether traditional marriage bureaux, small ads or technologically 'advanced' machine-aided matching – helping keep in place a stigma that would last into the next century. The layers of this stigma and the anxieties surrounding mediated dating will be explored in the next chapter through attention to media discourse.

3

Representations of the mediated dating industry

This chapter concerns representations and perceptions of mediated dating. It tracks the growing media interest in matchmaking and singles, drawing out a set of flashpoints that arose around what it meant in terms of gender, class and safety to meet strangers. Newspapers are at the heart of this analysis, since they brought together strands that were essential to the growth of mediated dating and moulded customer expectations. They ran feature and news articles that drew on relevant themes from social aspiration to danger, building up the image of dating as a truly modern pursuit, and providing a key forum for agency advertising. But the lifestyle and social features were tempered by the regular stream of stories about danger, fraud and crime in the personals, as well as the unscrupulousness of matchmakers, resulting in a constantly shifting and unstable status for dating agencies.

The interest of TV producers, journalists and editors in singles services rose sharply throughout the period, not necessarily in strict relation to the number of services provided, but rather as part of an overall expansion in media coverage of themes related to sex, gender and lifestyle. At the centre of this representational landscape was print, and national newspapers 'reflected and shaped' sexual culture on a number of fronts, including trends in understandings of romance.[1] As Adrian Bingham has demonstrated, sex, marriage and family demographics were major themes throughout the twentieth century in British newspapers. Singleness and dating overlapped to some extent with these, but tapped more clearly into post-1960s media debates over permissiveness, 'the Great Debate' and the 'subject of our times'.[2] Permissiveness had become 'the frame through which journalists observed the nation and they ceaselessly looked for new angles on this defining story of the age'.[3] Mediated dating offered several such angles: indeed, the sheer range of ways 'lonely hearts' and matchmaking services inspired or shaped representations in both culture and in discourse, from plays to metaphors, in different platforms and across complex moral registers, was striking. 'Lonely hearts' could be the topic of a play reviewed in the arts pages, considered in relation to complaints about a dating agency, a metaphor for the German motor trade in the business news, or the subject of personal reflection usually by a single woman in her thirties.[4] But in addition to running reviews on sinfoniettas and films about lonely hearts, newspapers' main interest lay in the claims of remarkable growth in the lonely hearts market. *The Times* noted in 1995, for instance, that the 'boom in introduction agency business during the past 15 years means there are now 90,000 clients compared with 50,000 in 1980'.[5] *The Daily Mirror* suggested that introduction agencies' reach was even more extensive, based on the same (uncited) source.[6]

In addition to reporting on the growing demand for singles' services, print media maintained a distinct relationship to the world of lonely hearts in other ways.[7] Broadsheet coverage helped establish singles' expectations of dating services, while also making space for first-person feature articles about the experience of using such services.[8] And with the publications that ran personals, print allowed readers to vicariously consume lonely hearts experiences, since many more people read the ads than placed them or responded to them. Print, then, was the forum in which mediated matchmaking unfurled its dimensions in terms of information, experience, the quest for encounter, and the invitation to daydream. Focusing on newspapers allows us to explore a set of frictions that arose as the media debated the legitimacy of the dating industry and interrogated points of contention. Television also offers important clues, thanks in particular to a set of documentaries that investigated mediated matchmaking, and these will also be discussed.

Coverage of mediated dating provides a unique point of departure for understanding the flux of ideas surrounding gender and romance in the period because it highlights the play of anxieties and opinions about women's status, money, class and danger.[9] The recurrence of these themes testified to an enduring confusion over what it meant to be sexually modern, and kept mediated dating stigmatized. Dating was often portrayed as an engagement with an ongoing sex war, with different rules of engagement and consequences for men and women. Much of the gendered discourse relating to mediated matchmaking suggested that single women and single men were destined to fail in mutually satisfying the other due to irreconcilable differences in desire and outlook.

Anonymity, illegibility and peril: anxieties about dating strangers

In *The Love Tapes*, Dateline's promotional documentary, there was a section dedicated to showing women how to negotiate the 'blind' element of the dates arranged through the agency: 'If you're the cautious type, you might not like the idea of a blind date, but you can of course ask for a photo before meeting or make a survey from a safe distance.' A woman was then shown peering out from behind a clothes rack at an outdoor market, and deciding against the somewhat shifty-looking man clearly waiting for her. 'But,' the narrator continued, casting doubt even on this precaution, 'looks, as everyone knows, can be deceiving.'

In addressing fears about the 'blind date', Dateline was engaging with a central trope in dating agency discourse, in which the clientele was seen as a conglomeration of unknown quantities. As a range of observers made clear, it was, on a basic level, impossible to be sure that the person you were meeting was single, solvent and sane. And there was a decided element of sexual danger, depicted in *The Love Tapes* in a scene in which a man was shown trying to put his hand under a woman's skirt: 'Of course there are always a few sharks, seeking sexual adventures.' The threat for the dater in London was also emphasized. As discussed in the introduction, the city's 'sexual exceptionalism'; its 'brighter lights', 'later hours', its alleyways, crowds and dens could be dangerous, and required women to be extra careful when meeting strangers. It also fuelled some powerful imaginative evocations, such as Frances Fyfield's *Blind Date* (1998), a dark thriller of misogynistic violence revolving around the meetings arranged by a scheming matchmaker. Combining the dangers of sex, city and strangers, *Blind Date* allowed Fyfield to exploit 'the menace of city life'.[10]

The blind date, then, was synonymous with the perils and excitements of commercial but anonymous matchmaking forums. The anonymity and uncertainty, as well as the unknown logics of the increasingly blind date-dependent matchmaking landscape, were rolled out in two main ways. The first was contextual, presenting blind dating as a necessary result of social development, and a pragmatic solution with exciting opportunities if carefully managed. The second focused on the equally inevitable result of crime, with the singles market, and London in particular, rife with the sordid effects of loneliness. John Cockburn pinpointed this duality accurately when he mused: 'What is the truth behind the lonelyheart ad? Is that plea a last ditch scream for help from someone who through emotional inadequacy finds themselves in a deep well of chronic loneliness? Or is it a rational response by the person whom through external and unavoidable circumstances, simply finds it difficult to meet others and begin more intimate relationships?'[11] For some, such as Joan Ball, head of Dateline rival Compat, the 'rational response' argument was a matter for 'messianic enthusiasm' and she was given the opportunity to express this view in *The Times*. Blind dates, Ball suggested, were the necessary antidote to increasing isolation: the anonymity of the modern single's life required an equally anonymous but pro-active approach.

Central to the idea that dating agencies were a natural response to modern social conditions was a vision of a vanished past. Quoted in *The Times*, Ball noted: 'Everyone used to mix such a lot more than they do now, in dance halls and social clubs and so on. But now people are more wrapped up in their own little worlds: they just go home and watch television.'[12] *Man & Woman* also set the rapid proliferation of mediated dating within a modern setting that required it. Thus an in-depth discussion of the whys and wherefores of the dating industry was headlined in terms of the contrast between past and present. 'Meeting the ideal partner may seem an impossible dream. Do marriage bureaus hold out the chance of finding love and companionship in the impersonal chaos of modern life?'[13] Often, though, when customers were quoted in press reports for their favourable views of agencies, they rephrased the idea of the 'impersonal chaos' of modern life as an awareness of the need to expand social opportunities, itself a 'modern' measure and perspective.[14] 'If you join to expand your circle and meet new people,' one dater told *The Guardian*, 'then something is more likely to develop from that in a natural way. It's all very civilised and modern.'[15] Matchmakers grasped this idea firmly, such as the head of the Picture Dating agency, who, as mentioned in the last chapter, called this a 'modern' way of meeting people. He was careful to explain that 'no one there is short of friends or short of people to go out with, they are just looking for someone different'.[16] The motive was the maximization of social potential, not a sign of weakness or failure, something which all matchmakers promoted in their branding and press quotes.

For others, the contrast between present and more ordered past was more problematic, and winked at other signs of troubling change. There was some concern about a new social order, in which a society unhinged from its community roots could also become unhinged from sexual prudence, mistaking lust for love and perhaps abandoning decency and morality entirely. 'Compared with our grandparents,' wrote a *Times* journalist in 1976, 'our increasing social and geographical mobility has vastly increased the numbers of our transitory encounters with other people, and so the number of opportunities for infatuations based on physical appearance.'[17] The appearance of Videomatch in 1978 seemed to corroborate fears about the mechanization, commercialization and generalization of lust in the guise of a matchmaking service. Following the launch of Videomatch, *The Guardian* worried about female sexual behaviour. 'One girl said [on her video profile that] she was interested in "screwing around" while another said she would not go out with coloured or foreign men.[18] These lapses in sexual morality and decency were presented as a function of the ease with which mediated dating services provided singles (and especially women) with strangers.

People in favour of older, more personal romantic mechanisms focused on the meaning of computer dating, the hallmark of a modern method in terms of technology and – with its lower price tags – an ethic of disposability. Those with a vested interest in more traditional approaches disparaged the computer's anonymity. 'Computers are so impersonal,' noted Rita Barker, matchmaker of the Ivy Gibson Bureau, in 1981:

> Suppose for example that one of my gentlemen indicates he likes sports. A computer will put down a little tick for sports. But who can say whether he plays squash, or tennis, whether he likes to sail, or prefers to go to the cricket matches? That sort of thing can only come out in personal interviews.[19]

Less interested observers, particularly earlier in the period when computers were still shrouded in a degree of mystery, also found in computer dating a concerning sign of modern life, in which delicate social matters had been brought within the control of machines so that anonymity had spread to both the form and function of modern dating.[20] In 1970, Jill Tweedie wrote in *The Guardian*, in an article headlined 'Stick that in your data dating program': 'Given this unromantic view of life, I've watched with astonishment the [way] the computer has moved into the [realm] of love.'[21] Meanwhile, a researcher at the University of Kent warned of the dangers of a society that allowed computers to make matches for them: 'no one in the world knows what chemistry is at work when two people fall in love, least of all a machine.'[22] As computers got smaller and became household goods, 'dating by machine' lost its novelty and its dystopian wonder, but Dateline's economies of scale and quasi-industrial matching function continued to provoke social analysis by turns concerned and positive.

If anonymity signalled both positive and negative associations with 'modern' life, including both social freedoms and the sinister experience of a bad 'blind' date, there was a sharper end of blind dating by lonely hearts ad or dating agency in the form of real crime. It was in the scrupulous reporting of lonely hearts criminality that newspapers built a narrative of sexual violence, disordered class interactions and preying criminality as strong as the more upbeat one of modern pragmatism, echoing older narratives concerned with sexual misdemeanour and violence discussed in the introduction.

The extent of the horror of what could happen when lonely hearts services brought together people from wildly different classes was made clear by the grisly murder of the GP Ann Mead in 1994, who was bludgeoned to death outside her home by a man she met through her *New Statesman* personal ad but was too embarrassed about to introduce to her friends. For the *Daily Mail*, this was cause for reflection not just about the 'modern disease' of alienation and anonymity but about the dangers of mixing with people lower down the social scale. 'Even without the violent end to their relationship', stated the *Mail*:

> anyone could have predicted that a highly-qualified doctor would be badly matched with a former civilian police worker with a record of marriage and relationship failures culminating in a thwarted attempt to enrol for a university degree at the age of 45.[23]

Typically, the *Mail* saw a tale of social decline – specifically the death of hobbies – behind the fact that 'women like Ann Mead are forced to go shopping for love in markets they would not normally consider'. *The Times*' conclusion was more measured. Ann Mead was very unlucky: 'anyone who ventures into the world of blind dating and marriage bureaux should be prepared for disappointment and deception ... [but not murder].'[24]

Escalating coverage of lonely hearts-related crime cemented the sense that using services to hunt for love was deadly dangerous as well as modern, and that these two were somehow linked. Out of 109 *Times* articles concerned with 'lonely hearts' in the 1990s, twenty-three reported on crime. By comparison, out of forty-eight in the 1980s, just four had a criminal hook. Crimes did not always occur on the blind date, but murderers were frequently found to have used lonely hearts services, particularly those engaged in gruesome sexual violence. The range of crimes connected to lonely hearts was bewildering, and mixed sexual criminality with class-bounding fraud. Within a three-month period in 1994, *The Times* reported on a gigolo who conned rich women through the small ads into buying race horses that he would then kill for insurance; the rape and murder of a '22-year old chambermaid' by a man 'now thought to have been met in the lonely hearts', a paedophile who found fellow paedophiles through the personals, while letters to women found in national personals pages were found in the caravan in which a ten-year-old girl was raped.[25] Although the print world of the personals – both as a host for classifieds and for news stories about them – was seen as dangerous in a way that was linked to distinctively modern social conditions, there were strong echoes of the Edwardian matrimonial press, which saw sensational cases like that of Henri Desire Landru, convicted in 1921 of murdering ten women after it was found he had spent seven years combing the personals.[26]

Occasionally the tale of sexual violence was reversed, as in the case of the Austrian 'black widow', who killed five men she met in the lonely hearts pages; another Black Widow emerged in 2003, dubbed 'every man's nightmare'.[27] But in general, women were reported in connection to fraud rather than violent crime – for conning men, or in the case of the mostly female matchmakers, conning customers. Generally, women were tricksters and gold-diggers, while men were rapists and murderers.

Given that they pooled anonymous people desirous of a range of sexual and romantic outcomes, it is perhaps not surprising that dating services came across as dangerous, arrayed in all the problems that could be imagined in relation to the meeting of strangers of different classes and sexes, problems exacerbated in urban settings. The sense that the dating pool of possible matches was fluid and without boundaries, sometimes troublingly so, nurtured another dominant thread in representations of matchmaking. This stemmed from the fact that meeting strangers, and being a stranger, allowed for a flexibility in self-presentation that made self-reinvention and the expression of social aspiration easier. The media seemed to be tapping into this idea by circling around the tropes of exclusivity, professionalism and the entrepreneurial approach to romantic destiny that were enshrined in the new breed of introduction agencies. Thus as well as revealing the dangers of dating socially illegible people, media coverage of mediated dating also portrayed it as a means for achieving the socially and the emotionally modern self. This portrait of newly fluid social boundaries was cross-cut by older models of class, which brought to the fore concerns about respectability that echoed those that characterized the late nineteenth-century matrimonial press.

Mediated dating and social status

Changing meanings of class in the twentieth century have been linked to structural economic changes, particularly the decline of manufacturing and the manual working class, the rise in its place of service industries in which increasing numbers of women worked part-time, and the expansion of the arena of consumption. To take one of many overviews, Patrick Joyce has summarized these arguments and their implications in terms of 'a movement from production to consumption as the new basis of structural divisions and unities in society'.[28]

Resonating with the idea of taste as matchmaker, this interpretation emphasizes the importance of cultural signifiers, alliances and sympathies in modern romance, and drove the success of some mediated dating businesses, such as the personals in *Time Out* and *City Limits*. Crucially, Joyce's overview also highlights the degree to which late twentieth-century treatments of class have been framed by notions of instability, and dominated by post-modern critiques of class based on the concept of decentred power in an era of consumerism, globalization and transnational popular culture.[29] Class became more negotiable as the coordinates of identity moved away from the external (church, work, civic societies) towards the self.[30] These arguments contribute to a reading of class as a malleable category, rhetorically suggestive but ultimately unfixed. This reading is particularly apt for considering how commentators as well as matchmakers discussed the conditions in which modern romance was felt to take place, conditions that were increasingly and logically leading people towards a pragmatic, consumerist approach to courtship. It wasn't that romantic pragmatism was new: as Simon Szreter and Kate Fisher have shown, the 'sensible attitude towards life and love' characterized working-class communities in the early-mid century, such as those in Lancashire mill towns.[31] This meant shunning cross-class relationships in favour of people with the 'same background, similar occupation and same interests'.[32] But new attitudes towards how one might treat partner-hunting as a modern consumer were appearing. If in 'space age' life, social identity and therefore destiny were becoming the responsibility of each individual, it made perfect sense, according to some observers, to treat the search for a partner as you might treat any other service. And, in these conditions, treating dating as a service that maximized options allowed one to think about romantic encounter as a means for exploring individual social potential no longer bounded by the old fixities of occupational class or even race. One woman who had found two husbands through the lonely hearts pages of what appears to have been *Singles* was invited to share her experience in *The Independent*. Her account fit the more experimental frame of personals rather than the agencies, and of her first husband she wrote, 'We were different generations, different races, different religions and from vastly different backgrounds, and it is hardly likely that we would have met any other way. I enjoyed a short but very happy marriage until my husband died suddenly.'[33]

On the level of language, too, class worked flexibly and suggestively. It could be used in different ways and used to suit different purposes, from forming a good slogan for an advert (*'your* type of person') to a means for setting the tone of a report in *The Times* to providing a simple descriptor in thorough accounts by chroniclers of the industry John Cockburn, Linda Sonntag and Colette Sinclair. In fact, 'class' was not necessarily mentioned, with markers of professional or lifestyle spending habits and discernment such as references to cars, leisure pursuits, geography, terms such as 'smart set' and, particularly from the 1980s onwards, many references to wine and Mediterranean food appearing instead.[34] *The Times* wrote about a woman whose clients 'pay £6,000 a year to meet the right people'.[35] Virginia Charles, founder of the expensive Farrar Grey agency (a made-up name chosen to sound smart, picked after a browse through the phone book), told *The Times* too about how people no longer met in supermarkets but in the auction rooms of Christie's and Sotheby's.[36] Yet in tracking the way social and professional hierarchies appeared in representations of mediated dating in Britain at this time, David Cannadine's insistence remains pertinent that class should not be treated as so unfixed or subject to varying approach that it ceases to be 'essential to a proper understanding of ... Britain'.[37] Indeed, by tracking back in time, we see some of the ways that more fixed understandings of class intersected with mediated courtship. A brief analysis of these will help reveal some of the key flashpoints associated with mediated dating in the late twentieth century.

Since the advent of the matrimonial agencies of the late nineteenth and early twentieth centuries, observers had been struck – both positively and negatively – by the potential of commercial, secular mediated matchmaking to create socially incongruous couples. As suggested earlier, some reformers interested in eugenic solutions to social ills saw the small ads as a salutary means for cutting across class barriers and heeding the healthier sex instinct in mating choice. But as discussed, the bulk of concern about the matrimonial market related to the class dimension of advertising for a spouse. The growing matrimonial press in the late Victorian and Edwardian period was seen as increasingly catering to a dreary lower middle class of clerks, socially lost in growing cities, while also destabilizing assumptions about social norms in which people courted and married people of the same class. The clerk class was mocked for taking a mercenary approach to the marriage market, as well as for aping a version of the upper-class Season. Sketches of the matrimonial press offered an opportunity to critique the centrality of economics in the marriages of the gentry too.[38]

Despite instances of upper-class spouse advertising in fashionable newspapers, the gentry was associated with networks of sociability and ritualized opportunities for mixing. Meanwhile, working-class communities continued to produce the 'bunny run' or 'monkey parade' – whereby young people met each other in public outings in the streets – until the 1960s.[39] The result was that matrimonial agencies or marriage bureaux, as we saw with some of the class-conscious advertisements in the *London Weekly Advertiser*, continued to serve members of the lower middle or working classes who found themselves afloat, either through romantic abandonment or through the vicissitudes of modern labour patterns. The 1970s were a decade of sharp growth in the British dating industry, but it was still the age of marriage bureaux like Ivy Gibson and Ida Reynolds, with more emphasis on processing large numbers of marriage hopefuls than on class exclusivity. Through the 1970s, the association between matchmaking and the lower middle classes remained strong. Thus the wording of *The Daily Mail*'s headline about the founder of the Middle Class Association: 'Middle class man seeks 50 lonely hearts', was revealing, exploiting a sense of contrast between the subject and actor – in fact, the man was advertising to create 'an incredible social document' as well as to find love.[40] Even for Heather Jenner, the upper-class founder of the most famous of mid-century marriage bureaux, the approach to class was flexible. Respectability and seriousness of intent mattered more than exclusivity of social category. Only the 'very peculiar', the too young and the too old would be turned away.[41] A Pathé film of Heather Jenner and her associate Mary Oliver in action in 1939 focused on the successful matching of 'the perfect secretary', while the man's occupation remained unmentioned.[42]

But as discussed in the previous section, the 1980s saw a shift in deployment of social status, as marriage bureaux remodelled themselves as 'introduction agencies'. Despite being more preoccupied with social elitism than the bureaux, these agencies were actually mining newly flexible social territory. New businesses such as Hedi Fisher, Sara Eden, The County Register and Drawing Down the Moon forged new industry norms with vocabularies of exclusivity – 'bespoke' and 'tailored' introductions were promised, catering to 'professionals'; 'your type of person' whether that was 'town or country'. But was this about class? The idea that 'people from different classes simply don't mix' was rooted, even for Balfour, in a reading of a professional landscape in which media and creative jobs had proliferated, rather than in any idea of hereditary destiny that was impervious to ambition. The veneer of social hierarchism that lay behind agency claims of 'exclusivity' was shored up by the media, whose own portrait of the glamour, speed and riches of the post-industrial, deregulated workplace in the 1980s and 1990s matched that of Balfour and her competitors' marketing materials. Indeed, newspapers frequently invited Mary Balfour, Penrose Halson and Heather Heber Percy of The County Register to comment on the situation for the 1980s and 1990s career woman and the predicament for the busy but still traditional male.[43] This kind of commentary affirmed the professionalized, affluent image of the new dating landscape, while the idea that women's growing share of the workplace and of rights in general had fostered sexual and romantic discord appeared to fascinate editors and producers.[44] Heber Percy recalled 'a huge amount of very positive publicity' when she launched The County Register in 1984, including interviews with Jeremy Paxman and Esther Rantzen.[45]

'Class' was used in a more orthodox way as a lens for reading the growth of mediated dating, and the social realities it suggested, by some. *The Daily Mail* – whose readership was 'popular', mostly working or lower middle class – portrayed introduction agencies as services for the well-heeled.[46] It described a video dating service's clientele as attracting some 'stable, middle class and fairly well off' clients. The dating entrepreneur himself was quoted saying, with striking specificity: 'We are catering exclusively for the middle classes, people who live comfortably in places like Bromley, Surbiton and Teddington.'[47] Tabloids took less interest in the dating industry than broadsheets or *The Mail*. Those stories that were selected for the tabloid readership were also explicitly interested in class, but in a different, more polarizing way. Thus in *The Daily Mirror*, there was indignation regarding a Hartlepool lonely hearts club 'suffering from men on the dole demanding "five-star brides" – "a well-paid job, their own home, sex appeal, kitchen skills – and be lovable with it"'.[48] There was an interesting regional angle too, as it was reported that the matchmaker found the local men so dastardly that 'she is putting women aged between 30 and 40 in touch with males in London – 247 miles away'.[49] *The Mirror* also reported with gleeful explicitness on the class hierarchy suggested by Heather Heber Percy's agency, The County Register, with the headline 'Posh splice: The woman who match-makes for the upper classes'.[50]

Inasmuch as tripartite class categories were relevant, mediated dating provided a prime opportunity for media outlets to rehearse the spending power and affluent industriousness of the new 'middle' class, a group whose aspirationalism had emerged as a key feature of the 1970s and 1980s, in domains from gentrifying houses to appetites demanding a new crop of fancy restaurants.[51] A typical *Times* headline of the decade ran like this: 'Business is booming, one matchmaker suggests, because people are more used to using service industries in other areas of their lives and expect instant results. Most of the leading companies say their clients are usually white middle-class professionals aged between 30 and 45.'[52] Such articles helped the matchmakers by contributing to the image of the new dating industry as a new middle-class domain for an age group decreasingly siphoned off in traditional families and ever more successful at work. Of the coterie of matchmakers favoured for quotes by *The Times*, most were based in London W1, bolstering the development of the upmarket, metropolitan image.[53] By the 1990s, Mary Balfour explicitly identified her agency,

Drawing Down the Moon, with a *Times* readership and focused her advertising there.[54]

Superficially, *The Times* seemed to identify itself as a naturally interested observer of the rise of the well-heeled agency because of its own affluent and educated readership. Yet the newspaper's increasingly frequent first-person explorations of these agencies sometimes served to puncture rather than uphold agency claims about social elitism. When one journalist tried out Dinner Dates, run by a matchmaker whose 'product is professional, eligible men', the mismatch was clear.[55] The agency provided 'the 1990s man who has everything. Everything except a mate'. She noted that those at the expensive dinner were a professional motorist, a doctor, an interior designer and a marine engineer, but the journalist concluded on a negative note: 'Paul offered me a lift home in his Porsche. In the world beyond our windscreen, a teenage couple slung arms clumsily around each other's jackets... I wondered why we had to dress up and pay £75 for the most natural human encounter of boy meets girl.' In stories such as these, *The Times* asserted the difference between the real meaning of class (it) and that of the matchmaking business and what could be seen as its dupes, willing to pay £75 for a basic human encounter.

Most coverage, however, was actually suggestive of the *flexibility* of what it meant to be an 'exclusive' agency customer in modern Britain. Being 'exclusive', particularly if you were a man, was attainable through aspirationalism, ambition, careerism – all within the individual's control (as Colette Sinclair's account makes clear, discussed in the next chapter, this could play out very differently for women).[56] Some newspapers were also interested in how the upper crust, both hereditary and professional, were grappling with contemporary conditions, but even here, language referring to social brackets was rooted in the individual's work ethic so that potential dates (men or women) become synonymous with their jobs. The result was an American-influenced patter. For instance, the American owner of Dinner Dates, was quoted in *The Times* saying: 'I've got a motor racing driver just your type. I've got a guy who imports Italian wine. I've got accountants. I've got terrific gentlemen.'[57] Two years later, William Cash reported from LA on a new phone-dating service, quoting matchmaker Nereda Gibbs discussing her clients: 'They are mainly doctors, Hollywood producers, lawyers and even judges who simply don't have the time to spend dating dozens of different people each week.'[58] And in an extended meditation on the role of dating agencies in modern British life, *The Guardian* mused that an aging, richer population would ensure that mediated dating would lose its stigma and 'will no longer be regarded as a final attempt for emotional also-rans but as an absolute necessity for those too busy to organise their own social lives.'[59] The emphasis on profession and wealth had become a key motif in British dating discourse.

Social and professional status was suggestive territory for exploring what it meant to look for intimacy within a patina of 'modern' trends and norms, and particularly the increasingly porous boundaries between professional and personal life. This was not necessarily a preoccupation with class in a clearly defined way. Rather, modern life seemed to mean a new orientation towards work, a greater consciousness – sometimes ostentatiously so – of time and time-poverty, and to provide a new set of tools for reading, and making sense of, potential matches. These were linked to new gradations of taste and experience emerging from consumerism, 'lifestyle' and the kinds of cultural passporting enabled by publications such as *Time Out*. But it was the image of the 1980s and 1990s professional that prompted the most widespread questioning of singles' relational capacity. New ways and metrics of approaching relationships were required, of which exclusivity seemed the most appropriate (and flattering) for people who had refigured their romantic isolation as a function of busyness and success rather than loneliness and need.

A sexual gulf? Dating as antagonistic encounter

The success or failure of courtship depends partly on the satisfaction of certain expectations about masculinity or femininity.[60] In the final part of this chapter, I want to turn to a third flashpoint: sexual acrimony and the pervasive idea that men and women were brought into an increasingly antagonistic relationship by dating. Returning to Scott's framework, this section reviews how the gendered relationality underpinning the quest for intimacy was seen as having been put under strain by women's changing status to the extent that romance and any older certainties associated with it were in danger of being fatally undermined. Tracing out this motif in matchmaking coverage helps illuminate the contradictions in understandings of women's advancement. 'Women's lib' was presented as a done deal while also decried or depicted as the main source of social chaos by a variety of voices that showed just how contested the goals and language of feminism still were into the 1990s.[61]

The explicitness involved in the negotiation of gender in mediated dating raised specific questions for onlookers. Had the institution of marriage changed to accommodate the new 'career woman' written about so much in the 1980s? Who exactly was the 'new man', and how did he fit with traditional romantic goals?[62] What did changing archetypes of gender mean for accountability and chivalry – often parsed as the financial burden – that had traditionally been expected in courtship?

But mediated matchmaking was increasingly seen as a woman's issue. Newspapers stressed data relating to soaring numbers of single career women or the later age at which they were having babies.[63] A number of high-profile books and television shows about single women and dating gave the media a prolonged opportunity to discuss the intersections between contemporary women, feminism and the realities of the dating landscape. By 2000, even the newspaper most attuned to sexism, *The Guardian*, agreed that careerist young women were the most likely to be single and lonely. With three times the number of singles in Britain since 1970, 'working women under 35 make up the biggest growth area in people joining matchmaking agencies, dinner groups and singles parties'.[64] Women were now at the discursive frontline of what was sometimes seen as the decline in social order caused by, among other social changes, feminism. As Susan Faludi demonstrated in *Backlash*, there had since the 1980s been a growing inclination to locate the need for dating agencies in a panoply of social problems caused by women's liberation.[65] Dating discourse, she argued, thrummed with 'myths' – including the idea of a man-shortage – that blamed feminism 'for making women miserable'.[66] Janice Winship has discussed the articles in women's glossies (of which only *Cosmopolitan* identified with aspects of the feminist movement) and men's magazines that implied there was a man-shortage, along with the idea that men were now too afraid to approach women, and at any rate were commitment-phobic. With its centre-right politics and dedicated interest in the fortunes of Britain's solos, *Singles* also weighed in on the results of feminism on dating. Although its analysis varied, it usually offered a sympathetic reading of what it saw as men's plight in the post-feminist dating domain. One typical article, 'Pity the single male', reasoned that 'In a society that is screaming about sexual discrimination (always against women)' single men's suffering were 'sorely overlooked'.[67] And because of women's increasing financial success, it was regularly emphasized that 'Men feel resentful . . .' at having to buy them drinks and dinner.[68]

If the effects of feminism on gender dynamics attracted a great deal of comment in the wake of the launch of Women's Liberation in 1970, the assumed polarity between the 'new woman' and her still-traditional male counterpart in the dating game crystallized in the 1980s and continued to inform analysis in the 1990s. In her memoir *Happily Ever After: How To Meet Your Match* (1998), Penrose Halson explicitly blamed feminism for making women miserable. One of her most prominent stories was that of Julia, an extremely successful professional woman who entered Halson's office with poise and elegance, only to crumple and cry.[69] She'd spent her thirtieth birthday alone eating an omelette after working late. She wanted a man and a family but had married her desk instead. This woman's name was Julia and from then on Halson categorized her clients into 'Julias' versus those with more pronounced wifely instincts. 'In 1986 my most highly paid thirty-something woman client earned £25,000. In 1998 the figure was £250,000 plus bonus', Halson wrote, followed by the story of a man who found that modern women 'think flirting is a dirty word' and flowers an insult. 'Small wonder that men may fear they're becoming redundant, or are going out of fashion,' she concluded.[70] Hedi Fisher, of the upper-crust London agency by the same name, also put the apparent rise of the career woman at the centre of her memoir of matchmaking over the years.[71]

The Daily Mail led the newspaper dating backlash, and featured a number of disillusioned women and concerned onlookers. In an article called 'The new spinsters [in caps]: Are men afraid of these women?'[72] one interviewee confessed: 'The preliminaries of dating remind me of a job interview. After a long day at work, I don't want to bother.'[73] A Relate counsellor provided analysis of this woman's issue, suggesting that single women had unfortunately lost the ability to love at all: they are 'not so much having problems within a relationship as having a problem establishing any relationship'. In 'A Singular Quest for Happiness: How the mating game has become the bitter obsession of the Nineties', *The Daily Mail* interviewed participants in a seven-part Carlton TV documentary called *Singles* (1993).[74] One female participant, Denise, said: 'I think this programme is a sign of the 1990s, which is why I decided to go on it. A lot of professional women in my age group have become quite independent and find it difficult to have a relationship'. Another, Monica, had clearly absorbed the image of a spinster dying alone among cats: 'I honestly felt I was scraping the bottom of the barrel going to a dating agency. To go in there was a complete disaster. But it is desperate being single at my age. I get pangs of panic that I am going to end up on my own...' Perhaps more tellingly, ITV's *The Truth About Women*, aired five years later and, according to cultural critic, lecturer and documentary film maker Victoria Mapplebeck, was 'full of "lifestyle soundbites and caricature" that "match perfectly" those of [Bridget Jones]' scored an impressive 8 million viewers.[75]

The women's paradox of miserable liberation was identified and critiqued by Mapplebeck in an extended report for *The Guardian*, with a depth that merits dwelling on here. Mapplebeck saw the positioning of women as failed bodies, condemned to loneliness and childlessness through their own careerism, as central to dating discourse in the 1990s. For her, programmes like the BBC's *Real*

Women located the '"realness" of women . . . in their pain. These "real women" were tough and witty in the face of "having a hard time of it" '.[76] Such portrayals were partly a backlash to feminism and partly a 'spectacle of angst' made possible by a new confessional zeal in the presentation of sex and relationships. Princess Diana was 'a Bridget Jones in reverse . . . her dating crisis became her trademark; she became the patron saint of the rejected'. The media's own dynamics of thrusting circularity played a major role in perpetrating what Mapplebeck called the 'career woman can't get a boyfriend panic' formula. Nick Fraser, the commissioning editor of BBC2's *Storyville*, confirmed that the 'relationship breakdown epidemic' was largely a media obsession with novelty, even if that novelty was favoured for its perceived fit with a more general national mood. Speaking to Mapplebeck, Fraser said: 'Documentaries feed into drama, and drama feeds back into the documentaries. It's on a loop. The medium just recycles itself. . . Commissioners are now looking at a lot of this stuff. It goes with the perceived "newness" of Blair's Britain.'[77]

The 1990s closed with a gender-polarized idea of how dating might fit the truly modern man or woman's life. The idea of 'the one' had inflected female-focused cultural narratives surrounding romance at least since the interwar period.[78] By the late 1990s, the quest for 'the one' remained a quest associated with women, but with those in their thirties who were poised between the joys of independence and affluence, and the miseries of counteracting biological destiny. What that hunt might look like went global thanks to Helen Fielding's *Bridget Jones' Diary* (1996) and the quartet of *Sex and the City*, which debuted on Channel 4 in 1998. Dating and relationships had become commercial gold.

This chapter has analysed the representational themes that framed and sometimes promoted the dating industry's development, suggesting that matchmaking coverage operated as a kind of proxy for a broader process of assessing shifts in social identity, romantic aspiration and gender. The flashpoints discussed in this chapter concerned the anonymity and social illegibility of potential dates, the instability and flexibility of social identity, and the emergence of competing sexual agendas. Taken together, these flashpoints return us to a key claim of this book: that the period after 1970 saw the development and refinement of a new emotional arsenal for use not only in managing expectations and rejection but in converting rejection into a productive, pro-active response. For underpinning each flashpoint was the awareness that failure rather than success was the more likely outcome of taking a punt on a blind dating service. In fact, according to the 1983 *Which?* report, the only way to approach such services was 'to treat it as a gamble, don't expect to win and if hearts come up trumps, then congratulations'.[79]

Dating services seemed to be constantly refining their offering, catering to specific needs, wants and types. Whether or not this meant their success rates improved as the industry matured in the 1990s is unclear. But the attitude to failure and success changed, with a paradigm emerging that put the onus on customers to use failure as a signal to work harder at success: how this played out comes to the fore in the analysis of singles' testimonies in the next and final chapter. Romantic failure was, perhaps, the fault of the agency or the unresponsive people in the lonely hearts pages. But it was also portrayed as a measure of how much labour – emotional, financial and administrative – the single was prepared to invest. As we saw at the close of Chapter 1, the approach to dating in the 1980s and 1990s seemed geared towards 'success' in terms that required business-style management of the process, shrewd calculation and finely honed, aspirational taste.[80] Books, articles and television programmes all marked how dating culture had shifted since the 1970s by emphasizing daters' use of the same terms they would use in choosing a car or other luxury good. Market-oriented language was used in a variety of ways, with different degrees of knowingness, and with different implications for the malleability and meaning of an individual's position in the social strata. But as well as encouraging a flexible, agentic approach to romantic destiny, this language also put pressure on singles to approach loneliness with an entrepreneurial, not a downbeat spirit and a 'how-to'/'can do' attitude. People could and perhaps should 'learn' how to improve their chances, to play the game better and to market themselves. In other words, to shepherd their own destinies and emotional lives; to 'take control', a formulation used repeatedly by case studies whose extended testimonies appeared in John Cockburn's *Lonely Hearts*.

The next chapter explores in more detail what it felt like to bring romantic fantasy into collision with flesh and blood lonely hearts, and – by no means always negatively – to experience the self as an object in a trade-fair of vital statistics and first impressions.

4

Mediated daters and the experience of matchmaking

'Every single man I met lied to me.'[1] For Pen Fudge, seventy-three at the time of writing to me in response to my *Saga* ad, mediated dating – which she undertook in the 1980s and 1990s – was a disaster from beginning to end.[2] A keen lace-maker, the nadir for Fudge came when the jealousy of a man she met in the 'small ads' led to him eating – physically ingesting – the lace motif she was working on at the time. 'He was telling me that now I would always be a part of him! Absolute madness.'[3] For Fudge, the men she met through mediated dating demonstrated just how sharply sexual agendas could clash. Her experience was one in which far from acting as a palliative for sexual difference, mediated romance set the stage for a gendered antagonism to which remaining single seemed preferable. The first-person testimonies examined in this chapter reveal a spectrum of approaches and feelings about how gender played out in the context of mediated dating, with few quite as negative as Fudge's. But as an example of miscommunication and sexual mistrust linked to the context of meeting, Fudge's account offers an apt entry point to the evidence considered here.

Singles developed, in tension with new psychological vocabularies of the self, an emotional pragmatism that accommodated the romantic failures that were becoming part of the instability of 'modern' relational life. The use of emotional self-management and armoury was particularly clear among customers of the matchmaking industry, since their dates were blind, arranged without prior confirmation of sexual chemistry, and therefore the most likely to disappoint or disconcert. In turning to daters' experience, however, this chapter illuminates how the tensions inherent in gender as a relational concept were played out in the 'applied' setting of courtship.[4] Moreover, although it attracts much public interest, dating itself is an intensely personal experience, with only two witnesses per date. The experience of those who went on mediated dates does confer 'authority' on the subject, since it is only through first-person accounts that we can learn what actually happened in these encounters.

One of the challenges of this section has been to categorize a heterogeneous group of subjects. In the last chapter, I argued that in the 1980s and 1990s, matchmakers and the media deployed the concept of social status as flexible, rooted in professional ambition and rank rather than heredity. We saw that although matchmakers emphasized the exclusivity of their operation, in practice they adopted a relatively non-discriminatory process aimed at making sales. In this chapter, the idea of 'exclusivity' breaks down further in two main ways. First, when customers were attracted to the promises of agents to provide an elite service they usually came away particularly disappointed, and second, the social heterogeneity of all types of customer, from lonely heart to West End dating agency, was evident. Although class, geographical milieu (metropolitan settings vs. smaller towns) and gender constantly inflected perceptions and uses of dating services, advertisers were mixed in terms of social class, emotional and social adeptness and need, educational and professional background, but their approach to mediated dating did not map in any obvious way onto these categories. In Cockburn's collection of 200 interviews of users of a single medium (personals), a faint pattern is discernible: women appeared to have more social capital than the men, whose jobs – clerks, local government officers – often went with more lonely existences. Yet taking all the first-person sources together, it is clear that there was not one type of mediated dater. However, the individuality with which singles made sense of their romantic quest did not preclude the emergence of a set of clearly sexual agendas arising from the experience of romantic clienthood.

Mediated dating: motivations and usages

The promise of control

We have seen how purveyors of dating after 1970 loaded it with promise in marketing materials and press appearances. Agencies strained to present commercial matchmaking as the domain of the busy professional, sometimes specifying alignment with the middle, upper middle and occasionally the upper classes. Meanwhile, computer dating was an efficient solution for the lovelorn but respectable everyman and woman, with no awareness of 'Clerks, shepherds, Peers of the Realm' because 'The Computer knows no class barrier, just people with a need'.[5] And the branding of *Time Out* and *City Limits* shaped the image of their typical advertiser. All of them positioned themselves against the omniscient stigma surrounding singles services and emphasized a 'modern' form of sociality that was realistic, adventurous and an appropriate response to a couple-centric society.[6]

Unsurprisingly the ways in which mediated daters explained and contextualized their use of singles services did not necessarily map onto the categories put in place by dating businesses and by cultural sources. Nonetheless, taking control over intimate life was seen by both men and women as a freedom that should be exploited. While they had mixed feelings about using mediated dating, singles explained that they saw it as a rational response to circumstance, while the more extended interviews cast recourse to matchmaking services as a solution to internal and external pressures to find a relationship, a symbol of maturing and personal growth as well as an end in itself. By engaging with the idea of options and choice, the testimonies considered here point back to Giddens's idea that expanded social options helped make sexual relationships more egalitarian, more 'plastic'.[7] However, while the expansion of social options enshrined in the business model of mediated dating offered a pathway for thinking pro-actively about the social self, it did not appear to help smooth sexual relations. More useful, I think, for interpreting singles' approach to mediated dating is Rachel Bowlby's theorization of the cultural meanings of modern shopping as a way of exerting 'freedom of choice'.[8] Bowlby writes:

> Instead of confinement, darkness, hidden controls, shopping in its positive guise appears as ... the proud symbol of modern mobility. People are no longer restricted to their traditional horizons, whether geographical, social or psychological; consumer choice epitomizes their liberty to move away from old constrictions, to indulge the freedom of new desires and demands and to take on different identities as they wish.[9]

Building on this image of consumption in its 'positive guise', this section explores the degree to which paying for romantic aid allowed people to experience the multi-faceted, forward-looking freedoms of consumer status elucidated by Bowlby. As we will see, being a romantic 'shopper' offered daters a novel means for self-fashioning and enabled them to both control their exposure to the sexual domain, and push back against the limitations of personal and social circumstances.

Romance has long been conceived in market metaphors; the economist Gary Becker's influential description of the 'marriage market' in 1974 enshrined the idea that people searching for partners deploy the economic principles of choice used in other markets.[10] The way people negotiate choice has also come to define a more recent sociology on love and courtship, further entrenching the conceptual similarities between shopping and dating. Thus Eva Illouz has theorized contemporary romance in terms of an 'architecture of choice' encouraging people to approach potential lovers as though at a buffet, the logics of consumerism problematically co-mingling with the demands of feeling.[11] Her account foregrounds the importance of the *search* for dates, a new 'field' whose 'invisible but powerful marketplace of competing actors' had made it the most absorbingly complex part of the romance process.[12] The result, according to Illouz, was that dating – despite encapsulating all the freedoms of sexual modernity – had become defined by ambivalence.[13] These formulations offer a frame for considering the feelings singles experienced as they faced the explicitly marketized milieu of mediated dating. But whatever its emotional or psychological after-effects were, the desire to have 'options' was central to the decision for many to become customers. The attractions of paying for a service that offered choice were often discussed in gendered terms, linked, for instance, to understandings of 'modern' women's work. For one female respondent to the Mass Observation Project (MOP), a dating agency was used 'to find myself partners to take to official dinners connected with my job'.[14] Meanwhile Linda Sonntag, whose mediated dating manual was partly based on personal experience, framed the advantages of advertising by what she saw as the diminution of social choice caused by an ever-more 'fragmented' society in which women 'who are highly successful in their chosen professions' found themselves shorn of choice.[15] And rising divorce rates had left another Mass Observer a 'single mother, and over 40 [with] no men in village'.[16] Younger women also pushed back against lack of options: a student librarian at Wolverhampton Polytechnic lived in a 'bedsit with girls in Ealing [and] had no way of meeting men' and was persuaded by friends to try computer dating.[17] For these women, the options that mediated dating collated and made available were seen as a key way of moving beyond limited social geographies.[18]

Beyond the professional sphere, daters – particularly (though not exclusively) those who lived in small towns – felt pressure to expand their 'social circle' as a way of enriching their lives as well as of meeting someone.[19] One woman, forty-nine at the time of writing, joined a 'pen-friend agency' when she 'realised that almost everyone I had ever dated came from my small south-western university'.[20] Men also joined agencies in response to the limited options in their hometowns: one, born in 1963 and thirty-eight at the time of writing in 2001, 'joined a dating agency ... I was living in a small town with a pretty limited social circle'.[21] More often, male MOP respondents explained their recourse to commercial solutions to romantic loneliness in terms of emotional and sexual want, aligning the decision with need rather than choice. One man, seventy-two and a retired chartered surveyor, reflected on his situation in the early 1970s, cognizant but locked out of 'a new culture afoot . . . the Pill; a revolution in the publishing world about what was pornographic and a plethora of sexually oriented magazines'. He concluded that: 'Something had to change in my life and I started to follow up contact advertisements', resulting in the longed-for sexual initiation.[22] A man who at thirty left college to begin work as a teacher 'felt very much on the shelf' and joined a Catholic introduction agency.[23]

If men and women pursued mediated dating from within different emotional frameworks of need and control, the idea of 'options' was also gendered. For many, particularly women, 'options' could be as much about who they were trying to avoid as whom they were seeking because of safety issues, as well as complex, gendered expectations around finances. Some women who 'found' themselves single after a marriage or a long relationship ended, joined agencies as a way of controlling their exposure to sexual partners (e.g. risky short-term 'affairs' with married men) as well as a way of moving on.[24] For interviewee Millie, a 74-year-old woman who met her third husband Michael (also interviewed) through Hedi Fisher, the agency was a refuge from predatory men, its female matchmaker imposing a reassuring order on sexualized male agendas.[25] Millie had found that 'Every person I come into contact with wants to know whether I'll go to bed with them ... Men seemed to think, if you were a divorced woman, you were missing sex or whatever, and that's all you were interested in'.[26] Millie paid £150 to join, 'a lot of money', but figured that 'if someone was willing to pay that amount . . .' then the chances are they would not be sexual aggressors.[27] Safety was also a concern for my interviewee Hilary, an academic journal editor aged sixty-three, who started her mediated dating career with an agency when she was in her late twenties because 'I felt that an agency would have much much more ... probably safety ... that there was somebody there that would help to filter out psychopaths'.[28]

For women, the threat of sexual danger was built into mediated dating, and confirmed in the news reports discussed in Chapter 3, but in fact none of my female sources recalled being threatened by the men they met this way. Instead, other disappointing masculine behaviours came to the fore and shaped women's thinking about how to approach singles services. Thus because agencies offered the personalized attention of a matchmaker, and were expensive, singles turned to them as a refuge from disappointments encountered through other, less tailored channels. Mary signed up to an agency when she found that her Solos singles holidays weren't providing attractive options but rather 'guys who ... I didn't see them as someone who I was going to spend the rest of my life, or any time at all with' – moreover, the company was increasingly catering to the thirties and forties age range 'at the cost of' older singles.[29] For Michael, joining an agency seemed the most respectable means for taking his widower's life in hand. Both he and Millie had frequented dances in north London as a primary way of meeting people but by the 1990s 'they [the dances] had all gone'.[30] Hedi Fisher had a 'good name', with lots of Jewish clients, and the woman who interviewed him, a 'Mrs Joyce Zane', was 'good'.[31] He remembered the interview as thorough and effective, fulfilling the brief he was prepared to pay for. She 'went over the things in the questionnaire and probed a bit further'.[32] For Millie, as we have seen, the agency signalled a stock of men with – above all – respectable intentions: 'I wanted someone not shorter than me, but I didn't care what they looked like' as long as they were 'honest', 'reliable', had 'all the good qualities'.[33] The matchmaker advised her that, after two failed marriages with them, she should avoid Jewish men, because she was 'too down to earth'.[34]

In allowing women to control the context in which their options were produced, mediated dating also offered a means for avoiding men who would drain their resources. In personal ads, this required clear syntax, which, in the case of *Singles* readers, was often flagged by men as a sign of shameless gold-digging. Their female counterparts had to explain forcefully why they were justified in doing so. Wrote one woman:

> "Professional" man is stipulated in order that unwashed unshaven and part dressed yobs don't appear for meals and also to intimate that the advertiser would like to meet a male with a wider topic of conversation than football and bars. The "successful" "solvent" etc. part of the vocabulary usually tells a story if you look a little further. It usually means they are sick to death of trying to live on a pittance … My ex-husband was so mean with his money …[35]

Taking semantic precautions, another female *Singles* reader's advertisement tellingly requested that men 'Read no further! Unless you are a good looking professional fella …'[36] The need to filter was extreme in Pen Fudge's experience, since 'most' of the men she met through the small ads

> were not working and hadn't for a long time yet they told me they had really good jobs when we talked on the phone. Several turned out to be married. Two were alcoholics, one had been in prison for a long time and finally one of them stole my car as he turned out to be a crack addict.

For this reason she later turned to an agency (although this didn't provide a happy solution either). Women also commented on the need to avoid the kinds of men who, in their sixties or even seventies were advertising for younger women with a view to 'looking for a carer for their declining years'.[37]

The concept of choice and options worked in two ways, then, for the mostly female singles discussed above: first, as a way of expanding social options in the context of demanding careers, single-sex or small-town environments, and second, as a means for controlling and filtering exposure to men who would take advantage financially or sexually. In the next section, I turn to another set of pragmatics, focusing on the traction these had with women's testimonies in particular, and highlighting how mediated dating was used as an instrument of personal growth, as well as for the fulfilment of explicit relational and familial preferences and intentions. These could be articulated in a spirit of explicit self-assertion that some onlookers saw as a troubling by-product of feminism. On this score there are some intriguing insights to be gained from Arlie Hochschild's analysis of late twentieth-century attitudes towards romance.[38] The relationships expertise that emerged in the 1980s and 1990s, argues Hochschild, circulated a 'paradigm' of instrumentalism that offered a 'blend' of feminism and 'commercial spirit'.[39] Women in particular were coached to develop 'an instrumental detachment' enabling them to face men as non-needy equals, conversant in the emotional 'coolness' required of the self-aware, self-protecting and balanced partner.[40] While my subjects did not necessarily achieve (or strive for) detachment, Hochschild's analysis nonetheless anticipates the use by British singles in this period of mediated dating for non-romantic ends such as self-development and social or sexual experience.

How men perceived women's approach to matchmaking also invites attention. Hochschild suggests that feminism was used to legitimate the claims put forth in commercial dating and relationships advice.[41] Here we see how – outside of the commercial sphere – men used feminism to *de*-legitimate women's approach to relationships, and what they saw as the disturbingly business-like nature of female singles' sexual approach. Noted the character Nick in the 1993 documentary *Singles*:

> 'British women have got a very very gentle side to them I think but that is disappearing because of some of the more militant feminine thoughts that are going around society today … I'm not saying I disagree with feminism, but there's such a big deal made today by women, "oh I'm independent"'.[42]

But, Nick wondered, 'What is independent really? How can you be independent – totally independent and have a loving relationship?' What exactly Nick had encountered as 'independence' remained unclear. Clearer was the sense that the women he was encountering were more interested in pursuing personal ends in a self-assertive fashion than in 'giving', and were therefore somehow representative of what he perceived to be feminism's destructive power.

A tool for personal growth

The Mass Observer who used computer dating when she was a trainee librarian found that: 'it was very good for me as I had to stop expecting Prince Charming to come along and lighten up a bit'.[43] The idea that dating lots of people was 'good for' her marked her movement away from aloofly waiting for 'the one', towards the conviction that experience was a good in itself whatever the outcome.[44] Attitudes such as these gave individual texture to the documentation of broader shifts in sexual behaviour discussed in Chapter 1, and highlighted how courtship – no longer tethered to marriage as an end point – took on a complex gradation of purposes that related as much to the questions of selfhood as of romantic commitment to someone else. Indeed in Cockburn's analysis of his 200 interviews with personals users, the use of dating for personal development, 'as part of the self-awareness movement', was a key part of their usage.[45] Linda Sonntag also captured the sense that the romantic experience on offer to mediated daters could, perhaps first and foremost, be seen as a valuable tool for self-development: 'Even if you don't meet anyone who changes your life, you will have changed your life yourself, by opening it up to new experience'.[46] The implication of this shift for women was marked: romantic experience was for the first time not something they needed to ration and avoid, but rather something that they could and should actively seek as an end in itself, reshaped as an instrument of self-realization.

Among Cockburn's interviewees, both women and men admitted to 'seeing [in the columns] an instrument that enhances their love lives'.[47] First, however, Cockburn categorized singles as 'single girls looking for lovers', while men were 'bachelors on the search'; cross-gender categories included divorcees and widows (including 'divorcees looking for replacement wives') and 'Affair seekers', 'sugar daddies' and 'toy boys'. Whereas some kind of sexual politics shaped many of the accounts considered in this book, Cockburn's study explicitly framed his investigation in terms of Women's Liberation and its effects, returning repeatedly to the idea of confusion over changing gender roles. Certainly, in his view, feminism structured the recourse to mediated dating:

> a large proportion of single women advertising in the lonelyheart columns are independent and achieving women who have learned that they can influence, if

not fully control, their lives and futures. Hence they go about their tasks of mate finding with the same kind of efficiency that they go about their careers.[48]

Cockburn's female interviewees stressed the pressures of what they felt to be biology in terms that were both traditional but also redolent of the new technocratic romantic vocabularies discussed in Chapter 1. Thus Susan, who advertised in *Time Out* and *Singles* answering six adverts or letters a week, was searching for Mr Right: 'I'm 31 now so I only have about seven childbearing years left. And I want at least two children.'[49] Like Colette Sinclair, the author of the dating memoir *Manhunt*, Susan had the listing style of the mediated dating habituée: the children 'have to be with the right man ... I need support and warmth and a caring relationship too. I want someone to love me and be here for me to love.'[50]

Commercial dating could also provide more than a tool for enhancing love life or personal development. For some, it offered an emotional emollient for restlessness and dissatisfaction more generally, becoming an internal rather than an external instrument embedded in the single's wider psychological ecosystem. Thus one woman told how after she'd placed an advert for the first time that:

> I knew that I'd never be lonely ever again. I get bored very easily, but I knew that however bored I got and however many people I would meet I could always turn to this resource. There are millions and millions of men and I never had any hesitation doing it.[51]

Loneliness, a feeling imposed by circumstance, and an innate tendency to 'get bored very easily', were both shaped by 'this resource'. But taken to extremes, the inward-facing instrumentalization of romantic choice could create anxiety and a sense of being emotionally and psychologically shelled out rather than enriched. One of Cockburn's female interviewees claimed to be addicted to lonely hearts advertising: 'I tried something dramatic to stop myself doing it ... I thought I would completely wipe out the past, kind of exorcise myself and that I would start to be a real person, not just a hollow shell that did this all the time.'[52] This account suggests that the realities of selfhood were not always able to keep pace with the modes of self-management implicated in being a 'modern' single. It is striking that for this woman, 'the past', normally taken to substantiate personhood, negated the person she wanted to be into the future. She made this clear in her means of 'exorcising' the lonely hearts addiction, symbol of the emptied-out person: creating a bonfire and burning all her correspondence.

I want now to turn to two more in-depth examples of how mediated dating could be experienced not simply as a response to an 'architecture of choice', but as a carefully calibrated method of psychological self-management and maturation, historically embedded in a landscape of changing sexual norms and options.[53]

For journal editor Hilary, born in 1952, the decision to deploy a commercial service and therefore take control was driven by a longing to gain independence, sexual confidence and experience. On her thirtieth birthday, in 1982 ('it felt like I was becoming old and mature') a male friend 'paid for an ad in *City Limits*, I did the wording'.[54] That it was presented as a birthday present suggests how exciting it was, an innovative piece of social and personal manoeuvring brimming with options suited to the sexually liberated woman of 1970s London – albeit one that wanted a partner and children – rather than a last resort for the desperate. 'I felt it was me taking charge, I felt I would like to have a committed partner and children . . .'[55] Hilary's *City Limits* ad did lead to her meeting her husband, with whom she had two daughters. But they eventually divorced after he 'got in touch with his homosexual side' – whether or not this result caused Hilary to reconsider the benefits of the medium of meeting was not clarified.

Prior to the *City Limits* advert, Hilary had used a dating agency. The reasons she elucidated for this went deep into her childhood, to a mother who, she said, always undermined her academic ambitions, her parents' miserable marriage and the sense of claustrophobia and failure associated with home life. After a period of being unwell, she had to sell her flat (on buying her own flat: 'my parents said it was a great mistake') and move home. Moving back in with her parents felt like an all-time low, conveyed in the disjointed wording of the recollection. 'There was a sort of sense of gosh . . . I am really . . . many of my friendships were such that I wouldn't have wanted to continue them . . . I had moved out of London and back into West Sussex and that was it really. That was why I did it really.'[56] By 'it' she meant joining a dating agency, which seemed to represent a step back into adult life, a taking back of adult control. 'It was very much . . . how am I going to get out of this . . . having come full circle, having had some adult life, ending up as a child again and I didn't like it.'[57] The choice of an agency was intuitive: more comfortable to her then than the more open-ended personals and Dateline because it offered a 'safety' net. Although the agency was technically a failure – she didn't meet her match – it catalysed a kind of sexual maturity by bringing into relief the type of person Hilary was not looking for, nor felt she was. In particular, it drew out what felt like irreconcilable differences between generations: 'These men were very conventional, very conservative, in a sense, belonging to the kind of society, the kind of social habits that were pre-1968 and sexual revolution. They were too old for me'. By contrast, *City Limits* was 'much more exciting and useful than the dating agency' – it was also full of socialist politics that agreed with Hilary's self-image – the socialism 'really came out'. The initial letters she exchanged with her future husband, a scholar of early modern Hindi, contained references to well-known socialist theoreticians. *City Limits'* lonely hearts offered a classic example of a left-learning metropolitan milieu: more politically homogenous than *Time Out's*, and contrasting sharply with the national *Singles, Private Eye* and the personals of regional papers. Left-leaning print culture enabled a form of romantic exploration that fit with Hilary's generational sense of being 'modern', and affirmed her political identity. The matchmaker's clientele might have been too traditional for her, but Hilary's use of both mediums suggests that the psychological need for a sense of her own agency as a daughter and a woman underpinned her use of a singles' service as much as the desire for a partner.

For Elaine, a mental health nurse who used Dateline before answering an advert in *Time Out*, third-party dating was also about expediting a romantic future that may otherwise have slipped away.[58] Although (as reviewed in Chapter 1) marriage age had risen since the early 1970s, and marriage rates were steadily dropping as cohabitation increased, the persistence of the monogamous heterosexual norm put pressure on Elaine. Turning thirty while single represented a watershed moment: 'I remember working on the ward with the ward sisters, who were 30, perfectly nice women, they had just resigned themselves to living in rented flats, never going to marry. I thought, ok this is desperate measures.'[59] And Dateline proposed an appealingly scientific method. Elsewhere, I have argued that the expansion of psychological expertise on one hand and new age 'science' on the other, helped carved out a historically specific niche for Dateline.[60] Indeed, for Elaine, 'I think perhaps in the 70s, if serendipity didn't work, you lived it and it didn't work, perhaps you were attracted to something scientific.'[61] That 'something scientific' was the core of Dateline's marketing around 1980, while its claims to be class blind (whether 'peer of the realm' or humble shepherd), also attracted Elaine.[62]

> I knew about those dating agencies but I thought they were expensive and for upper middle-class people ... They were too posh, for people who had been in Oxford and Cambridge. You need a level of confidence, you have to go and give a profile, you have to have something that can be introduced, and I think I didn't feel that.[63]

Dateline seemed less intimidating. She 'saw the ads on the Tube' and signed up, feeling more comfortable with the heterogeneous array of potential matches

Dateline offered than with the more exclusive outfits. Finally, for Elaine, like for Hilary, the pursuit of intimacy through mediation reflected a desire to avoid the unhappy past of their parents' generation. In Elaine's terms it was a 'big thing, do not end up like your mother – do not go there – happiness does not lie there': in her mother's case, an unhappy marriage and an unwanted child produced out of social expectation ('I was unwanted').[64]

The testimonies of a number of Mass Observers, Millie, Michael, Elaine and Hilary present different versions of mediated dating as a profound way of exercising agency; for Elaine, it was a private ('desperate') but necessary measure, while for the others, singles services jumped out as the only solution to romantic isolation, and – whether or not they led to marriage – opened up valuable new perspectives on life and selfhood.

Hesitations, discomforts and the question of the natural

Singles used mediated matchmaking for a variety of pragmatic reasons, and the accounts of these considered so far paint a fairly positive picture. But as the analysis continues, the dissatisfactions, clashes and discomforts that could also accompany mediated matchmaking become more emphatic. Here I want to move from the reasons people did date this way to look in more depth at the discomfort that could be associated with using these services. Tracing unease about matchmaking, among both users and non-users, brings us nearer to unpicking the key tension this book posits between the commercially revealed source of romantic production and the generation of romantic feeling itself. By the 1980s, consumption was, according to some scholars, 'a whole way of life', and as I have suggested, some of the language deployed by mediated daters was taken explicitly from the workplace and the market.[65] However, the testimonies considered below demonstrate the limits of how porous the 'logics of the market' actually were. Daters might have used marketized language to describe their approach, but their feelings were less amenable to such a framework, so that for many, the reconcilement of romantic clienthood with the constitution of a legitimate romantic setting did not appear to be possible. The following section is dedicated to probing this dissonance between the systematic and the authentic, and in doing so points to the complicated ways in which romantic feeling could be set against the unfurling of market processes.

Claire Langhamer, along with sociologists Beck and Beck-Gernsheim, Arlie Hochschild and Eva Illouz, have posited a fundamental tension in twentieth-century courtship between pragmatism in partner choice and 'true' love, or between 'routine, labor, and calculation [as the] enemy of romance' and the need for 'regular applications of effort and skilful management' in order to find and maintain a lasting relationship.[66] Applied to mediated dating, this tension was particularly noticeable, with singles acutely aware of the ways in which paying for a service and mediation by technology or matchmaker threatened to stifle proper romantic bonding. This sense was clear among both customers and those who hadn't used services. A number of respondents cited a preference for more 'natural' ways of meeting, assumed to be more likely to elicit more 'natural' grades of romantic feeling. One Mass Observer put it succinctly: 'I suppose dating agencies are allright [sic] for some people but I would prefer to meet someone in a more natural way in the ordinary course of events.' Others saw love as something you 'just know'; are 'hit' by, and of being like a 'chemical reaction between two elements, acid + alkali = neutral.'[67]

Love appeared, in this light, to be generally resistant to third-party matching. Another Mass Observer, a young woman of twenty-three, said she 'never used a matchmaker or felt the arrogance to play matchmaker for anyone else.[68] As a general rule I see relations and sexual relations as a private matter which is the business of no one else.'[69] For her, intervention in intimate matters was a form of god-playing. Machines were no better: 'I once used Dateline to find a partner,' noted one woman, 'and quickly learned that computers can not think in abstracts, e.g. about a person's personality.'[70] The unnatural was not simply to do with the intervention of a third party. It was also related to the apparently murky boundary between courtship and sex in dating services. Tellingly, a number of people who explained why they had avoided or never come into collision with a dating service seemed to think that dating services were a form of sexual service, eliding 'escorts' and matchmakers.[71] One observed, agencies 'Seem[ed] a good idea but asking for trouble' while others noted with bemusement their friends' experiences, emphasizing their sexual nature, a facet that stood out particularly to the older respondents: 'What she wanted was something extra,' recalled one woman, born in the 1920s, of a married friend. 'She got it.'[72] Sex, like commerce, was seen as an antithetical framework for the pursuit of true romantic bonds.

If some struggled to make sense of this 'unnatural' form of dating, and associated dating services with insalubrious or unrespectable strangers, then for others blind dating – in wrenching away social context – raised uncomfortable questions about the social value and standing of individuals. The stigma surrounding mediated dating was widespread, after all, and suggested that there was something wrong with people who had failed to meet people in the normal course of life. If 'lonely hearts' were thought to be for losers, then what did that make oneself as a customer? In wrestling with this question, some singles deployed complex manoeuvres to show that they were distanced from the process while participating in it. One extreme but revealing example of this approach was found in the account of a 42-year-old man who described how he and his friends placed an ad in *NME* music magazine 'for a laugh'.[73] This account is worth dwelling on because it shows the complexity of feelings deployed in responding to stigma – in this case shame, the desire to prove social mastery and the impulse to sexual judgement.

Advertising in *NME* was 'a laugh' because 'only really sad people do it' and 'what we wanted was the fun of getting letters back with photos of these women so we could laugh and sneer at their comments about themselves'.[74] Acknowledging the malign spirit of their trick hints at a kind of confession, but the account remains distant, using the manoeuvre as a narrative device for self-distancing rather than for engagement with personal ads as a valid way of meeting. The narrator tells how 'we were like little children', making up the name of Mark Scott, 'which we thought sounded dull and non-threatening' for their dating avatar. The ploy resulted in the receipt of forty letters in the first week and fifteen after. The joke continued somewhat darkly when 'Mark Scott' met up with a woman from London. He rang her up on speakerphone so his friends could listen in, and then arranged to meet her, saying he would wear a particular jacket. This 'was a lie because if when I got there and she looked a mess I would not identify myself and could slip away'.[75]

This account openly revolves around duplicity, tones of misogyny (the idea that women were there to be 'sneered at' and ditched if they 'looked a mess') as well as the feelings driving him and his friends to engage collectively in what amounted to a ritual shaming of the date. But the ploy went beyond a homosocial ritual, extending to a date. The testimony offers a flicker of mutual regard when the man recounts how he and Karen went to a pub and talked. But the date – and the whole testimony – was framed by the need to satirize the mediation of meeting women. Indeed this tale is presented as a lesson in how mediation can be manipulated and subverted. Not only were further meetings shunned when it transpired she was a 'devout Christian' but, having invited her home, Karen was shown further deliberate inconsiderateness. 'I knew I had no intention of seeing her again and I didn't care if she didn't like my mates or home.' A final reflection allows some consideration of the impact of his actions: 'I suppose I do feel sorry for her and the other women who my mates went out with' but the account is tied up with a retreat to self-distancing: 'but at the time it was just so funny to us'.[76]

For this man, lonely hearts was for 'losers', and he therefore positioned the women who advertised as strange or irregular; unnatural people to meet. Instead of offering an opportunity to encounter women on an equal footing of singleness, this story highlighted how mediation could be used to create and enhance sexual dissonance and otherness. As we will see in more detail in Mary's experience, the sense of encountering people who jarred with, not to say offended, one's sense of self-worth also came through in women's encounters with men. One 53-year-old Mass Observer from London wrote of her experience using Dateline: 'What a revelation. Most of them … didn't have the first idea how to deal with [women]. What shocked me was how uninteresting and unadventurous they were (a number said to me "you go on holiday alone?").'[77] Her independence and self-sufficiency, contrasted with the feebleness of the men, suggested that in the lonely hearts pages at least, men were moving away from idealized versions of masculinity, and were therefore not only unattractive but not the type with whom women saw themselves. Elaine recalled of her outings with Dateline, 'I don't know if it was just bad luck, the men I met were not terribly well educated …'[78] They didn't manipulate the service to over-determine the distance between themselves (the 'normal' party) and their dates, as the *NME* advertiser did. Nonetheless, for these women, singles services did seem to sharpen the sense that blind pairings produced disappointment and a sense of unbridgeable difference in the romantic encounter.

Dating as consumption

Expectations

The discomfort with mediated dating expressed in the preceding testimonies was somewhat localized, their sexual dissonance remembered through specific encounters with the opposite sex. As suggested earlier, however, dating services could also elicit a broader discomfort that stemmed from the friction between pragmatic self-positioning and money-spending on the one hand and the apparently 'natural' development of authentic feeling on the other. This section explores an analogous problem: to what degree did daters allow themselves to approach mediated dating as consumers? And what problems were posed when the searched-for partner was also evaluated in materialistic terms (income, professional background)? Colette Sinclair provided a stark reminder of the stigma attached to appearing mercenary, judged harshly by observers and cultural arbiters for openly seeking a man who could provide a luxury lifestyle, and for doing so through a methodical approach to dating agencies and ads. Heather Heber Percy, the matchmaker, commented that she 'seemed just out for money'.[79] Sinclair's memoir offers a rich example of the numerous levels in which consumer status, materialism and instrumentalization of the romantic quest could both shape and confuse the mediated dating experience.

Scholars have debated the extent to which romance and courtship (not necessarily in reference to mediated dating) have been colonized by market imperatives acting both within and outside the individual or couple. Eva Illouz has insisted that over the course of the twentieth century, romance became 'a potent idiom through which the culture of consumption addresses our desires'.[80] Matthew Hilton has identified consumption as a key means by which twentieth-century citizens 'moulded their political consciousness'.[81] Yet as Hochschild and Illouz, building on the theories of Fromm, Marcuse and the Frankfurt School, have made clear, the expanding field of late twentieth-century consumption moulded other types of consciousness too, including that which relates to the constitution of romance.

Here we might consider Colin Campbell's theory of modern hedonistic consumption, revolving around the changed nature of expectation. Unlike its 'traditional' predecessor, modern pleasure is sought 'via emotional and not merely sensory stimulation', using a set of 'modern' emotional skills that enables individuals to create, stoke and harness emotion on command.[82] Mirroring Weber, Campbell links such emotional skills to the rise of the Protestant ethic in early modern Europe. The Protestant ethic, with its insistence on emotional control, in turn equipped moderns with the tools required for the 'romanticism' – longing imbued with fantasy – that in Campbell's theory drives modern consumption. Campbell's work provides an intriguing departure for considering aspects of mediated dating. For if, as he claims, modern consumption revolves around the seduction of the 'romantic', meaning 'remote from everyday experience', 'imaginative', suggestive of 'grandeur' or 'passion', we might assume that mediated dating is an ideal fusion of the spirits of both consumerism and romance.[83] Certainly, those who bought romantic aid were not only seeking to answer an emotional need, but indulging in a host of options located within a rich imaginative terrain, heavily laden with the suggestion of future pleasure in the very emotional terms in which Campbell locates modern hedonistic pleasure. Yet what emerges in the following discussion does not follow the logic of modern hedonism in Campbell's sense. While the purchase of cigarettes and perfumes might be imbued with romantic feeling (evoking the 'exotic', for instance), and triggering pleasurable longing in advance of the actual unwrapping of the product, the purchase of actual romance itself in the form of dates left buyers acutely aware of the banal textures of the transaction: the social effort, the anxiety of etiquette, forced conversation. If it was possible to accurately anticipate and read the value associated with other goods and services, then buyers of mediated dates often felt the disappointment of having been mis-sold. The prince, in the words of one disillusioned MOP respondent, was too often 'a frog'.[84]

So for mediated daters, the purchase and unwrapping of the 'product' itself was often anything but romantic. In revealing too clearly the context of its production, and by over-determining expectations, matchmaking services frequently caused romance to evaporate, leaving a different set of feelings, from the tolerant to the wary to the fair-minded, in place. But Campbell suggests that the anticipatory part of consumption is integral to its pleasure, since 'the essential activity of consumption is ... not the actual selection, purchase or use of products, but the imaginative pleasure-seeking to which the product lends itself'.[85] We might ask: to what extent did 'imaginative pleasure seeking' shape the ways in which users of mediated dating platforms handled their expectations, compared to the sense that they were customers with consumer expectations *entitled* to satisfied expectations? After all, mediated daters in the 1970s, 1980s and 1990s made sense of their romantic clienthood in a context of growing consumer awareness and representation. Consumer representation bodies had multiplied since the First World War, but as Matthew Hilton has shown, the post-1950s period witnessed a flourishing of government-funded groups such as the Consumer Council (1963–70), the Office of Fair Trading (1973) and the National Consumer Council (1975).[86] By the late 1980s, the Consumer Association – publisher of the magazine *Which?* – reached peak membership of over one million.[87] There were more ways than ever for consumers to seek redress, and platforms in which to articulate their expectations and disappointments.

Unsurprisingly, the more money daters spent on a service, and the more ambitious or insistent the service's marketing materials, the greater the 'returns' they expected. Therefore for agency customers more than for lonely hearts advertisers, the relationship between their quest for love and their expenditure – between cost and benefit – was more taut. Agencies were expensive, costing up to £1,500 per year for a dozen introductions and raising expectations accordingly.[88] Michael remembered exactly how much he paid for Hedi Fisher's services in 1990: '£150 to register, £20 for an interview, £250 for marriage.'[89] The agencies' front office – sales staff and usually female matchmakers who purported to be excellent at assessing personal needs – further bolstered expectation.

Clients were wooed through their emotional pressure points, through a kind of ad-hoc psychological profiling, as Julia, the matchmaker at an 'exclusive' London agency, made clear. The experience of going in for an interview was intense and the customer's hopes were usually boosted in that setting, convincing them to pay on the spot for membership. Afterwards, the customer might express unease about the gap between promise and reality. Sinclair's account of two Hedi Fisher dates accentuated the banality of the disappointment: 'lots of promises but nothing at the end of it except two rather gruelling evenings, and a lot of hard work for me.'[90] Mary described the experience of the interplay between the psychologically and emotionally honed sales pitch, interview and reality in more detail: 'I suppose [the interview] convinced me that I would find people based on all the criteria I had offered up, that my expectations were to be matched with somebody with whom I was compatible were reasonable.'[91] Expectations were therefore intensely rigged, but the 'pleasure' of anticipation often became anxiety at having made a poor consumer decision and anxiety about potentially unreasonable expectations. After a particularly disastrous date, Mary adopted a corrective stance. Finding the company's matchmaking record with her 'very poor, very very poor', she felt she 'had to ring them up' and say '"this person needs to be taken off your books". I felt that he was totally inappropriate – not just for me …'[92] Likewise when Cockburn's interviewee Annie joined an agency the 'really inadequate guys' produced for her caused her to 'complai[n] to the agency by letter' because 'it costs a lot you know, it's not cheap'.[93]

Occasionally, the interview itself put clients off by collapsing their expectations under a poorly managed sell. One woman struck agencies off her list of options following an interview as uncomfortable in its implications as its atmosphere. It was 'chilly … I was so affronted to be thought a gold-digger'.[94] The result was that she became 'continually amazed by the thought of pairing up through an agency or a lonely hearts column'.[95] Another was also disappointed by both the content and form of her agency experience, whose opportunism was not sufficiently concealed.

> When I contacted the agency I was horrified to be told that I was rather old and might be difficult to match with anyone! However I was asked to go to a meeting with a principal of the agency. After she had met me she opined that I was lively and good.[96]

The matchmaker failed to facilitate any dates with 'frisson', so 'I decided that if I was going to meet another man (and I wasn't even sure if I wanted to) then it would have to be "naturally" through work or though friends'. When another

Mass Observer 'tried a dating agency called the DSS (divorced, separated and singles!) club' she found it 'so artificial and a complete failure, being approached by a few sad men I didn't fancy in the slightest'.[97] These testimonies do not suggest indulgence in hedonistic fantasy of the unknown, embellished by the pleasure of anticipating the emotional caramel of a romantic encounter. On one hand, they suggest the sense of disappointment of customers whose other purchases might have been monitored by the Consumer Association. On the other, agencies' failure to find them suitable matches left singles with a quality of dissatisfaction probably less present in the quest for a good automobile, one that was complicated by the networks of affect involved in this particular pursuit.

Lonely hearts ads were more often approached as an experiment – personal and social – and therefore with 'open-mindedness' rather than with consumer expectations. Divorcee Robert's breezy formulation was typical: 'my philosophy in all this [personals advertising] is be relaxed, open-minded and have a sense of humour. I think you really have to be like that . . ', while Maggie's approach was 'mild and exploratory'.[98] Lonely hearts ads may have been cheaper and more self-driven than agencies, less akin to a service and more like a personal project. But their chief offering of choice nonetheless encouraged advertisers to see themselves to differing degrees as customers and consumers too.[99] The dating industry did not necessarily lend itself straightforwardly to a consumer approach, consumer satisfaction, nor, perhaps ironically, to the fusion of romance and consumption theorized by Colin Campbell. But because it was structured by the assumption that many frogs preceded the prince, singles were acutely aware of their competitive advantage or disadvantage, and frequently used vocabularies of the market. The market-related language singles deployed was used either metaphorically or in reference to goods seen to be important to the process of romantic evaluation. I want to turn to this language now as evidence of the complexity with which singles identified as romantic clients, stressing materialism first in how men described the dating process, and then moving to a discussion of Sinclair's account.

Shopping for love: marketized language and the tensions of romantic clienthood

In the 1992 documentary *Singles*, Monica's date Jonathan echoed the sentiments of male *Singles* (magazine) readers in reducing the romantic quest to a (female) interrogation of material worth: 'What a woman is after is his man's balls – his home, his car, she wants everything and she'll make him pay for it ...' For

Jonathan, the sexual, the material, and the transactional all fell within a rubric of 'payment', with women exacting a cost that seemed to negate any pleasure in the union.[100] Just as Cockburn's interviewees found women 'daunting' sexually, Jonathan saw them in fundamentally adversarial economic terms. Nick, another subject of *Singles*, used the vocabulary of progressive self-awareness and sexual frankness in describing his ideal partner ('a soulmate, best friend, total companion, lover') but he also specified the desire for someone that 'likes good wine, eating at good restaurants, blow jobs'. Nick's elision of the sexual and the material into a kind of shopping list didn't explicitly denigrate the women he'd met, like the previous male subjects, but the sense emerged that a 'soulmate' could be broken into parts that had little to do with inner qualities. Taste played its role as matchmaker (good restaurants, good wine), but the woman also had to have an adequate sexual repertoire. A similar outlook was apparent in the BBC's *Man Seeks Woman* (1995), which stressed from the start the masculine fungibility of appetites: cars, women, sex, and cinemas were all desired from the same conceptual and visceral place. Pete was a self-described 'Italian stallion from Slough' who lived in a bedsit in Staines, and worked as a double glazer:

> I like to live life in the fast lane, restaurants, clubs, pubs, cinemas, you name it, I'm doing it and if I'm not doing any of that we're having sex, mad passionate sex, it's got to be to wild sex though, it's not boring stuff, it's highly physically demanding sex. So yeah, that's the kind of woman I'm looking for.

Sometimes specific brands became ciphers for the wider package. Monica from *Singles* was filmed as the Sarah Eden agency paired her with Richard, thirty-six. Richard said he didn't like women 'to dress from H&M and Top Shop' which went with wanting 'nobody intellectual or arty' but a 'real person'.

For Pete, it had 'got' to be 'wild sex', with life in the material 'fast lane'; Richard's looked-for partner wouldn't dress from Top Shop, and Nick wanted a 'total companion' but, like Pete and Richard, his description betrayed an internal checklist similar to the one he might have taken to buy a car. These requirements suggested that mediated dating lent itself to confusion about the nature of a possible romantic partner. The very articulation of what singles 'wanted' brought the romantic search closer to an act of shopping than mere metaphor, and reduced the sense that the single might at some point seek to enter into a dynamic relation with someone.[101] Having been invited, through the matchmaking process, to specify what the 'total companion' and the 'real person' meant, these men produced a list of specifiable parts suitable for the modern consumer. But the list, and the language they deployed, took them very far indeed from 'romance' as defined in the cultural terms discussed in the introduction, and far too from the often pragmatic but not materialistic attitudes brought to light in the studies by Langhamer and Szreter and Fisher.[102]

It was not just men who employed the language of materialism, as Colette Sinclair's memoir, *Manhunt*, makes clear.[103] Sinclair provided an extreme portrait of the ways in which consumer, sexual and professional discourse could be brought together for the female dater in the 1980s. In doing so *Manhunt* helps crystallize both how broader economic and cultural shifts in the 1980s could be refracted through the language and feelings surrounding romantic relationality, and how these could be experienced in a sex-specific way. As well as underlining the unique pressures and expectations assigned to female singles, Sinclair's exhaustive quest made clear that it was the extra labour of managing mediation itself, regardless of form, that could generate a clash between the self as consumer and the self as an emotional individual seeking out romantic feeling.

Sinclair saw the quest for a man in a multi-faceted way, but all the facets, including the emotional ones, were conceived of in terms of service-fulfilment. First, the man would be there to provide 'an ordinary family life with a father figure' for her daughter aged two. Personally, she 'needed someone to love, be loved by and to support us'. By 'support', she meant:

> comfortably-off ... an entrepreneurial type, independent of mind and means ... Alone together we might go to the theatre, cinema, discos, concerts. If he had his own interests like a boat somewhere it would be good, but he should not expect me to paint the hull every weekend.[104]

More urgently, however, Sinclair had a 'pressing overdraft', a fractious mother who was tired of offering free board, lodging and childcare, and the conviction that she 'could hardly go out to work with a small baby ... I would never earn enough to support us and pay for a nanny for her'.[105] Together, Sinclair and her mother hatched a plan:

> Mummie and I decided that somewhere out there, there was a suitably attractive, kind, comfortably off, dependable, family-minded man who would be only too happy to have me as his wife, and Moya has his daughter. The question was – where on earth to find him?[106]

Central to the unravelling of the *Manhunt* story – an unconventional one because her efforts did not yield Mr Right – was Sinclair's taste for luxury and the fine things in life. While class is explicitly discussed in her account of her early years, with emphasis on signifiers such as boarding school, an educated father and horse-riding, Sinclair's project of self-explication increasingly moved towards a catalogue of overtly materialistic tastes. These were partly a cipher for her own discernment and a way of defining herself. They also represented an instability at the core of her quest, evoked in Zygmunt Bauman's theory of modern ambivalence. Bauman argues that the modern emphasis on lifestyle and taste enables a marketized self-construction that is used as a self-protecting substitute for love. 'Through the market, one can put together various elements of the complete "identikit" of a DIY self ... [to] express oneself as a modern, liberated woman ... or ruthless and self-confident tycoon.'[107] Bauman astutely posits that the attraction of this kind of self-construction, especially among those seeking love, is that it replaces the 'torments' of the real, ragged self being rejected with a 'pleasurable act of choice between ready-made patterns'.[108] Indeed Sinclair's repetitive return to her attainment of luxuries read more like an attempt to remind herself that she was literally worth something: for instance, following her transformation from 'ugly duckling' to beauty she 'began to go out with the head boy of Lancing College, the public school on the hill. He took me to parties, there was laughing and kissing and lots of champagne. All quite smart and a lot of fun ...'[109] Later, in Brighton, she dated many men, including a married man who 'was wealthy and getting wealthier. I enjoyed his company, his attentions and his money. I looked good, had a ball and bought myself an MGb-BT'.[110]

At thirty, with three marriages behind her and a daughter, Sinclair's quest to meet Mr Right was introduced with an assurance that she was an attractive, diverse product herself.

> I am attractive for my age, now thirty-one, but not a dolly bird ... I have not skinny, not fat, a size twelve ... I possibly talk too much, but that's because I have a brain that moves even faster than my tongue ... I cry at movies ... but I can also be hard-headed ... I am many different things, a mass of contradictions, but the sum of the parts is not unpleasant.[111]

But we should not read such passages as indicative of an emotional economy purely motored by materialist, consumer-style considerations over the 'authentic' model of love and feeling. Rather they are a new kind of mixture of the two. To see Sinclair as purely materialistic would be to flatten the *tension* at the heart of mediated matchmaking that shaped her quest: between the methodical and the magical; the mercenary and the authentic; the planned and the serendipitous; the satisfaction of attributes and chemistry. A husband had to be 'only too happy to have me as his wife' and was not simply to be a source of financial security and shelter; he was to satisfy emotional as well as sexual conditions, and Sinclair insisted on an authentic sexual 'gelling'. Thus Sinclair's account highlights the confusion that could underscore romantic clienthood. If a partner was something you paid for, like any other service, could you be as specific in your requirements as you could for, say, one of the cars she so often referred to? While Sinclair tells us she wanted a caring, kind husband above all, and throughout the account rejects men for being rich but unkind, the language in which her project is set lapses repeatedly into what reads as a category error, signalled by the disconcerting elision of the professional, financial, cultural and physical aspects of a potential match. She appears unsure of her conceptual footing – romantically and emotionally – when she writes this disorderly list:

> He should be an entrepreneurial type, independent of mind and means. He should be taller than me, ideally 6 ft 4 inches, but 5 feet 11 inches would be fine ... He should not be bald, and I would prefer him to wear contact lenses (I do) if he needed help with his eyesight. He should have a good physique ... he should want to spend time with Moya ... being a family at home, or going on outings. Alone together we might go to the theatre, cinema, discos, concerts. If he had his own interests like a boat somewhere it would be good, but he should not expect me to paint the hull every weekend.[112]

Sinclair's vocabulary was also suggestive of the new forms of emotional pragmatism underpinning the (mediated) search for love. Thus beneath her hunt for luxury and the zealously systematic method undertaken, there was an earnest search for a committed partnership. Sinclair was repeatedly disappointed by the untempered materialism or shoddy manners she found in the men she met through the dating industry. Their flashiness betrayed unreliability or nastiness, their wealth often signalled a taste for sexual coercion, their high-paying jobs made them seem miserly in comparison, or bad father material. Caught between the desire for a stable commitment and an addiction to men as purveyors of luxury and security, Sinclair could be seen as a victim of the 'can-do/can-have' approach to the expanded field of dating options in the late 1980s. Certainly, she treated the search with determination, strategy, an open purse and a large store of effort, making herself the archetypal modern single. However, the disappointment of her return product signalled starkly the limits both of mediated dating and of treating the romantic quest in a consumerist fashion. Sinclair's case suggested that the effort required for finding that needle in the haystack could also merely exhaust a person's resources – emotional and financial – and corrode their self-confidence.

The date

Encountering the opposite sex

As we approach the date itself, we need to take stock of a final piece of context: singles' perceptions of the opposite sex – a significant factor in setting up the romantic encounter. As I have shown elsewhere, the romantic encounter between single men and women in the 1970s and 1980s could be fraught.[113] Cockburn's male subjects reveal the extent to which feminism negatively defined perceptions of the women they were encountering. To their male counterparts, some women seemed disturbingly alive to the possibilities of exerting control over their romantic lives. As Cockburn's narrative suggests, it was difficult for women to strike the right balance between 'not settling' and thereby showing diminished self-regard, and being demanding to only the correct degree. While Susan was simply answering the question Cockburn asked in a detailed manner, his commentary stressed the extremity of her expectation, noting 'perhaps Susan will find this exceptional man using the fine toothcomb technique, but she is also going to need a lot of luck to make that magic meeting happen'.[114] The suggestion was that Susan had fallen into the trap of being an excessively demanding single woman, reminding us of how slippery was the terrain single women had to navigate.[115] Meanwhile, Annie had 'very high standards'; she'd 'sooner be lonely for the rest of my life than partner some of the men I've met'.[116] Yet despite Cockburn's hinted disapproval, it's clear that the personals offered one way in which 'picky' women could exert as much control as they wanted over the process, foregrounding one of the key benefits women attributed to the use of internet dating cited thirty years later.[117]

Henry, fifty-six, a local government officer with 'basically masculine' interests, was one example of a man who found the encounter with 'modern' women – and specifically her sexual confidence – problematic. He rarely met women and craved affection – but while dates arranged through *Singles* offered 'respectable sensible' people of the kind he was looking for, the women were 'aggressive' and 'daunting'.[118] Another advertiser was also dismayed by how 'aggressive and forward' the women were:

> Honestly on several occasions I've been really daunted by them. They pick me up in their car and away we go to a restaurant. Then, during the evening they get very familiar. One woman I met was very much like that. In fact she became so familiar and physical it put me right off her.[119]

This interviewee had met 'over 80 women, and to be honest I have very little to show for it'. The tension between practice and feeling that this book argues for is evident in these accounts, as the decision to meet up to '80' women – only a recently available (and respectable) option for the ordinary single, and a bold embrace of the 'architecture' of sexual choice defining modern life – is marred by the encounter itself, with women who have suddenly become sexually 'daunting' in their modern guise.[120] Of course, such articulations of alienation between the sexes should not be read as entirely representative of wider historical realities of women's (or men's) attitudes; as the surveys discussed in Chapter 1 suggested, there was in fact relatively little divergence in attitudes towards relationships, for instance monogamy and casual sex, between men and women.[121] However, the trope of modern women possessing daunting sexual single-mindedness was widespread in the media (as well as in advice literature directed at women), and this discourse almost certainly shaped the way men such as Harry described their encounters with women.[122]

Other differences appeared to characterize the match-made encounter between men and women. Men appeared to suffer more from loneliness and social dysfunction than the women interviewed.[123] According to Cockburn, they were often single 'because their previous relationship has recently ended. They suddenly find themselves alone, and don't like it', raising questions such as 'how is sexuality to be managed ... where can emotional need be satisfied?'[124] Four main categories of men predominated: 'heartbroken'; 'unsettled types'; 'shy or short'; and 'busy people'. The most emotionally charged accounts came from the shy, who predictably found the clash between gender role expectation and personal inclination most painful. For Peter, forty-seven, a British Rail clerk, debilitating social unease led him to use personals.

> I [advertise] because I share what I think is a common problem. Some men who are a little bit on the shy side find it very difficult to make a cold-blooded meeting ... this is a good way of meeting because all the groundwork has been done ... I've always been a bit of a shy person ... a couple of years ago I even tried a hypnotherapist ... but that didn't work![125]

In the 1996 BBC documentary *Man Seeks Woman* male shyness and social awkwardness was brought into heart-rending focus in the case of Simon Emery, a bachelor who had been single 'all my life' and lived in a caravan on his parents' farm. Simon drove a three-wheeler, having been unable to pass the standard driving test (the car invited some disparaging comment from his dates) and found that 'I'm not one of these people who can give a straight chat up line ... I get lonely ... I'm no oil painting'. He'd been close to two women in his life but both had left him because of 'second thoughts and cold feet ... it really did knock my faith in human beings'.

The date in context

Having sketched out the perceptual context in which singles articulated their romantic aspirations, we are ready to turn to the date itself for a closer-range view of how these dynamics played out in the febrile romantic encounter.

Despite discomfort with the word, the emergence of the 'date' and the question of what to do on it had become pressing as the old system of 'calling' was replaced by excursions usually dependent on the male wallet (to the cinema, the café, the dance).[126] Of course, as the MOP Summer 2001 directive made clear, not all British courtships even in the post-1960s period involved spending money – for some, courtship was a 'certain amount of time lurking on badly lit corners'.[127] And in Britain, courtship practices up to the 1960s included gatherings such as the Monkey Walk and the Chicken Run in which young people participated in public rituals of display and performance, parading en masse to catch the eye of a member of the opposite sex.[128] Compared to the American emphasis on 'dating and rating', British courtships could be comparatively organic-seeming.[129] But by the late 1960s, both cinema and monkey walk, as well as the dance hall, were in decline as key courtship venues, with pub culture and coffee bars increasingly absorbing young people, as well as the private spaces of the home and bedroom with their record players and televisions.[130]

Moreover, as explored in Chapter 1, a number of contraceptive and legislative developments meant that the 1970s saw the emergence of new norms around courtship, key in which women as well as men were increasingly seeking experience for its own sake rather than as a path to marriage. This coincided with platforms such as Dateline and *Time Out* promoting a high quantity of dates; options that, as we saw earlier in this chapter, could be instrumentalized in a variety of ways. Crucially, unlike the terrain around mid-century courtship, this was a romantic landscape for professionals and older people – including growing numbers of divorcees – rather than teenagers. Not only were professional skills brought to bear on managing a mediated dating 'portfolio', as Cockburn's subject Susan put it, but eating and drinking in public were integral to such meetings, and required the type of planning that called on mature skills including logistical creativity and compromise.[131] As Cockburn noted, 'the place of meeting is always a major consideration . . . neutral ground is emphasised . . . Pubs, hotel bars, coffee shops and the like are favoured places.'[132]

As the century drew to a close, restaurants and bars had become integral to courtship settings. The centrality to the romantic process of dinner in the period under study can be read as an accumulation of norms around intimacy that had been in train since the 1920s in both Britain and the US, in which leisure expenditure was key, and couples were 'increasingly positioned within the public realm of consumption'.[133] In her 1997 study, Eva Illouz found that of the three categories of activity people assigned to the 'romantic moment', the gastronomic – and especially eating out – was the most common, followed by the cultural and touristic.[134] Dinners out carried deep associations with romance over and above other forms of shared leisure because of their ritualized consumption: restaurants 'enable people to step out of their daily lives into a setting saturated with ritual meaning'.[135] If meals were romantic because they were special occasions, 'out of' daily life, their importance for courtship also mirrored an expanding and diversifying catering industry, in which more exotic types of food, including European and Indian, began not only to enter the supermarket but to shape restaurant concepts, and in which pubs increasingly served dinner.[136] Along with the diversification and expansion of drinking options, the romantic landscape of leisure and consumption in Britain stretched in all directions. From the early 1970s, pubs were opened up and expanded to be more spacious and inviting, increasing their offering with more sophisticated food menus, a development which appealed to those less keen on 'propping up the bar' (women).[137] Meanwhile, the number of licenses granted for restaurants and hotels outpaced those of pubs by eight times between 1974 and 1979.[138]

In his polemical 1973 study of the American singles industry, *The Mating Trade*, John Godwin stressed the importance of setting from the outset, growing social and romantic isolation on the decline of 'downtown ballrooms' and the 'hotel cocktail dance'. He noted with envy the 'the splendid meeting places of the Old World', British pubs and European cafes, lambasting the expensive, socially awkward, intimidating options available to American singles in the form of bars – singles and otherwise.[139] Godwin was right to point to the British pub as a key venue for socializing as well as a setting for dates: alcohol in Britain was integral to the romantic encounter. Pubs were soon joined by wine bars, which signalled a new era in drinking culture, and further established the importance of alcohol to the courtship setting.[140] Wine bars – increasingly visible in the 1970s – were marketed to appeal as spaces that welcomed women and capitalized on the sophistication and diversity of wine that resounded with the Mediterranean trends seen in cooking.[141] Between 1965 and 1985, London gained 250 wine bars, and cities like Bristol also took up the trend. These were self-consciously aimed at women, with bans on staff that had previously worked in pubs, and a high proportion of female employees.[142] By the mid-1980s, a quarter of Britons, many of them women, were frequenting wine bars.[143] John Patterson, head of Dateline and *Singles* magazine, as well as the owner of a wine bar, Tiles, near South Kensington in London, linked women's increasing freedom in the sexual and financial spheres to their confident appropriation of these spaces. Writing in *Singles'* first issue, he lamented: 'I should have been born in the age of the wine bar. It is a fact that in London, and in most large cities in this country girls can now walk into a wine bar on their own without raising an eyebrow. And indeed they do.'[144] Certainly, Colette Sinclair's detailed account meticulously recorded the material significance of different drinks, indicating female connoisseurship, as well as the drinks' entry as a key part of the sequence of the date and indicator of the romantic outlook. A date with a man she dubbed Mr Poona Poona became progressively more disappointing when they found themselves at lunch where 'they were serving Andre's Californian champagne, available at Jack's discount store for $1.99 . . . and Sainsbury's claret, which also got the "oh gosh, how spiffing this is" treatment', to Colette's horror.[145]

Yet the flipside to women's apparently new alcohol-related freedom was that alcohol was increasingly an expected romantic and social emollient for dates, both courted and monitored for its ability to lower boundaries. For dating memoirist Paul Reizen, writing in the late 1990s, every date began in a bar, but he was repeatedly (and comically) thrown off by women who wouldn't get drunk. The scrupulously recorded opening scene of his memoir sees him waiting for a date in the Library Bar of the Lanesborough Hotel. A connoisseur both of bars and *Guardian* Soulmates dating, Reizen chooses this venue to impress the woman whose voice had a 'breathy resonance' he found exciting. Twenty minutes early, he had started on a 'world-class martini'.[146] The encounter, which starts as a disaster ('I struggle to keep the disappointment off my face') unfolds through the rituals demanded by the setting.[147] He offers a drink; the barman 'shimmers up before us', he 'watches her face as she studies the drinks list' and sinks into despair when she orders a 'ginger beer'.[148] He, instead, drinks four martinis and blacks out at the end of the evening. Another more successful date starts at 'Browns at six-thirty on a Wednesday evening', in which 'I find myself a position at the bar from where I can monitor the door, order a glass of house white and begin to get nervous'.[149] A 'knockout' walks in but once more refuses alcohol, leaving Reizen on the back foot: sexually desperate, frustrated, full of self-recrimination and longing for the now-vanished woman.

Women understood that the approach towards alcohol shaped the distribution of power on the date: as Pen Fudge recalled, 'I tried going out to bars but that was awful. I found to my cost that once alcohol is involved, things get out of hand on many levels'.[150] Depending on how it was handled, alcohol could also become a source of information about the sexual and moral delicacy of the male date. In 1977, Joan, a *Singles* reader, wrote a letter to the magazine in which she told how a date who 'saw her home' informed her

> that I had 'no right' to deny his access to my bed because I had let him buy me drinks. I pointed out that not only had he adopted an attitude of hurt male pride when I offered to buy a round, but that if he wanted to buy a woman I understood the going price in London was rather higher than two martinis, and I wasn't for sale.[151]

The question of payment

That Pen Fudge's boyfriend ate the lace she made served as a grotesque reminder of how rituals around ingestion could speak to wider questions of power and ownership. Certainly, it was over meals that the most concentrated power struggles took place. For many singles, a meal was a cipher for wider distortions in gender relationships seen to have emerged in the 1970s. *Singles* received so many letters about the issue of payment on dates that it ran a series on the morality and etiquette surrounding 'going Dutch' – paying an equal share on dates. 'These misunderstandings about who pays are becoming more frequent as more women become independent and earn more money,' the editor noted.[152] 'Men feel resentful that they are obliged to take a girl out, claiming women are taking advantage of them, while women often feel old conventions still apply when out on "a date"'. Men wrote furious responses to women who suggested that they deserved to be taken out, or complained that men made 'constant referral to the cost of living in relation to the prices of drinks etc'.[153] One man sought to justify the position of an aggrieved 'Miss A', however, noting she was 'rightly outraged at any man wishing to get emotional and physical satisfaction through her without adequate prior payment. She may have been trained by her mother not to need it, or can get it free from other girls'.[154]

Women's perceived changed economic power was at the heart of these disputes, and the dates themselves were the setting in which tensions over the gendered symbolism of the financial upper hand were played out. As scholars of the early and mid-twentieth century have outlined in relation to an earlier set of sexual and economic conditions, eating and drinking out in post-1970 Britain was tethered to its own complex system of gendered meaning, expectation and assessment. Although it describes the American context, Beth Bailey's analysis of dating as a means by which young people established themselves as 'commodities that afforded public validation of popularity, of belonging, of success' is helpful here.[155] If both the content of dates (restaurant, movie etc.) and the rank of the date him or herself were symbols of social capital, then mediated dating posed an interesting challenge to this system. After all, it was a stigmatized form of meeting that had little to offer in terms of social popularity – dates were strangers and people often kept quiet that they were meeting people this way.[156] There were internal economies of popularity, materially evident in the piles of post that younger women were shown to receive on placing an advert, for instance in the documentary *Singles*, and in the anguished letters to *Singles* (magazine) about being ignored. Yet compared to the more public forms of success and value that shaped traditional dating, the economy of worth and power attached to mediated dating in this period was a relatively closed one. Essentially, mediated dating was dating in private: dates were strangers both to the dater and their friends. Thus, stripped of the currency of public approval, mediated dating arguably put more pressure on the date itself and its material signifiers. Where and what you ate and how it was handled were the key sources of information about the other person. The meal provided the text that social knowledge could in more traditional contexts. For instance, my interviewee Marsha, an upper-middle-class woman, perused the personals sections of *Private Eye* and *Time Out* in the late 1970s, and went on one date arranged this way in 1979. They agreed to meet at the well-known London restaurant Joe Allen. 'It was quite trendy at the time', remembered Marsha, while the date was the sort of man who afterwards 'fancied a drink at the Savoy'.[157] The date itself lacked chemistry from the first moment, but Marsha 'wanted dinner' and felt comfortable with his tastes and manners, including the fact that he paid for dinner, which she had expected.

But the question of who paid on blind dates in the 70s, 80s and 90s was subject to far more ambiguity and flexibility not only because assumptions about male financial superiority were being continually challenged in many areas of discourse, but because nobody was watching. Who picked up the bill was subject to on-the-spot discretion and mood. If the pervasive idea from mid-century Britain and America was that 'a date centred around an act of consumption' and that 'one of the most important [conventions was] that the man pay the woman's way', then in post-1970 Britain, the picture had become murkier.[158] Some women preferred to share the bill; some to pay the whole thing or take it in turns, while some – such as Colette Sinclair – preferred an older, more American system in which their value was measured by how much the man would spend. As the letters pages in *Singles* made clear, many men resented women's expectations and actions, whether these were about sharing, footing entirely or avoiding the bill. Whatever singles' attitudes and feelings were towards the handling of food taken together, the meal was clearly a stage on which men and women both created and responded to a variety of tensions. The meal – in addition to other semi-public settings for consumption such as the pub – was therefore a rich source of information for both parties, as well as a lens for understanding how expectations, perceptions and technologies of mediated dating matched up to experience. With a rich selection of dates remembered in detail, we now turn to Mary's experience as a case study bringing together a number of the dynamics foreshortened by the romantic transaction of the evening meal.

Case study: Mary's dates

For some women, the decision to use an agency sat within a framework of independence that had been hard-won around life as a wife and mother and was therefore approached from a more defensive stance. If journal editor Hilary, former mental health nurse Elaine as well as Rose, a BBC administrator who had signed up to Heather Jenner at the urging of her grandmother, felt they had little to lose by giving it a go, Mary, born 1945, had accrued plenty to lose – emotionally and financially. As she made clear in her interview with me in her hometown in Essex, she was therefore highly sensitized to the disappointments of her mediated matchmaking career and learned she would rather be single than continue meeting the kinds of men the agency and holidays had presented to her.[159]

The sharpness of the tension between an adult, independent feminine self identity and the realities of match-made encounters is one reason Mary's account merits close attention. The other is that – as we draw to the end of this book – Mary's experience offers the chance to reflect on how disagreements and confusions elicited by the romantic encounter continued seemingly unabated two decades after the sexual upheaval of the 1970s. As a divorcee with three grown-up children, she was also meeting men in their fifties, and it is highly possible that a younger woman dating through an agency in the 1990s would have been confronted with different tensions. Among my respondents, however, Mary's account was most vividly anchored to the mealtime encounter of the date itself, and, crucially, depicted a scenario in which the fact of a woman able and keen to pay her way destabilized an expected balance of power and destroyed the possibility of romance taking root. In being self-directed, career-oriented, and financially independent, Mary embodied a dominant narrative of 1990s womanhood, but the men she met – although they were presumably aware that she was a professional divorcee from the information passed on by the agency – seemed unable to assimilate this fact. Thus Mary's testimony is valuable in suggesting that the lag between women's changing sexual and professional status, and the emotional response to it, particularly among men, persisted well past the point at which the male breadwinner model was thought to have been fully eroded.[160]

Mary's decision to sign up to an Essex-based agency in the mid-nineties, as she approached fifty, followed from a divorce and enrolment in an evening education course in 1993. Signing up to an upmarket agency felt like a sign of success and independence, even if – as we will see – positioning her desire to meet men as an addition to a life of hard-won independence produced a disillusioning experience of reality. She felt more comfortable with the company's thick parchment paper and calligraphy print than she did with personal ads which she found scruffy 'and I can't stand that'. Recalling the decision, Mary said she had:

> reached a point, where I thought I've done the hard work, I've got the qualifications, had the money to buy my own house. I was so chuffed at my excellent salary of the time, I went out and got myself a credit card, I thought I've got my own house, I can get a credit card . . . I signed up to [the agency]. I can't remember what I paid for membership, but it was a bronze, silver or gold payment. It was a policy ensuring a certain number of introductions over a period of time as well – I think I could afford the silver one, which was about 3 years. And from what I can remember I think that cost me and I am guessing truthfully – £700 pounds.[161]

Mary's experience of using an agency matchmaker unfolded almost entirely in the context of restaurants. But rather than affording a privileged view of the man's wallet, the meal was instead read for a wider series of meanings. Mary's memory of three restaurant dates arranged through the agency exhibit the confusion that could arise as men and women were culturally and temporally pulled further away from clear rules about spending money. And as an older woman, who took pride in her financial independence, Mary did not necessarily think that male culinary patronage boded well. Being based just outside of London, Mary had to travel by car to meet dates who also lived in a loose matrix outside the metropolis. As Colette Sinclair also emphasized in her memoir, having to drive some distance put extra pressure on the meeting itself.

One of the few men Mary saw more than once through the agency was 'a Buddhist' who had seemed promising on the phone. He was, however, more traditional in person.

> He paid for a meal the first time we met and the second time we met I paid for it and he didn't like it. He didn't like it at all . . . he'd taken to Buddhism later in life.

Was it karma? I don't know, but it just changed immediately. For his own sanity he took himself off to the toilet and came back not quite the same person as when he left the table.

This date's sensitivity on the matter of who paid signalled his unsuitability, which to Mary was bound up in a form of character weakness (he lacked 'courage'): 'He didn't have the courage or maybe felt it would be offensive I don't know – but he didn't phone me after that and I didn't phone him. Which didn't bother me, I mean, I didn't come away from that thinking I made a major faux pas.' For Mary, the tension between masculinity and femininity was not to be thrashed out over financial power relations, but decided in the way the two individuals aligned in terms of personality and values. Her date's preoccupation with paying was unfortunate, but a tangent to her central goal – in the end, it 'didn't bother' her that he had taken offence at her attempt to pay for dinner, since this indicated a broader incompatibility and it was best she learned of it sooner rather than later.

The unravelling of another potential liaison took place on a previous date at a restaurant, which instead staged tensions about physical rather than financial superiority. Having spoken on the phone, Mary had found this man 'obviously intelligent ... right age group etc. etc.'. In a spirit of equality, 'it was suggested amicably that we met half way between our homes, which was Chelmsford.' The power balance was tipped slightly in Mary's favour because she knew the restaurant he suggested. It was 'somewhere I'd been before ... so I knew [it] was up quite a rickety stairway. I said oh I've been there; it's quite a nice restaurant.' Her date then said there was something he had to tell her before they met. 'And you get that dread feeling,' Mary remembered. 'He said, "I've only got one leg, I do wear a prosthetic leg but ..."' Mary recalled how – rather than causing her to judge him badly – his disability triggered a habitual, professionally cultivated concern.[162] 'I know it sounds ridiculous but my job since 1986 had been within social services of Essex county council. Personally I was steeped in people's disabilities, people's financial difficulties. And I said, "will you be ok, there's rather a steep staircase up?"' Instead of impressing him, her knowledge both of the restaurant and of the possible mobility obstacles facing him annoyed him. Mary recalled how:

He took offence which told me something but it was my first date. Anyway we met, he made it up the stairs and had a pleasant meal. He bragged a lot about his home, he'd recently refitted his kitchen, he'd made all the cabinets himself out of pear wood. I didn't mind that, I admired him for being able to do that. We parted in the car park and he said, I'll ring you. But he didn't. Of course I was new to this and didn't know what to expect. So I rang him and he came out with what might have been legitimate reasons, my sister's ill etc. And I thought do I want anything to come of this? And it fizzled.[163]

Despite his touchiness and bragging, Mary was prepared to meet him again. The feeling was not mutual; the interaction of his disability and the physical setting of their meeting, up steep stairs, seemed to have broken the spell for him. Although in recollection it was clear the clues were there, at the time Mary had underestimated the degree to which a date could be thrown off balance by the appearance of a faint power shift from man to woman.

A third and final restaurant encounter was even more fraught: its tensions emerging from the initial phone call. He 'sounded almost too enthusiastic' when he rang up and suggested a 'venue' for a meal that 'just for a change wasn't Chelmsford' since he lived on the London side of Essex. Once more, deciding to meet required the weighing of mutual convenience and willingness to compromise. I thought, 'oh gosh it's going to be a bit difficult to find somewhere; it would have to be Billericay.' And once again Mary knew the place they decided on. But the man disrupted mealtime norms in a way that troubled Mary.

> He was bizarrely suggesting a late afternoon early supper ... I didn't mind because it was fairly local to me anyway. I said, 'oh that's fine' – it was something like half past five or something like that and he was waiting outside which I thought was quite polite really.

The reality was less salubrious.

> I'm thinking he'd just turned up. We went in, I knew the restaurant quite well, I used to go with my younger daughter when she had lunch off. The married couple who owned it and said hello to me then turned to him and said, 'oh hello again'.

Mary learned that the man had spent his day hanging around the restaurant.

> He'd come to the locality late morning, toured that area, gone to a local garden centre, bought himself a garden set, then gone to the restaurant, I suppose to make sure he knew where we were meeting, had lunch, then gone to somewhere else, then came back to the same place and had an afternoon tea. And as it transpired the whole time he'd been telling them about how he was going to meet 'this woman' – those were his words – for a meal early evening, based on the info the [matchmaking] company had told him.[164]

Although she didn't know at the time his movements or the way he was referring to their meeting, Mary found the fact that he had already been that day to the restaurant 'a bit odd, he played it down, said I've been in here already, and said he had been in the area, was making excuses'. The symmetry of the romantically exploratory meal had already been troubled by the fact that the date had been there already. But the real surprise, unequivocally negative, particularly in the context of the meeting, came next. It 'took my breath away', Mary recalled. Her date proceeded to ogle the 'extremely well endowed' waitress. When she came to take the order he 'focussed on a particular part of her anatomy, seemed to forget why we were there'.

His behaviour suggested sexual menace, disrespect and rejection all in one. But again Mary deployed her well-honed socio-emotional skills, and thought she'd 'better save the day and ask him about himself or say something about me'. But this attempt to get the date back on track didn't work, and she had to reprimand him. 'You could see his focus was elsewhere. And I said, excuse me, "am I boring you?" And he said, "did you see the tits on that?"' After being 'forced into having a coffee', Mary found herself in a confrontational position outside, telling him: 'I found your demeanour and your comments completely unacceptable, don't even think about contacting me.' She saw him not only as a personal offender, but as a risk to other women and a sign of the agency's negligence. The encounter prompted Mary to respond to the company's request for a report on the date in a particularly full way: 'let's say the piece of paper they sent for the report wasn't big enough. So they phoned me when they received my comments – I told them somebody like him shouldn't be on their books.'[165]

Mary's mealtime encounters showed how restaurants – as places for spending money – became an important theatre of assessment, staging a complex array of antagonisms and dynamics. However much Mary sought to meet on an equal footing she was repeatedly reminded that gendered expectations remained central, even if these were far from stable by the mid-1990s.[166] These dinners also underscored the ways in which mediated dating in particular sharpened conflicting agendas between men and women, by putting extra pressure on first impressions, manners and the impulse to pay. Ultimately, Mary's dinner experiences resulted in stark estimations of an unbridgeable gender gap which showed that 'men have totally different agendas depending on their own experiences – they don't have malicious intent but different reasons for facilitating a companion'.[167]

For some of the other women I interviewed, restaurants were also used for a variety of ends that actually pushed romantic harmony further away. For former BBC employee Rose, dinner was often a crude romantic gesture used to distract from less desirable reality (such as the man having another partner), something to make it 'worth my while, I think'.[168] Elaine, the respondent who later married a man she met in *Time Out*, was invited to dinner by a man she met through Dateline and instructed to bring a friend for a friend of his so that it would be a double date, but 'the friend would be awful, for my nice friend, I don't know why I went along with it'.[169] Ironically, when Elaine met her future husband, they avoided restaurants all together, opting instead for going 'round the corner to the local pub'. It is telling that the quality of the meeting and its aftermath eclipsed any details about what was consumed and who paid for it.

When Colette Sinclair signed up to agencies after becoming 'a bit exhausted' by countless dates arranged through the personals, she had become fatigued by the 'routine', of:

> vetting advertisements carefully, disregarding their wilder claims, not getting too carried away by possibilities, writing back to the ones I chose, waiting for their replies (or not hearing from them at all), meeting them, and all the palaver that follows that ...[170]

This evocation of fatigue caused by repeated cycles of self-presentation, arrangement, hope, rejection and failure went to the heart of contemporary courtship, and particularly mediated courtship.

For some, third-party dating was ultimately a success, allowing singles to personally grow, gain confidence and in some cases to meet a partner. But the cycle of trying and failing was ubiquitous, and was central to the ambivalent relationship not only between singles and the matchmaking industry, but also between romantic modernity – characterized by multiplicity of options and the freedom to pursue a range of relationship types – and the yearning for 'the one'. And there was more ambivalence in the contradictory relationship that lay between men and women; groups that sought each other out, but found that in practice their expectations were either not met, or resulted in acrimony. Disappointments ranged from revulsion at individuals or indeed whole groups ('men') to dead-end relationships. Mary's experiences showed how romantic hopes could fall apart when two strangers met across a table and a gender divide, while for Pen Fudge all the men she met through the small ads were 'disasters' who lied about their professional status and repeatedly betrayed her trust.[171]

But who was being blamed for the bigger failures of paid matchmaking, as well as for its smaller micro-disappointments – the mediation, the opposite sex, the matchmakers or the daters? How did people process and think about romantic failure? As consumers of a service, to what degree did they engage with the need to just keep going, refining the self and the process as they went?

One source of blame lay with the customer and their expectations. Several Mass Observation testimonies suggested that those who failed at agencies and lonely hearts had too-specific expectations: recall the observation by one female Mass Observer that in reality that 'tall dark businessman' she had enjoyed imagining 'becomes a frog'.[172] Colette Sinclair understood the perils of too-focused expectations, insisting that the only way to manage the quest for 'Mr Right' was to 'try everything', and that 'to find Mr Right you have to meet a lot of Wrongs first'.[173] Indeed, the balance of stress between individual emotional and administrative labour and the matchmaker's 'product' was increasingly shifting over the period towards self-responsibility. By the mid-2000s, mediated dating would emerge as a fully self-directed operation as online platforms gained prominence, flattening out the middle woman in favour of an algorithm, an interface and thousands of options. In some ways, Mary's narrative foregrounds this shift, returning repeatedly to the tension between individual responsibility and consumer expectation, and more particularly, unease around her own expectations. When her 'three-year subscription came to renewal ... I said no way, I'll never go down that road again'. Was the agency to blame? 'In fairness it was a mixture of things', Mary said. But the agency tried repeatedly to shift the responsibility for her dissatisfaction on her, insisting that she should 'broaden' the 'type of advertising' they could do for her since 'I suppose my interests, reading, certain types of novels etc., were too specific in hindsight'.[174] At the same time, Mary explained: 'I was saying what I needed, I put it in inverted commas, what I wanted, why look back on it and regret it ... I don't like putting blame on anybody – they were very successful ... Then again some people's expectations are just far less than mine.'[175]

Mary envisioned reassurance, expertise and the pleasure of being taken in hand so that she could meet a suitable 'companion'.

> I suppose I had in my head there'd be people sitting there saying, 'oh we've got just the woman for you' and another person saying 'oh we've got just the chap who came in the other day'. But I don't think it worked and I don't think they did it like that at all and that's what put me off.

Remembering, Mary blamed herself: 'I had a rose-tinted view of how it would work out.' Mary admitted she was looking for 'a background, no disrespect for anyone, I was looking for someone professional, a lawyer or whatever, or like yourself, an academic or whatever'. Mary's testimony accentuated unease surrounding her expectations, punctuated by ellipses of self-scrutiny, apology and assertion, suggesting confusion over whether the expectations were her fault, the matchmaker's fault or something to stand by.

> It sounds awful, you want to say 'oh I don't care what people are like as long as they're kind'. But actually when you look at it you have expectations in your head, and [the matchmaker] was good at teasing those out. Sometimes you haven't analysed those things yourself but when you stop and thinking about it you do have expectations.

As the histories of Elaine and the pair successfully matched through the Hedi Fisher agency show, mediated dating could offer rewards for perseverance. But the cumulative cost of that perseverance – repeated bouts of emotional labour expended on unappealing strangers, the stimulation and depression of hopes and expectations – was too great for some and they abandoned the attempt. Failure still rankled, though as mediated dating continued to expand, it became increasingly integrated into the course of normal courtship. However, the romantically framed sexual relationship at the heart of the encounter was not so amenable to integration. For even as the technologies and practices of self and sex were changing rapidly, feelings about gender and the romantic other often went against the grain, 'syncopated' with generation, personal history, economics and circumstance. The forms, norms and demands of modern relationality would shift further as the internet gained ground. But until the end of the pre-internet dating period, and possibly beyond, men and women continued to bring a patchwork of older, contradictory feelings about each other to the candlelit table. In many cases, these fatally disrupted the seamless modernity that mediated dating services purported to bring to the romantic quest, and helped constitute contemporary British singlehood as a position of profound sexual and emotional ambivalence, albeit one framed by novel forms of flexibility.

Conclusion

This book has mapped the social and cultural terrain of singleness in late twentieth-century Britain, uncovered the commercial landscape available to those willing to pay to find love and examined the faultlines that emerged within that landscape. In doing so it has argued for the emergence of contemporary single selfhood in Britain in the years after 1970. This was characterized by a range of new sexual and commercial options, distinctively modern forms of loneliness and by new pressures to couple up. Such pressures emanated from a variety of psycho-sexual discourses that were aimed with particular force at female singletons, and which caught women in a bind between a gender politics demanding they be fun and liberated, and one which saw emotional disorder and promiscuity as problematic. But both single women and men found themselves grappling with the seeming proliferation of relational options on the one hand, and the emotional realities and disappointments of exploring them (with commercial aid) on the other.

Focusing on the dating industry and its users, as well as the social and cultural pressures that shaped their quest, this book has sought to add to the historiography on gender, relationships, heterosexuality and dating in modern Britain in a number of ways. It argued that a complex set of lags and tensions between sexual change and feelings and attitudes towards gender were central to late twentieth-century heterosexual relational life. By a number of measures, sexual strictures broadly and drastically loosened in the post-1960s decades; singles were encouraged to explore themselves through sex, including non-committal sex, and dating services could be seen as befitting the 'space age'. But men and women still overwhelmingly sought committed monogamy and many male singles begrudged women's perceived increase in status and independence, blaming feminism for destroying romance. In economic and legislative terms, the equality gap between men and women narrowed. But as Chapter 4 showed, to those trying to forge romance with one another through blind dates, the affective gulf between them could feel very wide indeed.

By tracking twentieth-century discourses linking selfhood and sexuality, romance and individualism, we have seen how singles developed, in tension with new psychological vocabularies of the self, an emotional pragmatism that accommodated the romantic failures that were becoming part of the instability of 'modern' relational life. As we saw in Chapters 1 and 4, customers of the matchmaking industry deployed, or were expected to deploy, a rigorous programme of emotional self-management. This was partly because of broader changes in emotional culture and the prominence of tools and tricks for bolstering psychological well-being and exploring the self's needs, discussed in agony columns, psychologist's books and articles, lifestyle and sex-oriented magazines and singles services' marketing literature. But it was also because of the nature of mediated dates themselves, which were blind, arranged without prior confirmation of sexual chemistry, and therefore the most likely to disappoint or disconcert. Moreover, by revealing the workings of a market that traded in romantic desire, we saw how the attainment of romantic authenticity was actually made *less*, rather than more, possible through market intervention. At the same time, the quest for 'the one' was tempered by a desire to experiment, to keep an open mind, and to use managerial-style pragmatism in achieving romantic ends.

In being occupied with the three decades preceding the normalization of internet dating around 2000, this book has been organized by theme rather than by chronology. In Chapter 2 it analysed matchmaking services by decade, flagging up distinctive aspects of the industry in the 1970s, 1980s and 1990s – the co-existence of the conservative lonely hearts world of the *London Weekly Advertiser* and the sexually progressive one of *Time Out* in the 1970s; the rise in the 1980s of the introduction agency, marketed at singles too busy to find love, and in the 1990s the consolidation of singles narratives, particularly those directed at women, in the rise of 'must-she TV', best-selling fiction, and high-profile dating manuals.[1] Generally, however, this study has involved the period as a whole. This was partly to escape what Joe Moran has called 'decadology', a means of dividing up history that can misrepresent the unevenness, the waywardness, of change.[2]

Nonetheless, while the utility of 1970, 1980 and 1990 as breakpoints should be regarded critically, there is something of a decadal story here, with distinctive relational norms and contexts that invite some review in closing. Throughout this book, I have used 1970 as the start point of a new era, echoing the chronology put in place by historians of mid-century Britain and the so-called 'golden age' of marriage: Claire Langhamer, Alana Harris and Timothy Willem Jones and

Charlotte Greenhalgh have all given 1970 as the end-point to their recent studies. As Callum Brown and Hera Cook have persuasively argued, key cultural and contraceptive shifts in the 1960s, and particularly the late 1960s, were integral to the making of modern secular sexuality – these changes would take full effect in the 1970s as their studies, which run to 1975, suggest.[3] As for the importance of the 1970s as a threshold era in sexual relations, this book has been in agreement with Ben Mechen that – thanks to a number of political and policy changes – influential new discourses emerged that profoundly altered the status of sexual relationships.[4] This, together with the increased visibility of feminist discourse (including mockery of feminist demands) after 1970, had a profound impact on how people negotiated heterosexual relations. Within mediated dating, the high-profile launch of *Time Out*'s lonely hearts section in 1972 and the climate of sexual freedom and opportunity it seemed to suggest with its explicit and culturally eccentric ads, along with the consolidation of Dateline's success in the early 1970s, all signalled a new era. As discussed in Chapter 2, marriage bureaux continued to operate throughout the decade, but by the mid-1980s, the personals pages of *Time Out* and those of the national *Singles* magazine, along with a new crop of introduction agencies, suggested that dating had definitively moved towards being part of an exploratory lifestyle rather than a means for marriage. The 1970s was key to this process, with psycho-therapeutic, astrological and spiritualist currents helping to create a distinctive culture around sex and relationships that saw them become both more important (for self-actualization), and less codified, than ever.

As I have already suggested, consideration of sexual culture and gendered identities in Britain in the 1980s invites contextualizing within Thatcher's premiership. In this study, Thatcher's presence was felt as the pro-enterprise force facilitating the founding of dozens of introduction agencies – small businesses that also encouraged customers to bring enterprising tactics to bear on the quest for love.[5] In agency marketing rhetoric, more subtle effects of 1980s, pro-consumption culture emerged, with matchmakers promoting an 'exclusivity' that hinted at class elitism but was, in reality, more concerned with professional aspirationalism. This movement towards matching people on grounds of ambition, or professional achievement – as opposed to the more fixed tripartite class categories used to pair *London Weekly Advertiser* lonely hearts advertisers in the 1970s – suggested the emergence of a more flexible system of social categorization for use in assessing romantic suitability. But at the same time, the apparently classless emphasis on the spiritual and personal promise of sexuality advanced by the likes of Alex Comfort in the 1970s ebbed, making way for a strong interest in how the quest for romance could be better organized, hierarchized and instrumentalized. One effect of this was that the seepage of materialism into the romantic field became a more marked feature of singles discourse.

The late 1980s and 1990s saw the consolidation of these themes, and particularly the emergence of the 'single lifestyle' as a concept that included a bold and self-knowing approach to sexuality and dating, and that invited certain types of consumption (particularly of alcohol and food). Crucially, the 1990s was the decade in which dating services began to approach the mainstream. As discussed in Chapter 2, a number of national newspapers launched their lonely hearts services in the late 1990s, while the scale of interest by the media in mediated dating also changed, with singleness and singles services attracting for the first time a range of non-satirical broadcast investigations.[6] By the end of the decade, *Sex and the City* and Helen Fielding's *Bridget Jones' Diary* had affirmed singleness as a subject of sufficient global recognition and fascination to be commercial gold. Crudely put, between 1970 and 2000, singles' identity was moulded by a range of social, political and cultural factors into a key lifestyle phase, difficult and fun, normalized yet vexed, and above all, a highly gendered experience defined by asymmetries between men and women. As matchmaker Penrose Halson's memoir affirmed, the 1980s saw the emergence of the figure of the single woman who had chosen her career over her personal life alongside that of men who had also been seduced by careerism into neglecting relationships.[7] But in the 1990s, with the spread of popular representations of singleness and dating focusing on women in their thirties, singleness came to be seen as a women's issue in which biology had finally caught up with a generation that had apparently been taught to pursue their professional rather than their romantic fate. Thus, looking at 1970–2000 as a set of decadal micro-periods underlines the sheer number of new factors that shaped singles' experience in late twentieth-century Britain. While remaining cognizant of the depth of debate about whether historical change can or should be pinned to specific moments and dates, this book has offered an account of late twentieth-century British intimacy that sees the 1970s as a key transition point in the history of heterosexual experience, with the social, cultural and emotional currents that underpinned its radical changes structuring the options for what came next.

*   *   *

Two people with little to say to each other, nervously drinking red wine, knocking hands over the bread basket, and making banal comments about the *champignons*.

Such scenes, in which daters tested romantic potential over dinner, were a recurring image in dating documentaries such as *Singles* (1993). Two decades later, the Channel 4 programme *First Dates* (2013) would rise to prominence offering audiences the chance to watch strangers wrestle with gin and tonics, escargots and sea bream as they try to ascertain chemistry, while ITV's dating reality show phenomenon *Love Island* (launched in 2015) is punctuated by special dates that take coupled-up contestants out of the sun-drenched villa in which the programme takes place and into a perfectly staged table for two with 'champagne', chocolate, fruit and mood lighting.[8] On TV, food and drink is an entertaining prop but the meal is also gripping because it shows men and women grappling with complex and demanding social and gendered dynamics: dates derive their fascination for TV audiences – and particularly British audiences – because their format seems to exacerbate the tensions of competing sexual agendas as well as to create discomfiting degrees of awkwardness. (There is, of course, a layer of unreality or parody in both shows since neither the man nor the woman has to pick up the bill.)

But audiences also want to know: 'will it/does it work?' The question of whether blind dating works has been at the centre of matchmaking discourse since the late nineteenth century. Although we have seen how commercial mediation could work against daters' sense of the romantic grain, the bald question of whether it 'works' has been kept somewhat secondary. In closing, though, it invites attention. My answer in relation to the evidence considered in this book between 1970 and 2000 is that mediated matchmaking was rigged *against* working for customers. On one hand, this was a period in which women like Elaine and Hilary, born in the early 1950s, were able to move away from the seemingly repressive world of their parents by sleeping with multiple partners, embracing sex and dating, including mediated dating, as part of a lifestyle facilitated by the legislative and contraceptive advances of the 1960s and 1970s. But for many, including those born earlier in the century, older sensibilities overlaid and complicated the novelty of the new sexual landscape. Singles brought a patchwork of values and feelings about the proper role of men and women to the table, often, as we saw in the dates of divorcee Mary, clashing over them. This is one reason that, rather than melt the gap between romantic agents, matchmaking tended to exacerbate their differences.

Another reason for its tendency towards failure concerned the strain of managing and recovering from multiple blind dates. Mediated dating accentuated unrealistic expectations and hopes, generating encounters hamstrung by awkwardness and romantic dissonance, and amplifying the adversarial potential of the heterosexual encounter. The exposure to such encounters demanded the cultivation of an outlook on love that required rigorous strategizing, and which therefore jarred with persistent ideas about the authenticity and naturalness of romance. But however energetically they embraced it, the strategic approach to dating – exemplified in Linda Sonntag's account, or in many of John Cockburn's interviews – did not necessarily make singles more successful at finding a partner, as the Colette Sinclair memoir, oral history testimonies and a number of Mass Observation diaries made clear. Those who continued searching this way had to adapt to its realities and find ways to accommodate rejection, failure and repetition – the flipside of their apparent freedom and options. Some, like Colette Sinclair, did so by continually modifying their search tactics; others, such as Mary, did so through self-critique, wondering if their expectations were too high. Sinclair was a particularly fulsome example of the ways in which a dedicated course of blind dating could cause desensitization and emotional fatigue – afflictions that barred, rather than facilitated, the road to love.[9]

The same problems plague today's internet daters. In bringing strangers together, dating services continue to stage tensions between a wide variety of agendas – sexual, relational, romantic and gendered. But technology has drastically extended the pool of possible dates, and, according to scholars and commentators, radically transformed the dynamics and possibilities of romance.[10] The desire to pick apart the latter claim provided a starting point for this project, with the normalization of internet dating an obvious benchmark for considering earlier forms of mediated dating. Indeed, the present enormity of internet dating, and the apparent rapidity of its development after the switch to Web 2.0 in the late 1990s, had initially seemed an invitation to frame this project as a 'prehistory' of internet dating. But as the project developed, it soon became clear that the expansion of internet dating was an unsatisfactory rupture point, and that online dating was more accurately thought about as a sequel, or inheritor, of what came before. Far from transforming relations between men and women, online dating services could rather be seen as having served and cultivated trends and dynamics that had been in train for at least thirty years. After all, if internet dating is a clearing house for a spectrum of desires, aspirations and urges, these are possible only in a context of relative flexibility, one in which romance and sex are not assumed to be leading to marriage and family. To understand the present heterosexual romantic landscape, then, internet dating – including the rise of apps such as Tinder and Bumble – needed to be placed in a longer spectrum of singleness and mediated dating that tracked back, at the very least, to the first decade in which it was both possible and realistic to tease sex, romance and marriage apart. Thus although its focus throughout has been on a past era, this book can be seen as an insistence on the historicity of the experiences of, and structures faced by, contemporary British mediated daters, from the serious relationship-seekers of eHarmony and Match.com to those using dating apps to try out a range of intimate configurations.

In considering the bigger picture, it should be remembered that a relatively small fraction of Britons ever used singles services even at their pre-internet peak in the 1990s. In light of this, why does mediated dating matter, and why did it attract a visibility that far exceeded its social impact? Chiefly, mediated dating interested onlookers because it represented a cipher for the self as a 'modern' man or woman, and offered an opportunity for reflecting on a rapidly shifting, sometimes bewilderingly unstable romantic landscape. Indeed modernity, as it was invoked by commentators, experts and singles, referred to a populace facing a terrain of expanded sexual opportunities that invited new forms of control, self-management, experimentation, but also loneliness. This was a state of affairs in which mediated dating was both the perfect, or at least, the logical solution, as well as a symptom of malaise and alienation. Mediated dating also appeared to be the response to another seemingly quintessentially modern development: a growing demographic of single people who had either never married, not yet married, or were divorced. This multi-aged group was sufficiently broad, difficult to pin down, and composed of enough shifting sub-categories to attract a wide range of anxieties spanning lone motherhood, footloose men, childless career women, and the isolated and poor elderly.

In addition, the interest in mediated courtship, and single life more broadly, fed off the tensions and contradictions inherent in the topic, and it is to ambivalence, I think, that we must return to capture both the representational and the experiential spheres of mediated romance in late twentieth-century Britain. Crucially, singleness embodied the paradox of contemporary solo life, in which finding love was at once a reflection of self-determination, 'patience and perseverance' and a measure of the luck, fate and fortune implied by the very concept of finding 'the one'.[11] A number of contradictory notions reinforced this paradox. Serendipity and authenticity (the 'natural') were stressed alongside the sensibleness of taking control and outsourcing this need like any other. It also seemed that while singles faced the widest possible horizon of beneficial sexual choice, they were also failing to achieve the enduring gold standard of monogamous commitment. In sum, late twentieth-century singleness appeared inherently full of potential, and redolent of failure. Singles were acutely aware of these contradictions, observing in letters, MOP diaries, newspaper articles and interviews how they could, should or didn't fit within the social and cultural norms surrounding love, sex and romance.

Running throughout this book is a concern with the operation of a market whose 'architecture of choice' and offer of control undergirded the particular contradictions of mediated dating.[12] In brief, in buying the chance to rifle through a range of options, the dater herself also became one of many options to be rifled through and potentially dropped. This was the sharp end of the consumer approach. But to what degree did market logics actually infiltrate and shape the affect brought to bear on relationships – as scholars such as Eva Illouz, Beth Bailey and Rebecca Heino have insisted – by encouraging daters to treat the romantic 'field' as consumers?[13] By following the reasons singles gave for using services, and their experiences of doing so, this book has, in fact, suggested that however marketized the mediated dating process, the effect of this on the internal organization of feeling and desire was equivocal. Romantic aspiration may have been pursued in terms borrowed from the consumer sphere, but feelings, and romantic outcomes, did not align accordingly, as Sinclair's experience made especially clear. Some daters, of course, had internalized the competitive logic of choice, but this was seen as a mistake; one man described by Linda Sonntag 'had been doing [the personals] for years, and decidedly offputting it was too, because it seemed that he was still hoping the next post might bring a letter from somebody better'.[14] Indeed, as services became more mainstream, it became clearer that mediated dating was something to get right – daters should not buy too fully into the sense that people were products that could ever be upgraded and disposed of; nor should they be standoffish about dating multiple people. Mediated dating required aptitude and refinement of approach, pointing the way to the search-literacy demanded of internet dating portals in which users choose between algorithmic browsing; random matching, or flicking through pictures. The challenge, then as now, was to maximize effective usage of the services without losing the humanity integral to the romantic connection. Losing sight of the latter was not considered a fair price by daters to pay for the former.

There are a number of directions that future work on late twentieth-century intimacy and romance might take. Divorce was one of the drivers of the singles service clientele in the 1970s and after, and its impact on the single experience merits a more sustained enquiry. Moreover, as suggested in Chapter 4, post-1970s singles culture was marked by the influx of adults and professionals, rather than teens, into dating. Further investigating the differences between groups of daters, drawing out how being divorced or a single parent shaped not only dating experience but views and feelings about romance, would be a fruitful way of further digging below the demographic evidence documenting the rising divorce rate and number of single parents.

If marital history is one factor that could be further explored, then the ways in which age and generation intersect with the experience of romantic status in the late twentieth century also invites future research. Charlotte Greenhalgh's book investigating loneliness among the elderly population of Britain in the middle century offers up numerous avenues for exploration.[15] Focusing on the emotional and institutional terrain around widowhood, the study argues for the centrality of the experience of older people to a full understanding of selfhood and love in twentieth-century Britain. As lifespans increased in the latter part of the century, old age became an even bigger category, including a wider variety of relational pasts shaped by divorce and widowhood as well by the decision to not marry, or failure to do so. A study of late twentieth-century romantic solitude in old age would also shed light on how older men's and women's experiences differed.

A further avenue relates to a fuller investigation of the links between locality and attitudes to intimacy in post-1960s Britain. This study set out to scrutinize British, as opposed to English, sources, including national newspapers and magazines, and its call for oral histories was placed in a national magazine. Nonetheless, the focus that emerged was on England. There is certainly scope for a more sustained engagement with place: not only metropolitan versus non-metropolitan, but specifically tethered to locales around Britain – work by contemporaneous sociological scholars such as Pearl Jephcott, and by more recent such as Andrew Davies and Szreter and Fisher, emphasizes the richness of regional courtship cultures and attitudes to romantic intimacy.[16] In the later part of the century, the question of whether an increasingly globalized, centralized Britain created uniform romantic norms is pertinent – a future study might ask to what degree local customs, or simply locality, determined the meanings and experience of romantic status.

Similarly, there is scope for an exploration of other intersections: particularly that between dating and ethnic minority status – how did groups whose migration to Britain had substantially increased since World War Two, including Ugandan Indians, Pakistanis, Indians, Jamaicans and Nigerians, approach matchmaking and conceive of singleness in the post-1970s landscape? Successful agencies such as Suman (est. 1972), an Asian introduction service, suggest that there was a vibrant market in British ethnic minority introductions. And what about Jewish matchmakers, a number of whom ran mainstream services, such as Hedi Fisher, a Holocaust survivor and refugee from Hungary? Encounters between singles of different ethnic backgrounds in the period – a topic which surfaced occasionally in *Singles* and in newspaper first-person accounts – also merits closer attention, especially in light of persistent ethnic homogeneity in dating, with only recently changing patterns of cross-ethnic choice on dating apps beginning to emerge.[17]

And finally, from the 1960s onwards, the US was producing a far more developed discourse relating to singleness, dating and specifically mediated dating than was Britain. The flow of ideas about dating and romance from the US was rich and influential, from the findings of relationship 'scientists' William Walster and Elaine Hatfield to books interrogating the options for singles, and manuals for successful dating. The wealth of American sources documenting courtship culture in the post-1960s era could form the basis of a transatlantic study tracking the way ideas and feelings about courtship and romance developed in Britain. John Godwin's *The Mating Trade*, an exhaustive investigation of all aspects of singles culture in the US in the 1970s, was just one of dozens of books and magazines dedicated to investigating American mediated dating from the 1960s onwards.[18] Godwin's study alone throws up numerous fascinating avenues for future research, including a games club that operated in San Francisco in the 1970s, run by two women, in which singles interacted over a range of ingenious games including one in which two opposing sides had to debate the merits of each demand of the Women's Liberation Movement. This hints at even wider parameters of the courtship industry than this book has explored, and reminds us of the need to see the development of British dating culture as the result of a transatlantic current of images and ideas.

Ultimately, however, the primary contribution of this book has not been to exhaustively describe the matchmaking industry. It has been to show that the industry offers a novel purchase on the unique opportunities, contradictions and tensions that came to define heterosexual intimacy and single selfhood in late twentieth-century Britain. Dating brought ideas about romantically appealing models of masculinity and femininity into contact with actual men and women. Whether the customer got what they wanted or not, the period between 1970 and 2000 saw the entrenchment of the idea that it was singles' personal responsibility – emotionally, strategically and presentationally – to find what they were looking for. As the thickening tide of dating manuals in the late 1980s and 1990s made clear, agencies and personal ads could make it possible for singles to search, but it was up to them how successfully they did so. But however much they decided to *work* to bring it about, and however 'modern' this effort seemed to be, the sense that a more effortless romantic fate was out there somewhere hovered over the process. The mystery of the balance between pragmatism and destiny in contemporary approaches to love has remained unresolved.

Notes

Introduction

1 Interview with Elaine, 13 April 2016, London. All oral history testimonies took place with Zoe Strimpel.

2 Ibid.

3 In Britain, the percentage of adults married at any one time fell from sixty-five in the mid-1960s to fifty-three in 2006. The 1970s saw the fastest growth in the divorce rate. 'Divorces in England and Wales, 2010', Office of National Statistics, www.ons.gov.uk/ons/dcp171778_246403.pdf, p. 2 and Avner Offer, *The Challenge of Affluence: Self-Control and Wellbeing in the United States and Great Britain since 1950* (Oxford: Oxford University Press, 2006), p. 336. Verifiable statistics representing numbers of matchmaking companies at any time during this period are unavailable, and this problem will be discussed in depth later in this book.

4 'The lonely hearts merry-go-round', *The Daily Mail*, 2 November 1970, p. 2.

5 'Our eyes met across a small column', *The Guardian*, 31 January 2000, p. B6.

6 'Warning for lonely hearts caught in the love trap by dodgy dating agencies', *The Guardian*, 26 September 1992, p. 34; 'Our eyes met across a small column', *The Guardian*, 31 January 2000, p. B6.

7 Harry Cocks, *Classified: The Secret History of the Personal Column* (London: Random House, 2009), pp. 5–12; Harry Cocks (2004), 'Peril in the Personals: The Dangers and Pleasures of Classified Advertising in Early Twentieth-Century Britain', *Media History*, 10 (1), pp. 3–16: 11.

8 Gay men would become first adopters and innovators of digital technologies of sex and dating. The picture-based, real-time and geographically determined app Grindr would provide the template from which Tinder, then Bumble, Hinge and Happ'n would emerge. Kath Albury et al. (2017), 'Data Cultures of Mobile Dating and Hook-up Apps: Emerging Issues for Critical Social Science Research', *Big Data and Society*, 4 (2), pp. 1–11.

9 Laura Doan, 'A Peculiarly Obscure Subject', in Brian Lewis (ed.), *British Queer History, New Approaches and Perspectives* (Manchester: MUP, 2013), pp. 87–109: 88.

10 Matt Cook and Jennifer V. Evans (eds), *Queer Cities, Queer Cultures: Europe Since 1945* (London and New York: Bloomsbury, 2014); Brian Lewis (Ed.), *British Queer History, New Approaches and Perspectives* (Manchester: MUP, 2013); Matt Bunzl, *Symptoms of Modernity: Jews and Queers in Late-Twentieth Century Vienna*

(Berkeley: University of California Press, 2004); Matt Cook, *Queer Domesticities: Homosexuality and Home Life in Twentieth-Century London* (London: Palgrave, 2014); Geoffrey Chauncey, 'Privacy Could Only Be Had in Public: Gay Uses of the Streets', in Joel Saunders (ed.), *Stud: Architectures of Masculinity* (New York: Princeton Architectural Press, 1996), pp. 224–67.

11 Laura Doan, 'A Peculiarly Obscure Subject', pp. 91–2.

12 Nancy Jo Sales, 'Tinder and the Dawn of the Dating Apocalypse', *Vanity Fair*, 6 August 2015 (accessed online).

13 'Online dating? Swipe left', *The Financial Times*, 12 February 2016 (accessed online).

14 Cohen was responding directly to the Birmingham Modern British Studies Working Paper No. 1, 9 October 2014. https://mbsbham.wordpress.com/2014/10/29/deborah-cohen-response-to-working-paper-no-1/

15 Ibid.

16 E.g. Penny Summerfield (2004), 'Culture and Composure: Creating Narratives of the Gendered Self in Oral History Interviews', *Cultural and Social History*, 1 (1), pp. 65–93; see also Mike Roper (2005), 'Slipping Out of View: Subjectivity and Emotion in Gender History', *History Workshop Journal*, 59 (1), pp. 57–73.

17 Claire Langhamer, *The English in Love* (Oxford: OUP, 2013), p. 10.

18 Lynne Pearce and Jackie Stacey (eds), *Romance Revisited* (London: Lawrence & Wishart, 1995); Sharon Boden, *Consumerism, Romance, and the Wedding Experience* (Basingstoke: Palgrave MacMillan, 2003).

19 Brian Harrison, *Finding a Role? The United Kingdom 1970–1990*, The New Oxford History of England (Oxford: OUP, 2010), p. 209. For 1960s–70s 'sexual revolution' see also Arthur Marwick, *The Sixties: Cultural Revolution in Britain, France, Italy and the United States, 1958–1974* (Oxford: Oxford University Press, 1998); Hera Cook, *The Long Sexual Revolution: English Women, Sex, and Contraception, 1800–1975* (Oxford: OUP, 2004); Avner Offer, *The Challenge of Affluence*, pp. 303–35; Lawrence Black and Hugh Pemberton, 'Introduction: the Benighted Decade? Reassessing the 1970s', in Lawrence Black, Hugh Pemberton and Pat Thane (eds), *Reassessing 1970s Britain* (Manchester: Manchester University Press, 2013).

20 Cook, *The Long Sexual Revolution*; Callum Brown (2011), 'Sex, religion, and the single woman: the importance of a "short" sexual revolution to the English religious crisis of the 1960s', *Twentieth Century British History*, 22 (2), pp. 189–215.

21 Frank Mort, *Capital Affairs: London and the Making of the Permissive Society* (London: Yale University Press, 2010), p. 5; Alex Comfort, *Sex In Society* (Harmondsworth: Penguin, 1964); Michael Schofield, *The Sexual Behaviour of Young People* (London: Longmans, 1965); Geoffrey Gorer, *Sex and Marriage in England Today* (London: Panther, 1973); more recently Jeffrey Weeks, *Sex, Politics and Society: The Regulation of Sexuality Since 1800* (Harlow: Longman, 2012).

22 E.g. Weeks, *Sex, Politics*, pp. 326–7; see also memoirists, e.g. Lynne Segal, *Making Trouble: Life and Politics* (London: Serpent's Tail, 2007).

23 Pat Thane and Tanya Evans, *Sinners? Scroungers? Saints? Unmarried Motherhood in Twentieth-Century England* (Oxford: OUP, 2012) pp. 170–79; Ben Mechen (2015), *Everyday Sex in 1970s Britain*, PhD Thesis, UCL.

24 The longue durée argument is made in Mort, *Capital Affairs*, p. 5.

25 Michel Foucault, *The History of Sexuality*: Volume 1 (Harmondsworth: Penguin, 1981).

26 For a discussion of departures from Foucault in modern British history, see Mechen, *Everyday Sex*, p. 23.

27 Dagmar Herzog (2009), 'Syncopated Sex: Transforming European Sexual Cultures', *The American Historical Review*, 114 (5), pp. 1287–308: 1295; and Weeks, *Sex, Politics*, p. 393.

28 Josie McLellan, *Love in the Time Of Communism: Intimacy and Sexuality in the GDR* (Cambridge: CUP, 2011), p. 3; Weeks, *Sex, Politics*, p. 393.

29 Cook, *The Long Sexual Revolution*; Callum Brown, *The Death of Christian Britain: Understanding Secularisation 1800–2000* (London: Routledge, 2000) and Brown, 'Sex, Religion, and the Single Woman'; Alana Harris, *Faith in the Family: A Lived Religious History of English Catholicism, 1945–82* (Manchester: MUP, 2013); David Geiringer, *The Pope and the Pill: Sex, Catholicism and Women in Post-War England* (Manchester: MUP, 2019), 'The "Modern Girl" and Catholic Religious Life, 1940–1970', Institute of Historical Research paper, 18 November 2015; Timothy Willem Jones (2013), 'Postsecular Sex? Secularisation and Religious Change in the History of Sexuality in Britain', *History Compass*, 11 (11), pp. 918–30.

30 Brown, 'Sex, Religion', p. 194.

31 Katherine Holden, *The Shadow of Marriage: Singleness in England, 1914–60* (Manchester: MUP, 2007).

32 McLellan, *Love in the Time Of Communism*, p. 3.

33 For a conceptual consideration of these contradictions, and specifically the 'reification of monogamy', see Stevi Jackson and Sue Scott (2004), 'Sexual Antinomies in Late Modernity', *Sexualities*, 7 (2), pp. 233–48.

34 Marcus Collins, *Modern Love: An Intimate History of Men and Women in Twentieth Century Britain* (London: Atlantic, 2001); Weeks, *Sex, Politics*, pp. 395–405; Lesley Hall, *Sex, Gender and Social Change Since 1880* (London: Palgrave, 2000); Offer, *The Challenge of Affluence*; Ina Zweiniger-Bargielowska (ed.), *Women in 20th Century Britain: Social, Cultural and Political Change* (London: Routledge, 2001).

35 Ulrich Beck and Elisabeth Beck-Gernsheim, *The Normal Chaos of Love* (Cambridge: Polity, 1995), p. 14.

36 McLellan, *Love in the Time Of Communism*; Herzog, 'Syncopated Sex'.

37 Other sociological treatments of this include Eva Illouz's studies of romance under capitalism, e.g. *Why Love Hurts: A Sociological Explanation* (Cambridge: Polity, 2013)

and *Cold Intimacies: The Making of Emotional Capitalism* (Cambridge: Polity, 1997); Zygmunt Bauman, *Liquid Love: On the Frailty of Human Bonds* (Cambridge: Polity, 2003); Anthony Giddens, *The Transformation of Intimacy: Sexuality, Love and Eroticism in Modern Societies* (Cambridge: Polity, 1992). Key feminist contributions on gender and love include Simone de Beauvoir, *The Second Sex* (London: Everyman, 1993 [1949]); Shulamith Firestone, *The Dialectic of Sex: The Case for Feminist Revolution* (New York: Farrar, Straus & Giroux, 2001); Carol Ann Douglas, *Love and Politics: Radical Feminist and Lesbian Theories* (San Francisco: ISM Press, 1990), and the collection, especially Ti-Grace Atkinson, 'Radical Feminism and Love' (1972), in Susan Ostrov Weisser (ed.), *Women and Romance: A Reader* (New York: NYU Press, 2001).

38　A prominent attempt to historicize love both as a feeling and as a set of rituals is William Reddy, *The Making of Romantic Love: Longing and Sexuality in Europe, South Asia, and Japan, 900–1200 CE* (Chicago: The University of Chicago Press, 2012).

39　Joan W. Scott (1986), 'Gender: A Useful Category of Historical Analysis', *The American Historical Review*, 921 (5), pp. 1053–75.

40　Ibid., p. 1067.

41　Ostrov Weisser, *Women and Romance*, pp. 1–9.

42　Eva Illouz, 'The Lost Innocence of Love: Romance as a Post-Modern Condition', in Mike Featherstone (ed.), *Love and Eroticism* (London: Sage, 1999), pp. 161–87: 176.

43　Carol Dyhouse, *Heartthrobs: A History of Women and Desire* (Oxford: OUP, 2017); Stephen Brooke, '"A Certain Amount of Mush": Love, Romance, Celluloid and Wax in the Mid-Twentieth Century', in Alana Harris and Timothy Willem Jones (eds), *Love and Romance in Britain, 1918–1970* (London: Palgrave, 2015), pp. 81–100.

44　For the prominence in the mid- and late twentieth-century of romantic narratives featuring the ideal of 'the one', see Lucy Noakes, '"Sexing the Archive": Gender in Contemporary History', in Brian Brivati, Julia Buxton and Anthony Seldon (eds), *The Contemporary History Handbook* (Manchester: MUP, 1996), pp. 74–83: 77; discussion in Simon Szreter and Kate Fisher, *Sex Before the Sexual Revolution: Intimate Life in England 1918–1963* (Cambridge: CUP, 2010), p. 165; Judy Giles (1992), '"Playing Hard to Get": Working-Class Women, Sexuality and Respectability in Britain, 1918–40', *Women's History Review*, 1 (2), pp. 239–55.

45　Judy Giles, '"You Meet 'Em and That's It": Working Class Women's Refusal of Romance Between the Wars in Britain', in Lynne Pearce and Jackie Stacey (eds), *Romance Revisited*, pp. 279–92.

46　Clearly, the determination of intimacy thresholds is one feature of courtship and, as Illouz has suggested, can be directly shaped by the ways in which romance is evoked. But sex – its first appearance within a relationship; contraception; sexual practice itself – is not the focus here, partly for historiographical reasons that will be explored in more depth later.

47　Herzog, 'Syncopated Sex'.

48 In this book 'feelings' and 'emotion' are used interchangeably. 'Affect', in contemporary scholarly usage, signals a pre-linguistic surge that may or may not lead to an expression of feeling, and which can therefore remain elusive to the historian – the word is used here simply to indicate a domain of heightened feeling, e.g. that associated with the various stages of love. See discussion of these terms in Jan Plamper, *The History of Emotions: An Introduction*, (Oxford: OUP, 2015), p. 12, and Hera Cook (2014), 'From Controlling Emotion to Expressing Feelings in Mid-Twentieth-Century England', *Social History*, 47 (3), pp. 627–46.

49 See, for instance, Diana O'Hara, *Courtship and Constraint: Rethinking the Making of Marriage in Tudor England* (Manchester: MUP, 2002), and John Gillis, *For Better, For Worse: British Marriages, 1600 to the Present* (Oxford: OUP, 1985). In the early and middle twentieth century in America, economic metaphors were mapped onto teen courtship less from the point of view of marriage than popularity and social worth. Beth Bailey, *From Front Porch to Back Seat: Courtship in 20th Century America* (Baltimore: Johns Hopkins University Press, 1988).

50 In this it was continuing trends that Claire Langhamer has illuminated in her studies of mid-century courtship, especially *The English in Love*.

51 Mathew Thomson, *Psychological Subjects: Identity, Culture, and Health in Twentieth-Century Britain* (Oxford: OUP, 2006). See also Eva Illouz's discussion of 'the penetration of economics into the machinery of desire' in the post-permissive era in *Why Love Hurts*, p. 58, and Frank Furedi, *Therapy Culture: Cultivating Vulnerability in an Uncertain Age* (London: Routledge, 2003). For a further – though questionable – extension of the idea of marketplace logics in love, see Catherine Hakim, *Honey Money: The Power of Erotic Capital* (London: Allen Lane, 2011).

52 Maurice North, *The Secular Priests* (London: Allen and Unwin, 1972), p. 185.

53 Illouz, *Why Love Hurts*, p. 4.

54 Marie Stopes, *Married Love: A New Contribution to the Solution of Sex Difficulties* (London: Putnam, 1933); Paul Peppis, *Sciences of Modernism: Ethnography, Sexology, and Psychology* (Cambridge: CUP, 2013).

55 Jackson and Scott, 'Sexual Antinomies in Late Modernity', pp. 241 and 242.

56 On 'the one', see note 45.

57 The best unpicking of the conflicting messages around romance directed at women in the late twentieth century is still Janice Winship, *Inside Women's Magazines* (London: Pandora, 1987).

58 Illouz, *Why Love Hurts*, p. 59.

59 Langhamer and Dyhouse have emphasized that in mid-century romance storylines, true love and pragmatism often went together, especially in stories concerned with bagging a rich *and* handsome man. Langhamer, *The English in Love*, p. 52; Dyhouse, *Heartthrobs*.

60 Illouz, 'The Lost Innocence', p. 178.

61 Joe Moran (2004), 'Housing, Memory and Everyday Life in Contemporary Britain', *Cultural Studies*, 18 (4), pp. 607–27: 608.

62 Ibid.

63 Ibid.

64 For a brilliant account of the mediation of private life through economic forces in the American context, see Arlie Hochschild, *The Commercialization of Intimate Life: Notes from Home and Work* (Berkeley: University of California Press, 2003).

65 Hera Cook, *The Long Sexual Revolution*, esp. pp. 265–346; Pat Thane and Tanya Evans, *Sinners? Scroungers? Saints?*

66 The first of three ground-breaking National Survey of Sexual Attitudes and Lifestyles was published in 1990; see also studies like Michael Murphy (2000), 'The Evolution of Cohabitation in Britain, 1960–95', *Population Studies*, 54 (1), pp. 43–56; Jane Lewis and Kathleen Kiernan (1996), 'The Boundaries Between Marriage, Nonmarriage, and Parenthood: Changes in Behavior and Policy in Postwar Britain', *Journal of Family History*, 21 (3), pp. 372–87, esp. p. 373.

67 In addition, historians of post-war London have used a capital-centric idea of permissiveness suggested in the term 'swinging city', e.g. Frank Mort, *Capital Affairs* and Richard Hornsey, *The Spiv and The Architect: Unruly Life in Postwar London* (Minneapolis: University of Minnesota, 2010). See also Jerry White, *London in The Twentieth Century: A City and Its People* (London: Vintage, 2008).

68 Rosalind Brunt, '"An Immense Verbosity": Permissive Sexual Advice in the 1970s', in Rosalind Brunt and Caroline Rowan (eds), *Feminism, Culture and Politics* (London: Lawrence and Wishart, 1982), pp. 143–70: 144; *The Permissive Society: The Guardian Inquiry* (London: Panther Modern Society, 1969).

69 Marcus Collins, 'Introduction', in Marcus Collins (ed.), *The Permissive Society and its Enemies: Sixties British Culture* (London: Rivers Oram, 2007), pp. 1–40; David McGillivray, *Doing Rude Things: The History of the British Sex Film, 1957–81* (London: Sun Tavern Fields, 1992); Anthony Aldgate, *Censorship and the Permissive Society: British Cinema and Theatre, 1955–1965* (Oxford: Clarendon Press, 1995); Joseph McAleer, *Passion's Fortune: The Story of Mills and Boon* (Oxford: OUP, 1999). Beyond Britain, see, for instance, Elizabeth D. Heineman (2006), 'The Economic Miracle in the Bedroom: Big Business and Sexual Consumption in Reconstruction West Germany', *Journal of Modern History*, 78, pp. 846–77.

70 For a rigorous but not entirely convincing justification for focusing on sexual 'discourse' rather than the experience of intimacy, see Mechen, *Everyday Sex*, p. 42.

71 Annette Kuhn, *An Everyday Magic: Cinema and Cultural Memory* (London: IB Tauris, 2002); Jeffrey Richards, *The Age of the Dream Palace: Cinema and Society in 1930s Britain* (London: IB Tauris, 2010); Adrian Horn, *Juke Box Britain: Americanisation and Youth Culture, 1945–60* (Manchester: MUP, 2009); Carol Dyhouse, *Glamour: Women, History and Feminism* (London: Zed, 2010) and *Heartthrobs*.

72 Janice Winship, *Inside Women's Magazines*. Representation rather than reception was the key theme at a recent women's magazines conference, 'Consuming/Culture: Women and Girls in Print and Pixels', Oxford Brookes University, 5–6 June 2015.

73 E.g. Angela McRobbie, *Feminism and Youth Culture: From 'Jackie' to 'Just Seventeen'* (Basingstoke: Macmillan Education, 1991); Mica Nava, *Changing Cultures: Feminism, Youth and Consumerism* (London: Sage, 1992).

74 'Ordinary' here is used to mean people who were not well-off, activists, bohemians, or those working in the cultural industries or media; and quite often people with conservative leanings. 'Ordinariness' is far from a neutral term, however, as Claire Langhamer has made clear; and must be appreciated in relation to its historical and present uses for cultural, affective and particularly political ends. 'Who the Hell are "Ordinary People"? Ordinariness as a Category of Historical Analysis' (2018), *Transactions of the Royal Historical Society*, 28, pp. 175–95.

75 E.g. Sara Maitland, *Very Heaven: Looking Back at the 1960's* (London: Virago, 1988); Joan Bakewell, *The Centre of the Bed* (Bath: BBC Audio Books, 2004); Lynne Segal, *Making Trouble*; Molly Parkin, *Moll: The Making of Molly Parkin: An Autobiography* (London: Gollancz, 1993); Viv Albertine, *Clothes Clothes Clothes Music Music Music Boys Boys Boys* (London: Faber & Faber, 2014).

76 Jon Lawrence, 'Paternalism, Class, and the Path to Modernity', in Simon Gunn and James Vernon (eds), *The Peculiarities of Liberal Modernity in Imperial Britain* (Berkeley: University of California Press, 2011), pp. 147–65: 162–64.

77 Ibid.

78 Frank Mort, *Cultures of Consumption: Commerce, Masculinities and Social Space* (London: Routledge, 1996).

79 Ibid., pp. 2 and 3.

80 See Bauman on cloakroom communities in *Liquid Modernity* (Cambridge: Polity, 2000), pp. 199–202; Giddens, *The Transformation of Intimacy*; Illouz explores fungible relationships in *Cold Intimacies*, p. 109. For more recent historical work linking themes of economics, politics and sex in the 1980s, see Chris Moores (2014), 'Opposition to the Greenham Women's Peace Camps in 1980s Britain: RAGE Against the "Obscene"', *History Workshop Journal*, 78 (1), pp. 204–27; Laura Beers, 'Thatcher and the Women's Vote', in Robert Saunders and Ben Jackson (eds), *Making Thatcher's Britain* (Cambridge: CUP, 2012), pp. 113–32. See also work linking gay activism and governmental and popular perception of AIDS in the decade: Matt Cook, 'AIDS and Mass Observation', Mass Observation podcasts, 97, www.massobs.org.uk/podcasts/97-matt-cook-aids-and-mass-observation; Lucy Robinson, *Gay Men and the Left in Post-War Britain: How The Personal Got Political* (Manchester: MUP, 2007).

81 Cocks, 'The Cost of Marriage and the Matrimonial Agency in Late Victorian Britain' *Social History*, 38 (1), pp. 6–88.

82 Cocks, 'Peril in the Personals', p. 5.

83 Cocks, 'The Cost of Marriage', p. 66; Raymond Williams, *The Long Revolution* (Harmondsworth: Penguin, 1965), p. 204.

84 Matthew Rubery, *The Novelty of Newspapers: Victorian Fiction After the Invention of the News* (Oxford: OUP, 2009), p. 50.

85 Ibid., p. 51.

86 Ibid., p. 58.

87 Ann Fabian, *The Unvarnished Truth; Personal Narratives in Nineteenth Century America* (Berkeley: University of California Press, 2001), cited in Matt Houlbrook (2013), 'Fashioning an Ex-Crook Self: Citizenship and Criminality in the Work of Netley Lucas', *Twentieth Century British History*, 24 (1), pp. 1–30: 3.

88 Cocks discusses this at length in 'Peril in the Personals', especially pp. 10–12; for unease about female consumption in Victorian London, see Judith Walkowitz, *City of Dreadful Delight: Narratives of Sexual Danger in Late-Victorian London* (Chicago: University of Chicago Press, 1992) and Erika Rappaport, *Shopping for Pleasure: Women in the Making of London's West End* (Princeton: Princeton University Press, 2001).

89 Cocks, 'The Prehistory of Print and Online Dating', in I. Alev Degim et al. (eds), *Online Courtship: Interpersonal Interactions Across Borders* (Amsterdam: Institute of Network Borders: 2015), pp. 17–29: 26.

90 Walter Besant, 'In the City of Dreadful Solitude: a plea for a matrimonial bureau', *Review of Reviews* (February 1897), pp. 154–6.

91 Ibid.

92 See discussion of prosecution of Alfred Barrett of The Link in Cocks, *Classified*, pp. 3–23, for the longer stigma of degeneracy attached to the matrimonial advertisement, see Cocks, 'The Cost of Marriage', p. 69.

93 Cocks, 'The Prehistory of Print and Online Dating', p. 26.

94 Monica Whitty has extensively surveyed duplicity in online dating, e.g. with Adam Joinson, *Truth, Lies and Trust On the Internet* (London: Routledge, 2009).

95 Besant, 'In the City of Dreadful Solitude', p. 154.

96 Ibid.

97 Ibid.

98 Ibid.

99 Cocks, 'The Cost of Marriage', pp. 68–71.

100 This idea was played upon in popular novels and musicals, such as Florence Warden's *The Marriage Broker* (1907) and Arthur Anderson and Adrian Ross, music by Victor Jacobi, *The Marriage Market* (London, 1913), cited in Cocks, 'The Cost of Marriage', p. 75.

101 Ginger Frost, *Promises Broken: Courtship, Class and Gender in Victorian England* (Charlottesville: University of Virginia Press, 2015), p. 71.

102 'Magazines ABCs: Top 100 at a glance', *Campaign*, 12 February 2015, www.campaignlive.co.uk/article/1333599/magazines-abcs-top-100-glance.

103 Dorothy Sheridan (1994), 'Using the Mass-Observation Archive As A Source For Women's Studies', *Women's History Review*, 3 (1), pp. 101–13: 109.

104 John Tosh, *A Man's Place: Masculinity and the Middle-Class Home in Victorian England* (New Haven: Yale University Press, 1999); Terence Real, *I Don't Want To Talk About It: Overcoming the Secret Legacy of Male Depression* (Upper Saddle River, NJ: Prentice Hall, 1998).

105 The meaning of 'ordinary' in relation to Mass Observation is discussed extensively by Dorothy Sheridan in relation to the Mass Observation archive. 'Ordinary' is taken to indicate, both by Mass Observation creators and respondents what people are not, 'they are not academics, politicians, policy makers, published writers, professional historians, journalists, controllers of the media and other spokespersons – people who have certain sorts of power to define what history is'. Sheridan (1996) 'Damned anecdotes and dangerous confabulations: Mass-Observation as Life History', Mass Observation Occasional Paper No. 7, University of Sussex Library, pp. 10 and 11.

106 Sheridan, 'Damned Anecdotes' and 'Using The Mass-Observation Archive'; Annabella Pollen (2013), 'Research Methodology in Mass Observation Past and Present: "Scientifically, about as valuable as a chimpanzee's tea party at the zoo"?', *History Workshop Journal*, 75 (1), pp. 213–35.

107 John Cockburn, *Lonely Hearts: Love Among the Small Ads* (London: Guild, 1988), preface.

108 Cockburn, *Lonely Hearts*, vii. Cockburn himself admits that the 'false pretences' on which he met some female interviewees could be seen as 'unethical' and 'improper', but excused himself on the grounds that he was 'listening attentively to [their] stories … and provided a valuable therapy session'. He also reminded the concerned reader that he changed all names and also some professional or geographic details in some cases. Ibid., viii.

109 David Morley, *Home Territories: Media, Mobility, and Identity* (New York: Routledge, 2000), p. 3. See also Gavin Schaffer's discussion of television as a distancing device that enables viewers to think about their own (different) position: *The Vision of a Nation: Making Multiculturalism on British Television, 1960–1980* (Basingstoke: Palgrave MacMillan, 2014), p. 3.

110 Katherine Holden, *The Shadow of Marriage*.

1 'Live alone and like it?' Singleness in late twentieth-century Britain

1 Marjorie Hills, *Live Alone and Like It: A Guide For the Extra Woman* (London: Virago, 2005 [1937]). The book became a classic of the interwar period.

2   Katherine Holden, *The Shadow of Marriage: Singleness in England, 1914–60*
    (Manchester: MUP, 2007), pp. 6–9.

3   E.g. Langhamer, *The English in Love* (Oxford: OUP, 2013); Langhamer (2012), 'Love,
    Selfhood and Authenticity in Post-war Britain', *Cultural and Social History*,
    9 (2), pp. 277–97.

4   Jane Lewis, *The End of Marriage? Individualism and Intimate Relations* (Cambridge:
    CUP, 2002), p. 3.

5   Avner Offer, *The Challenge of Affluence: Self-Control and Wellbeing in the United
    States and Britain Since 1950* (Oxford: OUP, 2006).

6   From a sizeable American literature on the challenging effects of late twentieth-
    century individualism and career ambition on relationships, see Milton Regan,
    Family Law and the Pursuit of Intimacy (New York: NYU Press, 1993); on the
    privileging of individualism within intimacy, Arlene and Jerome Skolnick, *Family in
    Transition* (New York: Pearson, 1980). For a German case study, see Beck and
    Beck-Gernsheim, *The Normal Chaos of Love* (Cambridge: Polity, 1995).

7   *Singles* magazine's regular feature, 'Successful Single', underscored the magazine's
    view that through entrepreneurialism and pro-activity, singles could lift themselves
    up economically, socially and emotionally.

8   British demographic data is 'among the most complete in the world', David Coleman,
    'Population and Family', in Alan Halsey and Josephine Webb (eds), *Twentieth-Century
    British Social Trends* (Basingstoke: Macmillan, 2000), pp. 27–93: 27. For
    interpretations, see Michael Anderson (1985), 'The Emergence of the Modern Life
    Cycle In Britain', *Social History*, 10 (1),
    pp. 69–87; Jacqueline Burgoyne, 'Rethinking the Family Life Cycle: Sexual Divisions,
    Work and Domestic Life in the Post-war Period', in Alan Bryman et al. (eds),
    Rethinking the Life Cycle (Basingstoke: Macmillan, 1987), pp. 72–87; Jeffrey Weeks, *The
    World We Have Won: The Remaking of Erotic and Intimate Life* (London: Routledge,
    2007), pp. 87–107; Hera Cook, *The Long Sexual Revolution: English Women, Sex, and
    Contraception 1800–1975* (Oxford: OUP, 2005).

9   Geoffrey Gorer, *Sex and Marriage in England Today: A Study of the Views and
    Experience of the Under-45's* (London: Panther, 1973); NATSAL-1 findings in Kaye
    Wellings et al., *Sexual Behaviour in Britain: The National Survey of Sexual Attitudes
    and Lifestyles* (London: Penguin, 1994), and Anne Johnson et al., *Sexual Attitudes &
    Lifestyles* (Oxford: Blackwell Scientific Publications, 1994). NATSAL-2 findings were
    published in a number of articles addressing themes including risky sexual
    behaviour, use of alcohol, early sexual experiences and contraceptive use. For data
    sets and summary, see Anne Johnson et al., *National Survey of Sexual Attitudes and
    Lifestyles, 2000–2001*, UK Data Service, 10.5255/UKDA-SN-5223-1.

10 Liz Stanley, *Sex Surveyed, 1949–1994: From Mass-Observation's 'Little Kinsey' to the
    National Survey and the Hite Reports* (London: Taylor and Francis, 1995), pp. 8–9.

11 Brian Harrison, *Finding a Role: The United Kingdom 1970–1990* (Oxford: OUP, 2010), p. 211; Weeks, *The World We Have Won*, p. 104. For insistence on an earlier period of change in core sexual change in terms of reproductive norms, see Anderson, 'The Emergence of the Modern Life Cycle'.

12 Yehezkel Dror (1959), 'Law and Social Change', *Tulane Law Review*, 33 (4), pp. 787–802. See discussion in Jane Lewis, *The End of Marriage*, p. 23.

13 Beatrix Campbell, *The Iron Ladies: Why Do Women Vote Tory?* (London: Virago, 1987); for confusion over the new vocabularies of feminism in a political context see Joni Lovenduski (1996), 'Sex, Gender and British Politics', *Parliamentary Affairs*, 49 (1), pp. 1–16. For analysis of class and race-related debates around differing meanings of gender and feminism in the 1970s and 1980s, see Natalie Thomlinson, *Race, Ethnicity and the Women's Movement in England, 1968–1993* (Basingstoke: Palgrave, 2016); Thomlinson and Florence Sutcliffe-Braithwaite (2018), 'National Women Against Pit Closures: Gender, Trade Unionism, and Community Activism', *Contemporary British History*, 32 (1), pp. 78–100.

14 Weeks, *The World We Have Won*, p. 69.

15 Peter Worsley, *The New Introducing Sociology* (London: Pelican, 1987), p. 158; Michael Young and Peter Willmott, *The Symmetrical Family* (London: Kegan Paul, 1973), p. 13.

16 Ann Oakley, *The Sociology of Housework* (London: Robertson, 1974).

17 Elsa Ferri and Kate Smith (1996), *Parenting in the 1990s* (London: Family Policy Studies Centre). See also Arlie Hochschild, *The Second Shift: Working Parents and the Revolution at Home* (London: Piatkus, 1990), and Julie Brines (1993), 'The Exchange Value of Housework', *Rationality and Society*, 5 (3), pp. 302–40.

18 Krista Jansson, *British Crime Survey – Measuring Crime For 25 Years* (London: HMSO, 2007), p. 12.

19 Offer, *The Challenge of Affluence*, p. 317, table 13.1.

20 Health Statistics Quarterly (2009), Office of National Statistics (ONS), 42, p. 15.

21 Albert Halsey et al., *Origins and Destinations: Family, Class and Education in Modern Britain* (Oxford: Clarendon Press, 1980), p. 59; see discussion of definitional issues of singleness in Holden, *The Shadow of Marriage*, p. 10.

22 David Coleman and John Salt, *The British Population: Patterns, Trends and Processes* (London: Clarendon, 1991), p. 188.

23 Coleman and Salt, *British Population*, p. 217; second two figures from 'Families and Households' (2014), ONS, p. 10. www.ons.gov.uk/peoplepopulationandcommunity/birthsdeathsandmarriages/families/bulletins/familiesandhouseholds/2015-01-28.

24 *Single Person Households: Single Living, Diverse Lifestyles*, Mintel International (London, 1992).

25 Ibid., p. 1.

26 Coleman and Salt, *British Population*, p. 192.

27 'The lonely hearts marry-go-round', *The Daily Mail*, 2 November 1972, p. 2. The divorced customer base was also a central strand in John Cockburn's investigation, *Lonely Hearts: Love Among the Small Ads* (London: Guild, 1988).

28 'Divorces in England and Wales, 2010', ONS, p. 2. www.ons.gov.uk/ons/ dcp171778_246403.pdf.

29 Michael Anderson, 'The Emergence of the Modern Life Cycle', p. 78.

30 Mintel, *Single Person Households*, pp. 1 and 6.

31 For the experience of old age in mid-century Britain, see Charlotte Greenhalgh, *Ageing in 20th Century Britain* (Berkeley: University of California Press, 2018). The history and meanings of consumerism in Britain has attracted a large literature that spans the period since the late sixteenth century. Paul Glennie, 'Consumption Within Historical Studies' in Daniel Miller (ed.), *Acknowledging Consumption: A Review of New Studies* (London: Routledge, 1995), pp. 163–203. For accounts of consumerism in the twentieth century, informed by rising affluence, massification, and the rise of consumer rights, see John Benson, *The Rise of Consumer Society in Britain, 1880–1980* (London: Longman, 1994); Matthew Hilton, *Consumerism in Twentieth-Century Britain: The Search For a Historical Movement* (Cambridge: CUP, 2003); Offer, *The Challenge of Affluence*. Callum Brown blamed the 'death throes' of Christianity in the 1960s on expanding consumer choice. Brown, *The Death of Christian Britain: Understanding Secularisation 1800–2000* (London: Routledge, 2009), p. 196.

32 Mintel, *Single Person Households*, pp. 6 and 1.

33 Ibid., p. 2.

34 'Solitary pains and pleasures: Janet Watts examines whether her experiences match up to those portrayed in last week's report on people who live alone', *The Observer*, 20 September 1992, p. 48; 'Single file', *The Guardian*, 14 April 1993, p. A9; and for earlier discussions, 'Alone again, naturally', *The Guardian*, 14 October 1981, p. 10.

35 Excellent discussion of the rise of more qualitative marketing tools in the 1970s and 1980s designed to navigate shifting patterns of consumer behaviour in Anna Gough Yates, *Understanding Women's Magazines: Publishing, Markets and Readerships* (London: Routledge, 2002), pp. 60–64.

36 'The Bridget Jones Economy', *The Economist*, 20 December 2001.

37 *Singles*, 3 (August 1977), p. 16.

38 *Singles*, 38 (July 1980), p. 17.

39 Wellings et al., *Sexual Behaviour in Britain: The National Survey of Sexual Attitudes and Lifestyles*, fig. 2.2, pp. 43 and 98.

40 NATSAL-1, p. 98.

41 Gorer, *Sex and Marriage*, p. 47.

42 Lewis, *End of Marriage?*, p. 4.

43 Robert Millar, *The New Classes* (London: Longmans, 1966), p. 31; *The Permissive Society: The Guardian Inquiry* (London: Panther Modern Society 1969); Marcus Collins ed.), *The Permissive Society and its Enemies: Sixties British Culture* (London: Rivers Oram, 2007).

44 While sexual theories and sexual practice have alternatively outpaced each other throughout history, the late twentieth century – with its tardy decriminalization of homosexuality on one hand and the discursive din of permissiveness on the other – is certainly a period in which picking apart the relationship between the two is challenging. For a nuanced attempt at doing so, see Langhamer (2006), 'Adultery in Post-War England', *History Workshop Journal*, 62 (1), pp. 86–115: 88 and 89.

45 Lewis, *The End of Marriage?*, p. 4.

46 Offer, *The Challenge of Affluence*, p. 314.

47 John Gillis, *For Better, For Worse: British Marriages, 1600 to the Present* (Oxford: OUP, 1985), p. 3.

48 Janet Finch and Jennifer Mason, *Negotiating Family Responsibilities* (London: Tavistock/Routledge, 1993), pp. 29–97.

49 Lewis, *End of Marriage*, pp. 3–5; D.J. Van de Kaa (1987), 'Europe's Second Demographic Transition', *Population Bulletin*, 42 (1), pp. 1–59, Stephen Brooke (2014), 'Living in "New Times": Historicizing 1980s Britain', *History Compass*, 12 (1), pp. 20–32: 23.

50 Thorough discussion of similarities and differences between cohabiting and married couples in Jane Lewis, *The End of Marriage?* (Cambridge: CUP, 2002) pp. 29–43.

51 Bob Erens et al., *National Survey of Sexual Attitudes and Lifestyles II: Reference Tables and Summary Report* (National Centre for Social Research: April 2003).

52 NATSAL-2, table 8.8, p. 82 and table 8.10, p. 83. This figure for people seeking non-monogamous arrangements comes from adding those seeking a few regular partners; married, but living with a partner and with some sex activity outside the partnership; and married, with some sex activity outside the marriage.

53 For the stresses of marriage, particularly on women, of the working-class male breadwinner model, see Joanna Bourke, *Working Class Cultures in Britain, 1890-1960* (London: Routledge, 1994).

54 'Values and the changing family: a final report from the working party on values', Study Commission on the Family (London, 1982), p. 15.

55 Sharon Boden, *Consumerism, Romance and the Wedding Experience*; Chrys Ingraham, *White Weddings: Romancing Heterosexuality in Popular Culture* (London: Routledge, 1999); Celia Lury, 'A Public Romance: "the Charles and Di story"', in Lynne Peace and Jackie Stacey (eds), *Romance Revisited* (London: Lawrence & Wishart, 1995), pp. 225–38.

56 On romance narratives shaping national stories about Diana and Charles, see Lury, 'A Public Romance'.

57 Offer, *The Challenge of Affluence*, p. 311.

58 Lynne Pearce and Jackie Stacey (eds), *Romance Revisited*, pp. 9 and 11.

59 Susan Faludi, *Backlash: The Undeclared War Against Women* (London: Vintage, 1993), pp. 21–66.

60 Mathew Thomson, *Psychological Subjects: Identity, Culture, and Health in Twentieth-Century Britain* (Oxford: OUP, 2006), p. 250; see also Paul Heelas, *The New Age Movement: The Celebration of the Self and the Sacralization of Modernity* (Oxford: Blackwell, 1996); Nikolas Rose, *Inventing Our Selves: Psychology, Power, and Personhood* (Cambridge: CUP, 1996), and Rose, *Governing the Soul: The Shaping of the Private Self* (London: Routledge, 1999).

61 Emily Robinson et al. (2017), 'Telling Stories about Post-war Britain: Popular Individualism and the "Crisis" of the 1970s', *Twentieth Century British History*, 28 (2), pp. 268–304: 304. The authors argue that the social movements and discourse around class, gender and race of the 1970s marked the rise of a 'popular individualism' that was firmly in place before Thatcher rose to power.

62 Jon Lawrence, *Me, Me, Me: The Search for Community in Post-War England* (Oxford: OUP, 2019), p. 234.

63 Langhamer, *The English in Love*, 'Love, Selfhood', p. 293; for a similar chronology in the American context, see Stephanie Coontz, *Marriage, A History: From Obedience to Intimacy, Or How Love Conquered Marriage* (New York: Viking, 2005). Longer chronologies foregrounding individual satisfaction in love include Lawrence Stone, *The Family, Sex and Marriage in England 1500–1800* (Harmondsworth: Penguin, 1972); Alan Macfarlane, *Marriage and Love in England 1300–1840: Modes of Reproduction 1300–1840* (Oxford: Basil Blackwell, 1986); Marcus Collins, *Modern Love: An Intimate History of Men and Women in Twentieth Century Britain* (London: Atlantic, 2001).

64 Mathew Thomson, *Psychological Subjects*, p. 250; Nikolas Rose, *The Psychological Complex: Psychology, Politics and Society in England, 1869–1939* (London: Routledge and Kegan Paul, 1985), p. 3.

65 Illouz focuses on Freud's American Clark Lectures in 1909 as a key turning point, *Cold Intimacies: The Making of Emotional Capitalism* (Cambridge: Polity, 1997), pp. 5–16.

66 QD Leavis, *Fiction and the Reading Public* (London: Chatto & Windus, 1932), p. 221; Theodor Adorno, *The Jargon of Authenticity* (London: Routledge and Kegan Paul, 1973).

67 Alison Miller's illuminating study (2013) of tomboy bodies in 1930s America offers one variant of vernacularization, focusing on the development of an institutional 'vernacular' of sexology. 'Am I Normal? American Vernacular Psychology and the

Tomboy Body, 1900–1940', *Representations*, 122 (1), pp. 23–50. See also Emily Robinson et al., 'Telling Stories about Post-war Britain'.

68 Langhamer, 'Love, Selfhood and Authenticity', p. 278.

69 Thomson, *Psychological Subjects*, p. 252.

70 Ibid., p. 254; A.E. Dyson and Brian Cox, *The Black Papers on Education* (London: 1971), p. 86.

71 Frank Furedi, *Therapy Culture: Cultivating Vulnerability in an Uncertain Age* (London: Routledge, 2003), p. 10. For a discussion of anti-therapy culture discourse, see Hera Cook, 'Complaining About Therapy Culture', in Jonathan Reinarz and Rebecca Winter (eds), *Complaints, Controversies and Grievances in Medicine: Historical and Social Science Perspectives* (London: Routledge, 2012), pp. 56–75. Thomson argues that therapeutic practice spread relatively slowly in Britain until the late 1970s, when a boom occurred with 5,500 registered psychotherapists by 1999, up from 500 in 1976, *Psychological Subjects*, p. 252.

72 John Rowan, *Ordinary Ecstasy: Humanistic Psychology in Action* (London: Routledge, 1988), pp. 62 and 64.

73 History of 'personal growth' centres in Britain and the US, and detailed description of their activities also in Rowan, *Ordinary Ecstasy*, pp. 39, 7 and 137; see also Thomson, *Psychological Subjects*, p. 275.

74 George Weinberg, *Self Creation* (London: Raven Books, 1978); 'How to love and succeed', *Company*, 1 (October 1978), p. 47.

75 Leon Zussman, *Getting Together* (New York: William Morrow, 1978).

76 Marje Proops, *Dear Marje* (London: Coronet, 1977), pp. 39 and 40.

77 David Shumway, *Modern Love: Romance, Intimacy and the Marriage Crisis* (New York: NYU Press, 2003), p. 6; *Company*, 1 (October 1978), p. 85.

78 Cockburn, *Lonely Hearts*, p. 24.

79 Thomson, *Psychological Subjects*, p. 262.

80 Ibid. p. 263. However, as Lucy Delap has shown in her study of anti-sexist men's responses to feminism through support groups and co-counselling, therapy had not lost its politically revolutionary potential for the far left: Delap ((2018), 'Feminism, Masculinities and Emotional Politics in Late Twentieth-Century Britain', *Cultural and Social History*, 15 (4), pp. 571–93. See also Thomson on Laing, anti-psychiatry, 'humanistic' psychology and counterculture, *Psychological Subjects*, pp. 270–78.

81 Anna Gough Yates, *Understanding Women's Magazines*, p. 108.

82 Ibid., p. 27.

83 This idea particularly preoccupied US observers. Arlene Skolnick, *Embattled Paradise: The American Family in an Age of Uncertainty* (New York: Basic Books, 1991); Karen Lystra, *Searching the Heart: Women, Men and Romantic Love in Nineteenth Century America* (Oxford: OUP, 1989).

84 Bellah et al., *Habits of the Heart: Middle America Observed* (Berkeley: University of California Press, 1985).

85 Anthony Giddens, *The Transformation of Intimacy: Sexuality, Love and Eroticism in Modern Societies* (Cambridge: Polity, 1992); Zygmunt Bauman, *Liquid Love: On the Frailty of Human Bonds* (Cambridge: Polity, 2003).

86 Baroness Young, House of Lords, Debates, 29 February 1996, c. 1638.

87 Lewis, *The End of Marriage?*, p. 4.

88 Gillis, *For Better, For Worse*.

89 Alex Comfort, *The Joy of Sex* (London: Quartet, 1974), pp. 6–7, cited in Ben Mechen (2015), *Everyday Sex in 1970s Britain*, PhD thesis, UCL, p. 175.

90 Maurice North, *The Secular Priests*, p. 79.

91 Stephen Heath, *The Sexual Fix* (London: Macmillan, 1982).

92 North, *Secular Priests*, p. 81.

93 Germaine Greer, *The Female Eunuch* (London: Harper Perennial, 2006), p. 10.

94 *Dear Marje*, p. 40; Greer wrote of the strain of expectation on women to satisfy 'the jaded male appetite, for which no breast ever bulges hard enough and no leg is ever long enough. Freedom from the uncomfortable clothes that must be worn to titillate. Freedom from shoes that make us shorten our steps and push our buttocks out. Freedom from the ever-present juvenile pulchritude'. *The Female Eunuch*, p. 10.

95 North, *Secular Priests*, p. 75; Marcus Collins (1999), 'The Pornography of Permissiveness: Men's Sexuality and Women's Emancipation in Mid Twentieth-Century Britain', *History Workshop Journal*, (47), pp. 99–120.

96 Cited in North, *The Secular Priests*, p. 76.

97 Naomi Wolf's *The Beauty Myth* linked such implicit and explicit messages with pressure on women to conform to patriarchal tradition. Naomi Wolf, *The Beauty Myth* (New York: Chatto and Windus, 1990). This argument was also echoed in Faludi's *Backlash*.

98 Janice Winship, *Inside Women's Magazines* (London: Pandora, 1987), p. 81.

99 Ibid., p. 166.

100 Yates, *Understanding Women's Magazines*, p. 111.

101 Winship, *Inside Women's Magazines*, p. 89.

102 *Woman's Own*, (July 1983), pp. 24–5.

103 Ibid.

104 Ibid., p. 24.

105 *Company*, (January 1983), p. 4.

106 Ibid., p. 60.

107 *Company*, April 1979 and November 1978.

108 See male-authored quiz, 'Are you really permissive?', *Cosmopolitan*, 5 (August 1972), p. 47. Questions were not actually focused on sex, but include views on capital punishment, religion and mixed-race conception.

109 Winship, *Inside Women's Magazines*, p. 85.

110 'These women are dangerous', *Cosmopolitan*, 3 (May 1972), p. 95.

111 'Sarah Miles – The cool man-eater', *Cosmopolitan*, 2 (April 1972), p. 78.

112 E.g. 'I was a sleep-around girl', *Cosmopolitan*, 1 (March 1972), p. 72; 'The sexually obsessed Girl', 7 (October 1972), p. 71.

113 Cosmopolitan, 2 (April 1972), p. 55; then pp. 58 and 63.

114 Tania Modleski, *Loving with a Vengeance: Mass-Produced Fantasies For Women* (London: Routledge, 2007); Carol Dyhouse, *Glamour: Women, History and Feminism* (London: Zed, 2010) and *Heartthrobs: A History of Women and Desire* (Oxford: OUP, 2017).

115 It should be remembered that *Woman's Own* and *Cosmopolitan* had a substantial number of male readers, one-third of *Cosmopolitan*'s were men, and one million of *Woman's Own*'s five to six million readers were men in 1987, Winship, *Inside Women's Magazines*, p. 5.

116 *Dear Marje*, p. 7. Advice bodies included the National Family Planning Service, while information was available for those who knew where to look in a raft of surveys such as Gorer, *Sex and Marriage*, Michael Schofield, *The Sexual Behaviour of Young Adults* (London: Allen Lane, 1973), and Karen Dunnell, *Family Formation* (HMSO, 1976). Sex education, however, continued to be a highly vexed arena, however, as the vitriolic response to Dr Martin Cole's *Growing Up* video of 1971 shows. Disc sleeve, *The Joy of Sex Education* (BFI, 2009).

117 Adrian Bingham, *Family Newspapers? Sex, Private Life, and the British Popular Press 1918–1978* (Oxford: OUP, 2009), p. 57.

118 Marjorie Proops, *The Daily Mirror*, 7 July 1963, p. 13, cited in Bingham, *Family Newspapers*, p. 80.

119 Adrian Bingham (2012), 'Newspaper Problem Pages and British Sexual Culture Since 1918', *Media History*, 18 (1), pp. 51–63: 53 and 54; see also Cyril Bainbridge and Roy Stockdill, *The News of the World Story: 150 Years of the World's Bestselling Newspaper* (London: Harper Collins, 1993), p. 133; Stafford Sommerfield, *Banner Headlines* (Shoreham-By-Sea: Scan Books, 1979), p. 106.

120 Angela Phillips, 'Advice Columnists', in Bob Franklin (ed.), *Pulling Newspapers Apart: Analysing Print Journalism* (London: Routledge, 2008), pp. 102–12: 103. There was a classed dimension to advice culture in the newspapers: according to *The Independent*'s columnist Virginia Ironside, broadsheet readers were more interested in 'giving than in receiving advice', ibid.

121 *Dear Marje*, p. 7; The magazine *Self and Society*, launched in 1973, pitched itself against the serious under-provision of psychotherapeutic help for the two in five with mental problems, Thomson, *Psychological Subjects*, p. 103.

122 *Dear Marje*, p. 8.

123 *Dear Marje*, p. 10.

124 Elaine Hatfield and William Walster, *A New Look at Love* (London: Addison-Wesley, 1978).

125 Ibid., vii.

126 Ibid., ix.

127 *Encyclopaedia of Love & Sex: A Comprehensive Guide to the Physiology of Sex, the Art of Loving, and the Psychology of Love* (London: Marshall Cavendish, 1972).

128 *Man & Woman*, Part 1 (1970), cover.

129 Ibid., p. 1.

130 Ibid., both p. 3.

131 Ibid., p. 9.

132 Ibid., p. 28.

133 Ibid., p. 217.

134 Ibid., p. 216.

135 Bernard Murstein, 'A taxonomy of love', unpublished manuscript (Connecticut College, 1977). The idea was developed further in the 1980s: e.g. Robert Stern and Michael Barnes (eds), *The Psychology of Love*
(New Haven: Yale University Press, 1988), pp. 13–37; Zick Rubin (1970), 'Measurement of Romantic Love', *Journal of Personality and Social Psychology*, 16 (2), pp. 265–73. For the runaway growth of personality testing in contemporary society, see Annie Murphy Paul, *The Cult of Personality: How Personality Tests Are Leading Us to Miseducate Our Children, Mismanage Our Companies, and Misunderstand Ourselves* (New York: Free Press, 2005).

136 Discussion of parapsychology in Francis Wheen, *Strange Days Indeed: The Golden Age of Paranoia* (London: Fourth Estate, 2009), p. 187; Penny Thornton, *Romancing the Stars: Astrology of Love and Romance* (London: Aquarian Press, 1988), p. 10. For a comprehensive discussion and historiographical overview of the New Age movement in the 1970s and 1980s, see Paul Heelas, *The New Age Movement: The Celebration of the Self and the Sacralization of Modernity* (London: Wiley, 1996).

137 Thornton, *Romancing the Stars*, p. 10.

138 On the London Village: 'About Brian Snellgrove', ezinearticles.com/expert/Brian_Snellgrove/1427473

139 Nicholas Campion, 'Horoscopes and Popular Culture', in Bob Franklin (ed,), *Pulling Newspapers Apart*, pp. 253–63: 255.

140 British credulousness in the face of seeming psychic powers has attracted lightly mocking social analysis such as that by Francis Wheen in *Strange Days Indeed*, and earlier, Theodor Adorno, *The Stars Down To Earth And Other Essays on the Irrational In Culture* (London: Routledge, 1994).

141 'Use your stars to have a good affair', *Cosmopolitan*, 9 (November 1972), p. 70.

142 *Singles*, 22 (March 1979), p. 9.

143 'Discrimination', in 'Survival for singles in the married jungle', *Singles*, 10 (March 1978), p. 10; 'couples philosophy' in reader letter, *Singles*, 12 (May 1978), p. 5.

144 *Singles*, 12 (May 1978), p. 5.

145 W.T. Stead 'In the city of dreadful solitude: a plea for a matrimonial bureau', *Review of Reviews* (February 1897), p. 154.

146 William Booth, *In Darkest England and the Way Out* (London International Headquarters of the Salvation Army, 1890), p. 233.

147 'Caught in the Foot-Benn crossfire', *The Times*, 13 November 1981, p. 2.

148 The 1970s saw a number of spiritualist appraisals of the loneliness 'epidemic' in the Anglosphere: see, for instance, Ronald Rolheiser, *The Loneliness Factor: Its Religious and Spiritual Meaning* (Denville, NJ: Dimension Books, 1979), who mused that: 'To be human is to be lonely', p. 9; Ira Tanner, *Loneliness: The Fear of Love* (New York: Harper and Row, 1973).

149 For interview with Nexus and London Village founder, and footage of both offices and operations, see *Lonely Hearts* (Thames, 1977).

150 Furedi, *Therapy Culture*, p. 21; for a culturally significant fictionalized account of urban alienation and loneliness published at the end of the period under study see Michel Houellebecq, *Atomised* (London: Vintage, 2001).

151 Emile Durkheim, *On Suicide* (London: Penguin Classics, 1996 [1897]).

152 Georg Simmel, *The Philosophy Of Money* (London: Routledge, 2004 [1900]). See also Erich Fromm, *The Sane Society* (London: Routledge, 1991 [1955]); Melvin Seeman (1959), 'On the Meaning of Alienation', *American Sociological Review*, 24 (6), pp. 783–91; for an overview of the sociological literature on modernity and alienation, see Devorah Kalekin-Fishman and Laura Langman (2015), 'Alienation: The Critique that Refuses to Disappear', *Current Sociology Review*, 63 (6), pp. 916–33.

153 Jonathan Raban, *Soft City* (London: Fontana, 1975), p. 9.

154 Ibid., p. 10.

155 Ibid., p. 147.

156 Ibid., p. 150.

157 Ibid.

158 Ibid.

159 Ibid., p. 137

160 Ibid., p. 139.

161 Amy Froide, *Never Married: Singlewomen in Early Modern England* (Oxford: OUP, 2005), p. 45.

162 Ibid., p. 2.

163 Holden, *Shadow of Marriage*, p. 26.

164 Ibid., p. 27.

165 Ibid., p.45.

166   Peter Townsend, *The Family Life of Old People* (Harmondsworth: Penguin, 1963), cited in Holden, *The Shadow of Marriage*, p. 45.

167   Peter Townsend, *The Family Life of Old People*, p. 192.

168   1961 census, Summary Tables, table 24, 'Institutions: Age and Marital Condition of inmates', cited in Holden, *The Shadow of Marriage*, p. 47.

169   Suzanne Gordon, *Lonely in America* (New York: Simon & Schuster, 1976). For an overview of the explosion in sociological research on loneliness, see Amy Rokach (2004), 'Loneliness Then and Now: Reflection on Social and Emotional Alienation in Everyday Life', *Current Psychology*, 23 (1), pp. 24–40.

170   Robert Putnam, *Bowling Alone: The Collapse and Revival of American Community* (New York: Simon and Schuster, 2000).

171   1951 Census, General Report, p. 87 and table 35, cited in Holden, *Shadow of Marriage*, p. 47.

172   Barratt Homes, 'Building a legend' (c. 2012), marketing pamphlet, p. 10.

173   *Singles*, 41 (Oct 1980), p. 7.

174   Mintel, *Single Person Households*, pp. 2, 41 and 42. New schemes for co-sharing houses for the elderly have since appeared, see, e.g. 'Cohousing: "It makes sense for people with things in common to live together"', *The Guardian*, 16 February 2016, accessed online.

175   Mintel, *Single Person Households*, p. 43.

176   'Single minded', *The Guardian*, 28 September 1976, p. 11.

177   Irma Kurtz, *Loneliness* (Oxford: Blackwell, 1983); 'anguish of loneliness' chapter in Marje Proops, *Dear Marje*, discussed below.

178   Irma Kurtz, *Loneliness* (Oxford: Blackwell, 1983), p. 4.

179   Ibid.

180   Deborah Cohen, *Family Secrets: Shame and Privacy in Modern Britain* (Oxford: OUP, 2013).

181   Ibid., p. 247.

182   Kurtz, *Loneliness*, p. 44.

183   Adams, *Single Blessedness: Observations on the Single State in Married Society* (London: Heinemann, 1976).

184   Ibid., p. 88.

185   Ibid.

186   Katherine Whitehorn, *Cooking In A Bedsitter* (London: Penguin, 1974); Tracey Thorn, *Bedsit Disco Queen: How I Grew Up and Tried to Be a Pop Star* (London: Virago, 2003).

187   *Singles*, 59 (April 1982), p. 5.

188   *Singles*, 4 (September 1977), p. 30.

189   *Singles*, 37 (June 1980), p. 19.

190   Pierre Bourdieu, *Distinction: A Social Critique of the Judgement of Taste* (London: Routledge, 2010), p. 367.

191 *Singles*, 1 (May 1977), p. 15.

192 Ibid.

193 Ibid.

194 'Tony Lake', obituary, *The Independent*, 17 April 1993, p. 15.

195 *Singles*, 1 (May 1977), p. 15.

196 Ibid.

197 Ibid.

198 *Singles*, 1 (May 1977), p. 16, and ibid., 2 (June 1977), p. 9.

199 *Singles*, 4 (September 1977), p. 23.

200 *Singles*, 4 (September 1977), p. 22.

201 Ibid.

202 Ibid., p. 23.

203 The shift in terminology from 'marriage bureaux' to 'introduction agency' in the 1980s reveals a telling change of emphasis, again in step with a move from a traditional concern with marriage towards a more open-ended conception of lifestyle. The shift is evident in the terminology used in the diagram, 'Circumstances/Personality', *Singles*, 3 (August 1977), p. 34, and will be explored further in the next chapter.

204 Proops, *Dear Marje*, p. 97.

205 *Singles*, 4 (September 1977), p. 34.

206 Yates, *Understanding Women's Magazines*, pp. 136–41.

207 Illouz, *Saving the Modern Soul: Therapy, Emotions, and the Culture of Self-Help* (Berkeley: University of California Press, 2008), p. 202; mediated dating, particularly computer dating and lonely hearts advertising, was by no means a middle-class-only pursuit, though – as this advert in *Singles* makes clear, all types were sought: 'Rough, tough, adventurous working-class wanted (trucker? Copper?)', John Cockburn, *Lonely Hearts*, p. 10.

208 'Our eyes met across a small column ...' From small ads to agencies, dating is big business these days – and young women are its keenest customers', *The Guardian*, 31 January 2000, p. B6.

209 Ibid.

210 'Bridget Jones: now all over TV: Helen Fielding's book has a lot to answer for ... soon you won't be able to switch on without seeing a thirty-something confessing all in a soap doc', *The Guardian*, 23 March, 1998, p. C10.

211 Cockburn, *Lonely Hearts*, p. 2.

212 Ibid., p. 5.

213 Ibid.

214 Ibid., p. 9.

215 Ibid., p. 28.

216 Ibid., p. 45.

217   Ibid., p. 58. Economic metaphors became widely used in American sociological studies of newspaper lonely hearts in the 1980s, taking part of a longer history of dating and marriage market metaphors: see Beth Bailey, *From Front Porch to Back Seat: Courtship in 20th Century America* (Baltimore: Johns Hopkins University Press, 1988), and recently, Moira Weighel, *Labor of Love: The Invention of Dating* (New York: Farrar, Straus and Giroux, 2016).

218   Cockburn, *Lonely Hearts*, p. 99.

219   Ibid., p. 74.

220   Ibid., p. 72.

221   Ibid., p. 81.

222   Ibid., p. 102.

223   Ibid., p. 103.

224   Ibid., p. 192.

225   Linda Sonntag, *Finding the Love Of Your Life Using Dating Agencies and Small Ads* (London: Piccadilly, 1993), p. 1.

226   Ibid.

227   Ibid., p. 29.

228   Ibid., p. 105.

229   Ibid., p. 118.

2 The matchmaking industry, 1970–2000

1   For first-person memories of the London Village services, see 'London Village – Social Whirlwind of the 1970's' [sic], 19 Aug 2015, lvrevisited70.wordpress.com and *Lonely Hearts* (Thames), 1977.

2   On British computer dating, see Zoe Strimpel (2017), 'Computer Dating in the 1970s: Dateline and the Making of the Modern British Single', *Contemporary British History* (published online). dx.doi.org/10.1080/13619462.2017.1280401.

3   John Cockburn mentions 'shudder' devices in a section titled 'The Commercial Cupids of the Future', in *Lonely Hearts: Love Among the Small Ads* (London: Guild, 1988), p. 245.

4   This is not accurate if *Mr and Mrs*, a 1960s game show, is to be counted.

5   'Every picture tells a story to the new love machine', *The Guardian*, 29 May 1978, p. 2. Video dating services continued to try their luck through the 1990s; e.g. 'Video Dating Ltd', advertised in, for instance, *The Times*, 16 May 1992, p. 8.

6   *The Daily Mail*, 'DJ's dial-a-date', 29 January 1981, p. 11.

7   Newspaper coverage of dating bureaux, agencies and personal ads throughout the 1970s, 80s and 90s included statistics but original sources were never cited beyond 'estimates' based on figures released by the agencies themselves. The ease with which matchmakers could keep data murky – e.g. through privacy arguments and non-

regulation – yet release figures flattering to themselves for marketing purposes, are recapitulated later among internet dating firms. Match.com, for instance, was sued for touting misleading marketing statistics based on false or inactive profiles: 'Customers sue Match.com', *Dallas Business Journal*, 4 January 2011. www.bizjournals.com/dallas/news/2011/01/04/matchcom-customers-sue-their-matchmaker.html. Its own lawyers had approached rival firm Plenty of Fish about unsubstantiated claims, admitting, however, that confidentiality might preclude full disclosure: 'Match.com picks fight with competitor Plenty of Fish', Gigacom.com, 28 April 2010. gigaom.com/2010/04/28/match-com-picks-fight-with-competitor-plenty-of-fish/.

8   Articles referring to new services or increased numbers of customers include, for instance, 'Marriage: cupid from the computer', *The Times*, 25 March 1972, p. 16. This article discusses Compat, a new rival to Dateline, in the context of a growing client base. New singles forums or dating agencies included Hedi Fisher, set up in 1968; Nexus (1974); Company (1976); and Dateline's *Singles* Magazine, in 1977.

9   'The lonely hearts merry-go-round', *The Daily Mail*, 2 November 1970, p. 2.

10 Ibid.

11 'Divorces in England and Wales, 2010', Office of National Statistics (ONS), www.ons.gov.uk/ons/dcp171778_246403.pdf, p. 2.

12 Avner Offer, *The Challenge of Affluence: Self-Control and Wellbeing in the United States and Great Britain since 1950* (Oxford: OUP, 2006), p. 336.

13 Cockburn, *Lonely Hearts*, p. 127.

14 'Singled out in the sunshine', *The Guardian*, 8 July 2000, p. F20.

15 E.g. Helping Hand in Birmingham.

16 It is worth remembering here and throughout, as Adrian Bingham has made clear, that newspapers do not necessarily correlate to readers' lives or interests, *Family Newspapers? Sex, Private Life, and the British Popular Press 1918–1978* (Oxford: OUP, 2009), p. 10. The divorcee experience of lonely hearts was far from absent, finding vent in agony columns and special interest magazines such as *Singles*, in a variety of self-help books, and in many personal ads.

17 There were twenty-four articles mentioning 'lonely hearts', meaning singletons in search of a partner, in *The Times* between 1970 and 1980, versus twelve between 1960 and 1970. There were ninety-five such articles in *The Guardian* between 1970 and 1980 versus thirty-two in the previous decade, and ninety-one in *The Daily Mail* versus forty-seven.

18 Although agencies were proliferating, and more people were advertising in lonely hearts pages, media attention exaggerated the sense of growth. As suggested in the introduction, lonely hearts businesses remained relatively marginal through the 1990s. A 2000 survey estimated they were the domain of fewer than one in five single people. 'The great date challenge', *The Daily Mail*, 19 October 2000, pp. 62–63.

19 Cockburn claimed that the expansion of regional lonely hearts sections was significant in *Lonely Hearts* (p. 7) but it appears that in fact the personals sections of many regional newspapers remained extremely limited – throughout the period *The Birmingham Post*, for instance, which had a substantial multi-page classified section only ran personal ads occasionally and usually not more than one, alongside sporadic individual adverts for local matchmakers. With more fanfare, however, *The Jewish Chronicle* launched its lonely hearts section in 1996. 'JC Introductions helps singles find true love', *The Jewish Chronicle*, 5 December 1997, page unmarked.

20 'Forget love, it's market forces, darling', *The Observer*, 14 February 1999, p. 1; 'Science to watch people by: biologist Robin Dunbar talks to Andrew Brown about lonely hearts ads, Shakespeare and what makes us human', *The Guardian*, 15 May 2003, p. B8.

21 Interview with Dunbar, 10 March 2015, Oxford.

22 *Singles*, 10 (March 1978), p. 3.

23 Cockburn, *Lonely Hearts*, p. 22.

24 Cockburn, *Lonely Hearts*, p. 7. ; 'Why time is running out for the sexists', *The Guardian*, 20 November 1974, p. 11.; *Singles*, 4 (September 1977) carried 230.

25 'Boom time in the lonely heart trade', *The Daily Mail*, 27 November 1985, p. 12.

26 This practice continues on a small scale, with Heather Heber Percy still placing ads in 'select' publications for clients of The County Register; see also the small but persistent section in the elite literary journal, *The London Review of Books*.

27 Ivy Gibson, 'A Trans-Atlantic bridal broker', *The New York Times*, 10 March 1981, accessed online, www.nytimes.com/1981/03/10/style/a-trans-atlantic-bridal-broker.html. 'Lonely billionaires roam globe for luxury love therapy', *Bloomberg* online, 24 January 2011, www.bloomberg.com/news/articles/2011-01-19/lonely-billionaires-roam-globe-seek-luxury-love-therapy-a-craig-copetas.

28 Frances Fyfield, *Blind Date* (London: Bantam, 1988).

29 'Searching for the perfect partner', *The Observer*, 13 September 1981, p. 29.

30 See, e.g. *London Weekly Advertiser* (*LWA*), 3–9 March 1976. On Ida Reynolds' agency, see 'Singles: merry olde matches', *Washington Post*, 15 May 1981, www.washingtonpost.com/archive/lifestyle/1981/05/15/singles-merry-olde-matches/9a47421c-2d14-4138-a067-11c09ebb0b90/.

31 *LWA*, 6 January 1972, p. 36.

32 Claire Langhamer (2007), 'Love and Courtship in Mid-Twentieth-Century England', *The Historical Journal*, 50 (1), pp. 173–96: 185.

33 Moya Woodside (1946), 'Courtship and Mating in an Urban Community', *Eugenics Review*, 38, pp. 29–30: 30.

34 Ibid.

35 *LWA*, 6 January 1972, p. 36.

36 Comparisons with the self-presentational norms that hardened with the rise of internet dating twenty years later are intriguing: it is now unacceptable or strategically ill-advised to refer to past relationships or to present vulnerability to avoid seeming needy. See, for instance, Doug Zytgo et al. (2014), 'Impression Management Struggles in Online Dating', Proceedings of the 18th International Conference on Supporting Group Work, Sanibel Island, Florida, pp. 53–62: 57.

37 *LWA*, 6 January 1972, pp. 39 and 36.

38 Ibid., p. 37.

39 Ivy Gibson advert, *LWA*, 6 January 1970, p. 37; ibid., p. 36; ibid.

40 *LWA*, 5 January 1971, p. 36.

41 *LWA*, 10–16 March 1976, p. 53. Liz Jobey was explicit about the untrustworthiness of matchmaker figures in 'Searching for the perfect partner', *The Observer*, 13 September 1981, p. 29. Harry Cocks has drawn attention to the hyperbolic claims of late Victorian and Edwardian matchmakers: The Matchmaker (est. 1926) claimed to be 'the Most Successful Agency in the British Empire', Matchmaker (April 1927, masthead), cited in Harry Cocks, 'Peril in the Personals', p. 7.

42 Publishers of lonely hearts offered workshops and advice, e.g.: 'Need help with your personal ad?', *LWA*, 10–16 March 1976, p. 53.

43 Interview with Elliott, 1 May 2015, London, and interview with Suzie Marwood, 13 July 2015, London.

44 'Computer dating firm "built up on porn"', *Daily Telegraph*, 21 April 1983, p. 3.

45 'Time Out celebrates its 50th anniversary this month', *Time Out*, 25 September 2018, timeout.com.

46 'Time Out celebrates', 2018; 12 January and 22 March 1973 it ran between twenty-six and thirty-eight lonely hearts adverts per week (this was up to 160 the week 19–25 November 1976) compared to around thirteen in the *New Statesman* and *Private Eye*. The greater cultural significance of *Time Out*'s lonely hearts is evident in the *Guardian* piece exploring its anti-sexist advertising policy: 'Why time is running out for the sexists.'

47 Interview with Elliott, 2015.

48 Interview with Marwood. A discussion of factors likely to have shaped *Time Out*'s readership, such as the effects of immigration and gentrification, is in Jerry White, *London in the Twentieth Century: A City and Its People* (London: Vintage, 2008), pp. 341–55.

49 Pierre Bourdieu, *Distinction: A Social Critique of the Judgement of Taste* (London: Routledge, 2010), p. 243.

50 Ibid.

51 Adrian Horn, *Juke Box Britain: Americanisation and Youth Culture, 1945–1960* (Manchester: MUP, 2009), pp. 115–42; Bill Osgerby, *Youth in Britain Since 1945* (Oxford: Blackwell, 1998), pp. 82–96. See also Jerry White's discussion of the

cultural influences such as the music recording industry in creating London in particular as a 'swinging city', *London in the Twentieth Century*, pp. 342–43.

52 *Time Out*, 6–12 April 1973, p. 74.

53 *Time Out*, 4–10 May 1973, p. 57.

54 Interview with Irene Campbell and Jane Rackham, 13 July 2015, London.

55 Interview with Marwood, 2015.

56 Ibid.

57 *City Limits*, 26 February–4 March 1982, p. 81; ibid.

58 *Time Out*, 4–10 May 1973, p. 57.

59 Interview with Campbell and Rackham, 2015.

60 Interview with Balfour, 17 October 2014, London.

61 *Time Out*, 18–24 May 1973, p. 73.

62 Ibid.

63 Interview with Garfield, 31 March 2015, London. The expansion of higher education after the 1963 Robbins Report may have led graduates to pursue professional futures in London. See e.g. Ann-Marie Bathmaker, 'The Expansion of Higher Education: A Consideration of Control, Funding and Quality', in Steve Bartlett and Diana Burton (eds), *Education Studies: Essential Issues* (London: Sage, 2003), pp. 169–89.

64 Interview with Elliott, 2015.

65 Interview, 2015.

66 Cockburn, *Lonely Hearts*, p. 22.

67 *The Guardian* was particularly attuned to *Time Out* news: see level of detail in 'Why time is running out for the sexists'.

68 Staffers in the 1970s included feminist activists such as Beatrix Campbell who decamped to *City Limits* in 1981 in a revolt over unequal pay at *Time Out*.

69 Interview with Elliott, 2015.

70 'Why time is running out for the sexists', *The Guardian*.

71 Ibid.

72 Ibid.

73 Interview with Marwood.

74 Interview with former lonely hearts advertiser Elaine, 13 April 2016, London.

75 Pauline Chandler, 'head of *Singles*', quoted in Cockburn, *Lonely Hearts*, p. 11; ibid.

76 Ibid. The expansion in the universities sector meant that the category of 'graduate' became a widespread metric for assessing background in dating ads, in London and outside.

77 E.g. 'Warmth, the economics of home heating', *Singles*, 19 (December 1978), pp. 35–37.

78 Interview with Elliott, 2015.

79 The national market for newsagents was 18.42 million sales per month as of 1977, and 'all good newsagents' numbered around 35,000 in the mid-1970s, Simon

Mowatt and Howard Cox, *Revolutions from Grub Street: A History of Magazine Publishing in Britain* (Oxford: OUP, 2014), p. 109. Because it was independently published by firms that have changed name or dissolved since, circulation figures have so far proved unattainable. Based on circulation figures for comparable magazines, *Singles* probably had a print run of about 100,000 in the late 1970s.

80 Cockburn, *Lonely Hearts*, p. 7.

81 *Singles*, 2 (June 1977), p. 2.

82 Bingham, *Family Newspapers*, pp. 213–23.

83 *Singles*, 1 (May 1977), p. 6.

84 Cockburn, *Lonely Hearts*, p. 11.

85 Strimpel (2017), 'In Solitary Pursuit: *Singles* Magazine and the Search for Love, 1977–1983', *Cultural and Social History*, 14 (5), pp. 691–715.

86 John Gillis's term, *For Better, For Worse: British Marriages, 1600 to the Present* (Oxford: OUP, 1985).

87 Harry Cocks (2013), 'The Cost of Marriage and the Matrimonial Agency in Late Victorian Britain', *Social History*, 38 (1), pp. 66–88; see also Jennifer Phegley, *Courtship and Marriage in Victorian England* (Westport: Praeger, 2011), and Ginger Frost, *Promises Broken: Courtship, Class, and Gender in Victorian England* (Charlottesville: University of Virginia Press, 1995).

88 Claire Langhamer (2007), 'Love and Courtship in Mid-Twentieth-Century England', *The Historical Journal*, 50 (1), pp. 173–96: 184.

89 'Searching for the perfect partner', *The Observer*, 13 September 1981, p. 29.

90 'Finding the right partner', *The Guardian*, 12 November 1969, p. 9.

91 *The Daily Mail*, 2 November 1970, p. 2.

92 Smaller ones included Nexus, Clover Leaf Companions, Kay's Agency ('the careful matchmakers'), and regional agencies such as Jane Stephens in Birmingham and Avenues in Essex.

93 'Following fearlessly in Mel Gibson's footsteps', *The Independent*, 28 May 1993, p. 40.

94 No clear date of establishment appears to be available for Helena International. Heather Heber Percy, founder of The County Register, referred to Helena International, run by Helena Amram who later left the UK in financial meltdown, as a contemporary, interview, 18 March 2015, London.

95 'Why wine bars?', *Singles*, 35 (April 1980), p. 8.

96 Brian Harrison, *Finding a Role? The United Kingdom 1970–1990, The New Oxford History of England* (Oxford: Oxford University Press, 2010), pp. 347–8.

97 Ibid., p. 350.

98 Ibid., p. 351.

99 Penrose Halson, *Happily Ever After: How To Meet Your Match* (London: Pan, 1999); Hedi Fisher, *Matchmaker, Matchmaker* (London: Book-Line, 1993).

100 Olive Robinson and John Wallace (1984), 'Part-Time Employment and Sex Discrimination Legislation in Great Britain: A Study of the Demand for Part-Time Labour and Sex Discrimination in Selected Organizations and Establishment', Dept. of Employment Research Paper, 43, p. 3.

101 The strain of patriarchalism in the dating world was more explicit, widespread and remarked upon in the US, thanks in part to best-selling books like Ellen Fein and Sherrie Schneider, *All the Rules: Time-Tested Secrets for Capturing the Heart of Mr. Right* (New York: Grand Central Publishing, 1995).

102 *Which?*, August 1983, p. 362.

103 'One advert and a wedding story', *The Times*, 11 February 1995, p. 1.

104 Interview, 2014.

105 'Mooning around for a soul-mate', *The Independent*, 14 December 1987, p. 12.

106 This wording was still in place in The County Register's marketing pamphlet, 2015.

107 Colette Sinclair, *Manhunt* (London: Sidgwick & Jackson, 1989), p. 164.

108 *The Times*, 4 June 1994, p. 26.

109 *The Times*, 11 June 1994, p. 26.

110 Ibid., 6 June 1992, p. 14.

111 Bourdieu, *Distinction*.

112 Ibid., xxv.

113 Ibid.

114 Ibid., p. 243.

115 Kay's Agency advert, *LWA*, 3–9 March 1976, p. 64.

116 Bourdieu, *Distinction*, p. xxv.

117 'Faint heart ne'er won fair trading', *The Guardian*, 5 May 1977, p. 1.

118 HC Deb 26 November 1980 vol. 994 cc. 545–2l; 'Searching for the perfect partner: Liz Jobey gets involved in the world of marriage bureaux', *The Observer*, 13 September 1981. The 1977 investigation followed a 1975 call by the OFT for more information: it had received 300 complaints in the 18 months up to December 1975 but did not consider this sufficient evidence for intervention. 'Fair deal on dating sought', *The Guardian*, 27 December 1975, p. 5.

119 'Faint heart ne'er won fair trading', *The Guardian*, 5 May 1977, p. 1.

120 HC Deb 26 November 1980 vol. 994 cc. 545–52. See Matthew Hilton on the appearance of new government-backed consumer bodies since WW1, a trend that accelerated in at mid-century, with the Office of Fair Trading set up in 1973 and the National Consumer Council from 1975. *Consumerism in Twentieth-Century Britain: The Search for a Historical Movement* (Cambridge: CUP 2003), p. 2.

121 'Why lonely hearts clubs went broke', *The Guardian*, 23 May 1982, p. 4.

122 'The price of bliss', *The Guardian*, 24 July 1981, p. 8.

123 Heber Percy's disdain for less thorough vetting was particularly strong in relation to personals, which had 'no checks'. 'I think the classified ads are dangerous', interview, 2015.

124 ABIA website, www.abia.org.uk/advice/the-ABIA-code-of-practice.

125 'Why lonely hearts clubs went broke', *The Guardian*.

126 For the persistence of suspicion about agency practices, see 'Love for sale: the dating agency industry is a lucrative one where profits often come before lonely hearts', *The Guardian*, 26 August 1997, p. A4.

127 Name has been changed. Interview with Julia, 10 July 2016, London.

128 See Hedi Fisher on the lack of men under 35 and excess of 'middle-aged widows', *Matchmaker, Matchmaker* (London: Book-Line, 1993), p. 17.

129 Interview with Julia, 2016.

130 Ibid.

131 Fisher, *Matchmaker*, p. 17.

132 Interview with Julia, 2016.

133 'Faint heart ne'er won fair trading', *Guardian*.

134 Marie Hicks, 'Computer Love: Replicating Social Order Through Early Computer Dating Systems', *Ada: A Journal of Gender and New Media Technology*, 10. adanewmedia.org/2016/10/issue10-hicks.

135 'Marriage: cupid from the computer', *The Times*.

136 'The marriage market', *The Guardian*, 30 January 1968, p. 7; *Singles*, 21 (February 1979), p. 4.

137 'The marriage market', *The Guardian*.

138 Marie Hicks, 'Computer Love'; 'Advertising and marketing,' *The Times*, 29 December 1971, p. 13.

139 Britain's computer dating scene took shape alongside, though on a smaller scale to, the one in the US.

140 'We'll make you a believer' advert, *Singles*, 1980.

141 Ibid. For a discussion of the Space Age as 'inextricable from the self-ascribed technomodernity of the 20th century', see Alexander Geppert (ed.), *Imagining Outer Space: European Astroculture in the Twentieth Century* (London: Palgrave, 2012), p. 5.

142 'We'll Make You a Believer'.

143 Ibid.

144 Gene Shalit, the American journalist who first covered Operation Match, marvelled at the powers of 'The Great God computer' in 'New dating craze sweeps the campus', *Look Magazine*, February 1966, pp. 30–35. For the computer's mystique around 1980, see Sherry Turkle, *The Second Self: Computers and the Human Spirit* (London: Granada, 1984); Joseph Weizenbaum, *Computer Power and Human Reason: From Judgement to Calculation*

(Harmondsworth: Penguin, 1979); Ted Friedman, *Electric Dreams: Computers in American Culture* (New York: NYU Press, 2005); Hubert Dreyfus, *What Computers Can't Do: The Limits of Artificial Intelligence* (New York: Harper Row, 1972); Fred Turner, *From Counterculture to Cyberculture: Stewart Brand, the Whole Earth Network, And the Rise of Digital Utopianism* (Chicago: University of Chicago Press, 2006).

145 Donna J. Drucker (2013), 'Keying Desire: Alfred Kinsey's Use of Punched-Card Machines for Sex Research,' *Journal of the History of Sexuality*, 22 (1), pp. 105–25, and Drucker, *The Classification of Sex: Alfred Kinsey and the Organization of Knowledge* (Pittsburgh: University of Pittsburgh Press, 2014).

146 Margaret Boden, 'Purpose, Personality, Adventure: A Computational Adventure', in Geoff Bunn (ed.), *Psychology in Britain: Historical Essays and Personal Reflections* (Oxford: Blackwell, 2001), pp. 353–63.

147 James Butcher, Julia Perry and Jungwon Hahn (2004), 'Computers in Clinical Assessment: Historical Developments, Present Status, and Future Challenges', *Journal of Clinical Psychology*, 60 (3), pp. 331–45: 332.

148 'We'll make you a believer' advert.

149 For the emergence of the 'psy' disciplines and the extension of therapeutic models across private and public spheres, see Nikolas Rose, *Inventing Our Selves: Psychology, Power, and Personhood* (Cambridge: CUP, 1998); Rose, *Governing the Soul: The Shaping of the Private Self* (London: Free Association Press, 1999); and into romance, Eva Illouz, *Saving The Modern Soul: Therapy, Emotions, and the Culture of Self-Help* (Berkeley: University of California Press, 2008).

150 'The marriage market', *The Guardian*.

151 Hicks, 'Computer Love'.

152 'Nothing immoral in tourist dating, Boac says', *The Times*, 13 September 1969, p. 3.

153 Ibid.

154 Hicks, 'Computer Love'.

155 Cited in ibid.

156 'Computer dating firm "built up on porn"', *The Daily Telegraph*, 21 April 1983, p. 3.

157 'Report on computer date firm', *The Times*, 29 August 1970, p. 2.

158 'A first date for match of your life', *The Guardian*, 15 October 1989, p. 40.

159 Ibid.

160 Paul Bonner and Lesley Aston, *Independent Television in Britain, ITV and IBA 1981–92: The Old Relationship Changes* (Basingstoke: Palgrave, 1998), p. 276.

161 'The marriage market', *The Guardian*.

162 'Marriage: cupid from the computer', *The Times*.

163 Ibid., *Singles*, 10 (March 1978), p. 19.

164 Simon Garfield, former editor of *Time Out* (1988-1989) recalled seeing people drop letters off. Interview, 31 March 2015.

165 Cockburn, *Lonely Hearts*, p. 24.

166 Ibid., p. 25.

167 Ibid., p. 27.

3 Representations of the mediated dating industry

1   Lucy Delap (2010), review of Bingham, *Family Newspapers? Sex, Private Life, and the British Popular Press 1918–1978, Journal of British Studies*, 49 (1), pp. 224–6: 224.

2   *The Daily Mail*, 6 May 1971, pp. 18–19, cited in Adrian Bingham, *Family Newspapers?*, p. 122.

3   Ibid.

4   Novels with an intrigue revolving around lonely hearts adverts included detective thriller *Lonely Hearts* by John Harvey (London: Mandarin, 1989), and *Take One Young Man* by Vivien Kelly (London: Arrow, 1999), in addition to TV shows, plays, film and visual art. The sinfonietta that took its cue from lonely hearts was the Lonely Hearts' song cycle by Dominic Muldowney which 'takes for its text some of those intriguing, sometimes sad advertisements in the magazine *Time Out*' (*The Times*, 9 March 1990, p. 18).

5   'Lonely hearts can lose a fortune when they play the dating game: Dating agencies', *The Times*, 13 February 1995, p. 22.

6   'Why we can't just fall in love any more', *The Daily Mirror*, 14 February 1995, p. 7.

7   Harry Cocks (2004), 'Peril in the Personals: The Dangers and Pleasures of Classified Advertising in Early Twentieth-Century Britain', *Media History*, 10 (1), pp. 3–16.

8   'Why I hang up on the lonely heart callers', *The Daily Mail*, 20 June 1987, p. 12; 'Searching for the perfect partner', *The Observer*, 13 September 1981, p. 29; 'Passion fruitcakes', *The Times*, 23 February 1991, p. 6.

9   Harry Cocks' elucidation of these anxieties in the Victorian and Edwardian matrimonial press points to the striking endurance of a set of concerns about sex, gender and the hard-to-regulate world of print personals. Cocks, 'Peril in the Personals'; *Classified: The Secret History of the Personal Column* (London: Random House, 2009).

10 P.D. James endorsement, inside cover of Frances Fyfield, *Blind Date* (London: Bantam, 1988).

11 John Cockburn, *Lonely Hearts: Love Among the Small Ads* (London: Guild, 1988), p. 2.

12 'Marriage: cupid from the computer', *The Times*, 25 March 1972, p. 16.

13 *Man & Woman: The Marshall Cavendish Encyclopaedia of Adult Relationships* (London: Marshall Cavendish, 1970), 7 (88), p. 2460.

14 Giddens places the multiplication of sexual and social options for both men and women at the centre of his account of the transfiguration of 'modern' personal life,

Anthony Giddens, *The Transformation of Intimacy: Sexuality, Love and Eroticism in Modern Societies* (Cambridge: Polity, 1992), p. 8.

15 'What a difference a date makes', *The Guardian*, 17 October 1991.

16 Linda Sonntag, *Finding the Love Of Your Life Using Dating Agencies and Small Ads* (London: Piccadilly, 1993), p. 188. For an urban perspective on what it meant to 'go out with' people in the 1970s and 1980s, see Jerry White on the expansion of clubland across geographies and classes in *London in The Twentieth Century: A City and Its People* (London: Vintage, 2008), pp. 341–51.

17 'Mysteries of choosing a partner', *The Times*, 12 August 1976, p. 12.

18 'Every picture tells a story to the new love machine', *The Guardian*, 29 May 1978, p. 2.

19 'A trans-Atlantic bridal broker', *The New York Times*, 10 March 1981. www.nytimes.com/1981/03/10/style/a-trans-atlantic-bridal-broker.html.

20 E.g. Michael Raban, *Soft City* (London: Fontana, 1974).

21 'Stick that in your data dating program', *The Guardian*, 1 December 1970, p. 7.

22 'Danger when computer plays Cupid', *The Times*, 23 August 1973, p. 4.

23 'Commentary on Ann Mead', *The Daily Mail*, 7 July 1994, pp. 42–3.

24 'Risks of the dating game', *The Times*, 6 July 1994, p. 15.

25 'Nine years in jail not enough, child molester tells judge', *The Times*, 6 September 1994, p. 6. Other examples include 'Sex attacker admits savage killing of mother and girl, 4', a story in which the victim of killer and rapist Robert Napper was 'found to have placed an ad in a lonely hearts column in local paper'; *The Times*, 10 October 1995, p. 3; and 'Lovelorn war veteran is fined for stalking', *The Times*, 22 October 1997, p. 3. The war veteran had 'met lover through lonely hearts' then harassed her with photographs. In 'babysitter burnt in acid attack on the wrong target', the perpetrator had arranged a date with two sisters he met in the personals, *The Times*, 3 March 1998, p. 3.

26 Cocks, 'Peril in the Personals', p. 8.

27 'This woman is every man's nightmare... They can sleep safe tonight knowing she has been taken off the streets', *The Times*, 16 December 2003, p. 1; 'Lonely hearts trickster – Black Widow', *The Daily Mirror*, 18 August 2000, p. 11.

28 Patrick Joyce (ed.), *Class* (Oxford: OUP, 1995), p. 3.

29 Ibid., p. 4.

30 Zygmunt Bauman, 'Sociology and Postmodernity', in Joyce (ed.), *Class*, pp. 74–83.

31 Simon Szreter and Kate Fisher, *Sex Before the Sexual Revolution: Intimate Life in England 1918–1963* (Cambridge: CUP, 2010), p. 191.

32 Ibid.

33 'Be flexible and friendly – and don't give up', *The Independent*, 10 July 1993, p. 41.

34 Some of these new vocabularies were enshrined in Ann Barr and Peter York's best-selling *The Official Sloane Ranger Handbook: The First Guide To What Really*

Matters In Life (London: Ebury, 1984) and in Peter York's more scholarly treatment of subcultures, including those of the new and old wealthy, *Style Wars* (London: Sidgwick & Jackson, 1983).

35 'Playing Cupid to the upper classes – Interview', *The Times*, 25 June 1998, p. 23.

36 'Flirty ways to find a lover – Valentine', *The Times*, 12 February 1994, p. 3.

37 David Cannadine, *Class in Britain* (New Haven: Yale University Press, 1998), p. 2.

38 Harry Cocks (2013), 'The Cost of Marriage and the Matrimonial Agency in Late Victorian Britain', *Social History*, 38 (1), pp. 66–88: 75.

39 Andrew Davies, *Leisure, Gender and Poverty: Working-Class Culture in Salford and Manchester, 1900–1939* (Buckingham: Open University Press, 1992), pp. 102–8; Jacqueline Sarsby, *Missuses and Mouldrunners: An Oral History of Women Pottery Workers at Work and at Home* (Milton Keynes: Open University Press, 1988), pp. 71–5.

40 'Middle class man seeks 50 lonely hearts', *The Daily Mail*, 23 November 1977, p. 19.

41 'Finding the right partner', *The Guardian*, 12 November 1969, p. 9.

42 Marriage Bureau 1939, British Pathé, www.britishpathe.com/video/marriage-bureau-1.

43 Featuring Mary Balfour: Linda Grant, 'Why are we single?', *The Independent on Sunday*, 10 October 1993, p. 21, and 'FIT and paying her way, the 90s woman', *The Daily Mail*, 9 September 1998, p. 30; for Penrose Halson, see, e.g. *The Daily Mail*, 'Four weddings and a bureau', 6 February 1999, pp. 12–13.

44 Anna Gough Yates, *Understanding Women's Magazines: Publishing, Markets and Readerships* (London: Routledge, 2002), pp. 95–118; Susan Faludi, *Backlash: The Undeclared War Against Women* (London: Vintage, 1993), pp. 19–61. Many of these busy singles were women, particularly 'career girls', and many were divorced women. For women's role in increasing divorce, see Avner Offer, *The Challenge of Affluence: Self-Control and Wellbeing in the United States and Britain Since 1950* (Oxford: OUP, 2006), pp. 270–356. It appeared that divorced women formed a larger part of personals advertising than divorced men. According to Pauline Chandler, spokeswoman for *Singles*, 53 per cent of female readers were divorced compared to 29 per cent of men, 'Dear lonely heart: Femail's sociological survey into the thousands of courageous people looking for love among the small ads', *The Daily Mail*, 12 January 1988, pp. 18–19.

45 Interview with Heather Heber Percy, 18 March 2015, London.

46 Bingham, *Family Newspapers*, p. 20.

47 'Romeo and Video! New dating firm puts clients on camera', *The Daily Mail*, 29 April 1982, p. 21.

48 'Love comes last as the men on the dole go hunting for a bride', *The Daily Mirror*, 19 October 1971, p. 9.

49 Ibid.

50 *The Daily Mirror*, 23 July 1998, p. 33.

51 On gentrification, see Jerry White, *London in the Twentieth Century*, p. 340; Joe Moran (2007), 'Early Cultures of Gentrification, 1955–1980', *Journal of Urban History*, 34 (1), pp. 101–21. On restaurants, see Michael Elliott, *Heartbeat London: The Anatomy of a Supercity* (London: Firethorn, 1986), pp. 142–45. On the 'new' affluent types of the 1980s, including those in artistic, media and financial industries, see Andy Beckett, *Promised You A Miracle: Why 1980–82 Made Modern Britain* (London: Penguin, 2015), especially prologue, and Peter York, *Style Wars*.

52 'Dating with danger?', *The Times*, 3 February 1989, p. 21.

53 E.g. Select Friends, Heather Jenner, Katharine Allan and Helena International.

54 Interview, London, 14 October 2014.

55 'Only the lonely and rich', *The Times*, 8 August 1990, p. 16.

56 For resonances with Thatcher's rhetoric about class, see Cannadine, *Class in Britain*, pp. 171–80 and Florence Sutcliffe-Braithwaite and Jon Lawrence, 'Margaret Thatcher and the Decline of Class Politics', in Ben Jackson and Robert Saunders (eds), *Making Thatcher's Britain* (Cambridge: CUP, 2012), pp. 132–48.

57 'Only the lonely and rich', *The Times*, 8 August 1990, p. 16.

58 'Life and Times: how to ring changes in your love life', *The Times*, 7 February 1992, p. 5.

59 'What a difference a date makes', *The Guardian*.

60 Srezter and Fisher, *Sex Before the Sexual Revolution*, p. 117.

61 'Women's lib' was assumed to have had ubiquitous successes in conservative publications such as *Singles* and *The Daily Mail*.

62 Anna Ford, *Men: A Documentary* (London: Corgi, 1986).

63 Faludi, *Backlash*; for the centrality to the British press of a more overt form of biological determinism, see discussion of the pin-up in Bingham, *Family Newspapers*, esp. p. 204.

64 'Our eyes met across a small column. . .: From small ads to agencies, dating is big business these days – and young women are its keenest customers. Raekha Prasad investigates modern matchmaking', *The Guardian*, 31 January 2000, p. B6.

65 Faludi, *Backlash*, pp. 89–125.

66 Ibid., p. 8.

67 *Singles*, 21 (March 1978), p. 13.

68 *Singles*, 47 (April 1981), p. 25.

69 Penrose Halson, *Happily Ever After: How To Meet Your Match* (London: Pan, 1999).

70 Ibid., p. 107.

71 Hedi Fisher, *Matchmaker, Matchmaker* (London: Book-Line, 1993).

72 *The Daily Mail*, 26 March 1992, pp. 24–25.

73 Ibid.

74 *The Daily Mail*, 7 April 1993, pp. 18–19.

75 Victoria Mapplebeck, 'Bridget Jones: now all over TV: Helen Fielding's book has a lot to answer for … soon you won't be able to switch on without seeing a thirtysomething confessing all in a soap doc', *The Guardian*, 23 March 1998, p. C10.

76 Ibid.

77 Ibid.

78 See, e.g. Simon Szreter and Kate Fisher, *Sex Before the Sexual Revolution: Intimate Life in England 1918–1963* (Cambridge: CUP, 2010), p. 165; Judy Giles (1992), '"Playing Hard to Get": Working-Class Women, Sexuality and Respectability in Britain, 1918–40', *Women's History Review*, 1 (2), pp. 239–55.

79 *Which?*, August 1983, p. 362.

80 See also Strimpel, *The Man Diet: One Woman's Quest to End Bad Romance* (London: Harper Collins, 2013).

4 Mediated daters and the experience of matchmaking

1 Personal correspondence, 12 December 2015.

2 Pen Fudge is this interviewee's real name: permission to use it was volunteered and confirmed by Ms Fudge over email, 5 May 2017.

3 Correspondence with Pen Fudge, December 2015.

4 Joan Scott's influential explanation of why relationality lies at the heart of gender, Joan W. Scott (1986), 'Gender: A Useful Category of Historical Analysis', *The American Historical Review*, 921 (5), pp. 1053–75.

5 Dateline advert, *Singles*, 18 (November 1978), p. 41.

6 For the frequent use of 'modern' in describing the context and practices of mediated dating, as well as the behaviour and attitudes of 'post'-feminist women, see, e.g. *Singles*, 44 (January 1981), 'Singular topics', ibid., p. 8; 'Don't think I am some old fashioned "fuddy duddy", in fact I'm a modern 27 year old', Letters; 45 (February 1981); ibid., p. 5; 'Old-fashioned values', ibid., 58 (March 1982), p. 6. 'Modern' is also used frequently by Linda Sonntag in *Finding the Love Of Your Life Using Dating Agencies and Small Ads* (London: Piccadilly, 1993), e.g. pp. 108–9, 118; and by John Cockburn in *Lonely Hearts: Love Among the Small Ads* (London: Guild, 1988), e.g. pp. 2, 5, 9, 226. Much of the historiography on twentieth-century love, sex and social change takes for granted the term 'modernity'. For Alison Light, 'modernity' characterized a type of sexed conservatism visible after the First World War, while Alana Harris and Timothy Willem Jones take the era of sexual 'modernity' to mean the period after the publication of Marie Stopes' *Married Love* in 1918, with Alex Comfort's *The Joy of Sex* marking the completion of the transformation into a 'modern' paradigm. In *Modern Love*, Marcus Collins takes as 'modern' the whole twentieth century, with the intellectual foment concerning 'mutuality' in the late

nineteenth and early twentieth century signifying its start. Langhamer cites the middle decades of the twentieth century as a moment in which people became aware of how their relationships fit within a sense of 'private modernity'. Examples of a wide literature on political modernity focused on the early to mid-century include Ben Jones and Rebecca Searle (2013), 'Humphrey Jennings, the Left and the Experience of Modernity in Mid Twentieth-Century Britain', *History Workshop Journal*, 75 (1), pp. 190–212, or for an overview see, e.g. Martin Daunton and Bernhard Rieger (eds), *Meanings of Modernity: Britain from the Late-Victorian Era to World War II* (Oxford: Berg, 2001). Alison Light, *Forever England: Femininity, Literature and Conservatism Between the Wars* (London: Routledge, 2013); Alana Harris and Timothy Willem Jones (eds), *Love and Romance in Britain, 1918–1970* (London: Palgrave, 2015), p. 2; Claire Langhamer, *The English in Love* (Oxford: OUP, 2013), p. 4; Marcus Collins, *Modern Love: An Intimate History of Men and Women in Twentieth Century Britain* (London: Atlantic, 2001).

7   Giddens, *The Transformation of Intimacy: Sexuality, Love and Eroticism in Modern Societies* (Cambridge: Polity, 1992), p. 2.

8   Rachel Bowlby, *Carried Away: The Invention of Modern Shopping* (London: Faber, 2000), p. 3.

9   Ibid., pp. 3–4.

10 Gary Becker (1973), 'A Theory of Marriage: Part I', *The Journal of Political Economy*, 81 (4), pp. 813–46.

11 Eva Illouz, *Why Love Hurts: A Sociological Explanation* (Cambridge: Polity, 2013), p. 59.

12 Ibid., p. 57.

13 Ibid., p. 97.

14 Mass Observation Project (MOP from here on), Directive Replies (DR from here on), G226, Summer 2001.

15 Sonntag, *Finding the Love of Your Life*, page not numbered (iii?), and p. 4.

16 MOP, DR, R1227, Summer 2001.

17 Ibid., S1983.

18 In her useful overview of the geographical literature linking space, sexuality and leisure, Cara Aitchison points out the dominance of queer, consumer and cultural themes (literature, film, street culture, body fashion). My subjects did not seem to experience their geographical situation as defined in these ways, however, so while I acknowledge its richness, my engagement with this body of work is limited at this juncture. Cara Aitchison (1999), 'New Cultural Geographies: The Spatiality of Leisure, Gender and Sexuality', *Leisure Studies*, 18 (1), pp. 19–39. For examples of work exploring how space shapes sexuality and vice versa, see David Bell and Gill Valentine (eds), *Mapping Desire: Geographies of Sexualities* (London: Routledge, 1995). There is a tenuous overlap with the geographical demands of arranging dates

in Rob Shields' study of the locations in which specific sexual agendas have been pursued, 'Dirty Weekends and the Carnival of Sex', in *Places on the Margin: Alternative Geographies of Modernity*, (London: Routledge, 1992), pp. 105–17. For historical treatments of gender (rather than sexuality) and space, see Claire Langhamer, *Women's Leisure in England, 1920–1960* (Manchester: MUP, 2000) and Judy Giles, *The Parlour and the Suburb: Domestic Identities, Class, Femininity and Modernity* (London: Bloomsbury, 2004), and for the historiography on sexuality and the city, see, e.g. Harry Cocks, *Nameless Offences: Homosexual Desire in the 19th Century* (London: IB Tauris, 2003) and Matt Houlbrook, *Queer London: Perils and Pleasures in the Sexual Metropolis, 1918–57* (Chicago: University of Chicago Press, 2005).

19   MOP, DR, H2840, Summer 2001.

20   Ibid., G2640.

21   Ibid., H2840.

22   Ibid., B1509.

23   Ibid., B1989.

24   Ibid., M1979.

25   Names of all interviewees apart from Pen Fudge have been changed.

26   Interview with Millie and Michael, 9 February 2016, London.

27   Ibid.

28   Interview with Hilary, 19 October 2015, London.

29   Interview with Mary, 16 December 2015, Essex.

30   Interview, 9 February 2016.

31   Ibid.

32   Ibid.

33   Ibid.

34   Michael was Jewish. Millie didn't fit Michael's requirements either: she smoked and was (twice) divorced, yet Michael saw this as 'lucky' – part of his satisfaction with the whole process. Michael had preserved the questionnaire and brought it along to the interview.

35   *Singles,* 18 (Nov 1978), p. 8.

36   *Singles,* 12 (May 1978), p. 45.

37   MOP, DR, M1395, Summer 2001.

38   Arlie Hochschild, *The Commercialization of Intimate Life: Notes From Home and Work* (Berkeley: University of California, 2003).

39   Ibid., p. 23.

40   Ibid., p. 24; see also Illouz's discussion of 'therapeutic modes of self control', in *Why Love Hurts*, p. 149.

41   Hochschild, *Intimate Life*, p. 23.

42   *Singles* (Carlton, 1993).

43 MOP, DR, S1983.

44 For links between self, growth and sexual encounter in the 1970s, 80s and 90s, Mathew Thomson, *Psychological Subjects: Identity, Culture, and Health in Twentieth-Century Britain* (Oxford: OUP, 2006), and Ben Mechen (2015), *Everyday Sex in 1970s Britain*, PhD thesis, UCL. For a feminist cultural studies perspective on how sexual, rather than romantic, experience became enshrined in British culture, see Angela McRobbie on the 'new sexual contract', *The Aftermath of Feminism: Gender, Culture and Social Change* (London: Sage, 2009), esp. pp. 83 and 84. For polemical analysis of female instrumentalization of sexuality through inverse feminism, see Natasha Walter, *Living Dolls: The Return of Sexism* (London: Virago, 2010). For the American context, see Ariel Levy, *Female Chauvinist Pigs: Women and the Rise of Raunch Culture* (London: Simon & Schuster, 2005), and more conservatively, Wendy Shalit, *Return to Modesty: Discovering the Lost Virtue* (New York: Free Press, 1999).

45 Cockburn, *Lonely Hearts*, p. 24.

46 Sonntag, *Finding the Love of Your Life*, introduction, page not numbered.

47 Cockburn, *Lonely Hearts*, p. 87.

48 Ibid., p. 62.

49 Ibid., p. 74.

50 Ibid.

51 Ibid., p. 207.

52 Ibid., p. 231.

53 Illouz, *Why Love Hurts*, p. 59.

54 Interview with Hilary, 2015.

55 Ibid.

56 Ibid.

57 Ibid.

58 Interview, 13 April 2016, London.

59 Ibid.

60 Zoe Strimpel (2017), 'Computer Dating in the 1970s: Dateline and the Making of the Modern British Single', *Contemporary British History*, 31 (3), pp. 319–42.

61 Interview, 13 April 2016.

62 Dateline advert, *Singles*, 18 (Nov 1978), p. 41.

63 Ibid.

64 Ibid. For an influential account of the complexities of recapitulation and differentiation in mother–daughter relationships between the generations in this period, see Carolyn Steedman, *Landscape For a Good Woman: A Story of Two Women* (London: Virago, 1986).

65 Frank Mort, *Cultures of Consumption: Commerce, Masculinities and Social Space* (London: Routledge, 1996), p. 2.

66   Eva Illouz, *Consuming the Romantic Utopia: Love and the Cultural Contradictions of Capitalism* (Berkeley: University of California Press, 1997), p. 192.

67   MOP, DR, J1890, Summer 2001. Ibid., W1457; Ibid., H276; Ibid., N2912; Ibid., R860.

68   Ibid., B2917.

69   Ibid.

70   Ibid., D2824.

71   E.g. ibid., H1806 (male).

72   Ibid., G1416, and P2138.

73   Ibid., P2915.

74   Ibid.

75   Ibid.

76   Ibid.

77   Ibid., R2247.

78   Interview with Elaine, 2015.

79   Interview with Heather Heber Percy, 2015.

80   Illouz, *Consuming the Romantic Utopia*, pp. 2–24.

81   Matthew Hilton, *Consumerism in Twentieth-Century Britain: The Search For a Historical Movement* (Cambridge: CUP, 2003), p. 1.

82   Colin Campbell, *The Romantic Ethic and the Spirit of Modern Consumerism* (Oxford: Basil Blackwell, 1987), p. 77.

83   Ibid., p. 1.

84   MOP, DR, B2917, Summer 2001.

85   Ibid., p. 89.

86   Hilton, *Consumerism in Twentieth-Century Britain*, p. 2.

87   Thirty Years of 'Which?', *Consumer's Association, 1957–1987* (London: 1987), cited in Hilton, *Consumerism In Twentieth-Century Britain*, p. 3.

88   Fee for four introductions charged by the elite agency Julia worked for, cited in interview, 10 July 2016, London.

89   Interview with Michael and Millie, 2016.

90   Colette Sinclair, *Manhunt* (London: Sidgwick & Jackson, 1989), p. 157.

91   Interview with Mary, 2015.

92   Ibid.

93   Cockburn, *Lonely Hearts*, p. 75.

94   MOP, DR, C2844, Summer 2001.

95   Ibid.

96   Ibid., M1979.

97   Ibid., T1843.

98   Cockburn, *Lonely Hearts*, p. 162.

99   Illouz, *Why Love Hurts*, p. 54.

100   *Singles* (Carlton, 1993).

101 For the classic text on how linguistic tropes structure thought and feeling, see George Lakoff and Mark Johnson, *Metaphors We Live By* (Chicago: University of Chicago Press, 1980). See also discussion specifically on the reciprocal relationship between the shopping metaphor often used to describe mediated dating, and the experiences of users, in Zoe Strimpel (2013), *Meat Market or Brave New World? How Women Go Shopping For Dates Online*, MPhil thesis, University of Cambridge, pp. 11–14, and Rebecca Heino et al. (2010) 'Relationshopping: Investigating the Market Metaphor in Online Dating', *Journal of Social and Personal Relationships*, 27 (4), pp. 427–47.

102 Simon Szreter and Kate Fisher, *Sex Before the Sexual Revolution: Intimate Life in England 1918–1963* (Cambridge: CUP, 2010); Langhamer, *The English in Love*.

103 Sinclair, *Manhunt*.

104 Ibid., pp. 28–9.

105 Ibid., p. 28.

106 Ibid., p. 29.

107 Zygmunt Bauman, *Modernity and Ambivalence* (Cambridge: Polity, 1991), p. 206.

108 Ibid., p. 207. For theoretical analysis of the relationship between tastes, status and historicity, see Mike Savage, 'Status, Lifestyle and Taste', in Frank Trentmann (ed.), *The Oxford Handbook of the History of Consumption* (Oxford: OUP, 2012), pp. 551–68.

109 Sinclair, *Manhunt*, p. 21.

110 Ibid.

111 Ibid., p. 28.

112 Ibid., p. 29.

113 Strimpel (2017), 'In Solitary Pursuit: *Singles* Magazine and the Search for Love, 1977–1983', *Cultural and Social History*, 14 (5), pp. 691–715. Despite a widespread media discourse positing 'masculinity in crisis' and endemic 'sex war' at this time, which intensified throughout the 1980s and 1990s, it is important to avoid over-determining any link between the tensions that emerged in mediated dating to this wider discourse, mainly because the idea of 'sex war' or 'masculinity in crisis' obscures the complexities and contradictions within sexual relationships, and therefore how they functioned, imposing something of a crude framework on the individual experiences discussed here. However, given the prominence of such discourse, my subjects' own perceptions and vocabularies might have reflected some of its tropes. For a discussion both of the idea of 'masculinity in crisis' in the 1980s and 1990s, and of the dubiousness of the claim, as well as that of a 'new breed' of rapacious single women, see Collins, *Modern Love*, pp. 208–12, and pp. 212–14; Roger Horrocks, *Masculinity in Crisis* (Basingstoke: Macmillan, 1994); Lynne Segal, *Slow Motion: Changing Masculinities, Changing Men* (London: Palgrave, 1997).

114 Cockburn, *Lonely Hearts*, p. 75.

115 Faludi dissects this in *Backlash: The Undeclared War Against Women* (London: Vintage, 1993); see also the discussion of women's relationship advice literature in Arlie Hochschild, *The Commercialization of Intimate Life: Notes from Home and Work* (Berkeley: University of California Press, 2003), pp. 22–9.

116 Cockburn, *Lonely Hearts*, p. 80.

117 Strimpel (2013), *Meat Market*, pp. 23 and 56–61.

118 Cockburn, *Lonely Hearts*, p. 95.

119 Ibid., p. 95.

120 Ibid., p. 94.

121 Marcus Collins makes this point in *Modern Love*, pp. 212–14.

122 This is not to say that the women that men like Harry met were *not* more sexually confident than they might have been a decade or two before; the rolling out of life with contraception, as well as the development of other discursive and practical shifts in norms around sex in the 1970s certainly enabled many women to build a new sexual repertoire of experience and taste, as, for instance, Jeffrey Weeks suggests in *The World We Have Won: The Remaking of Erotic and Intimate Life* (London: Routledge, 2007); Mechen, *Everyday Sex*, p. 22.

123 Studies of masculinity have taken increasing account of distinct male psycho-sexual and social problems, though these have been particularly linked to the world wars. Lesley Hall (1985), '"Somehow Very Distasteful": Doctors, Men and Sexual Problems between the Wars', *Journal of Contemporary History*, 20 (4), pp. 553–74; Joanna Bourke, *Dismembering the Male: Men's Bodies, Britain and the Great War* (Chicago: University of Chicago Press, 1996). Mike Roper (2007) unpacks the constructedness of masculinity concisely in 'Between the Psyche and the Social: Masculinity, Subjectivity and the First World War Veteran', *Men's Studies Press*, 15 (3), pp. 251–70. For a more recent analysis based in everyday contemporary life, see Patricia McDaniel, *Shrinking Violets and Caspar Milquetoasts, Shyness, Power, and Intimacy in the United States, 1950–1995* (New York: NYU Press, 2003).

124 Cockburn, *Lonely Hearts*, p. 86.

125 Ibid., p. 88.

126 Beth Bailey, *From Front Porch to Back Seat: Courtship in 20th Century America* (Baltimore: Johns Hopkins University Press, 1988), p. 58.

127 Quoted in Claire Langhamer, *The English In Love*, p. 180.

128 Simon Szreter and Kate Fisher, *Sex Before the Sexual Revolution,* p. 137; Andrew Davies, *Leisure, Gender and Poverty: Working-Class Culture in Salford and Manchester, 1900–1939* (Buckingham: OUP, 1992), pp. 104–5.

129 Willard Waller (1937), 'The Rating and Dating Complex', *American Sociological Review*, 2, pp. 727–34. The lower profile of expenditure in British courtship, compared to America, is likely related to the fact that Americans were richer in the

post-war period; US incomes led those of the British about one generation since 1950. Avner Offer, *The Challenge of Affluence: Self-Control and Wellbeing in the United States and Britain Since 1950* (Oxford: OUP, 2006), p. 7.

130 See Brooke, "'A Certain Amount of Mush'", p. 91; and for television's role in encouraging a retreat indoors, often atomized, Joe Moran, *Armchair Nation: An Intimate History of Britain in Front of the TV* (London: Profile Books, 2013), pp. 1–13.

131 Cockburn, *Lonely Hearts*, p. 69.

132 Ibid., p. 137.

133 Claire Langhamer (2007), 'Love and Courtship in Mid-Twentieth-Century England', *The Historical Journal*, 50 (1), pp. 173–96: 194.

134 Illouz, *Consuming the Romantic Utopia*, pp. 121 and 125.

135 Ibid., p. 128.

136 John Benson, *The Rise of Consumer Society in Britain, 1880–1980* (London: Longman, 1994), e.g. pp. 35–8. On restaurants' boom decades in the 1960s and 1970s: 'Steak men see ways of diversifying', *The Times*, 19 April 1967, p. 28; 'Restaurants – The way we were: why the British diner has never had it so good', *The Independent*, 15 November 1997; for a broader discussion of the evolution of the British restaurant industry which stresses the importance of the 1970s in the proliferation of restaurants, books and other food-related products, see John Burnett, *England Eats Out: A Social History of Eating Out in England From 1830 to The Present* (Harlow: Pearson/Longman, 2004), pp. 288–315.

137 The average pub carpet order expanded from 75 yards in 1974 to 130 yards in 1979, David Gutzke, *Women Drinking Out in Britain Since The Early Twentieth Century* (Manchester: MUP, 2016), p. 103; on women, *The Economist*, 9 November 1985, cited in Gutzke, *Women Drinking*, p. 103.

138 Ibid.

139 John Godwin, *The Mating Trade* (Garden City: Doubleday, 1973), p. 22.

140 For the parameters of drinking in earlier periods, such as those defined by temperance, religion and the spirits and brewing trade, see the classic Brian Harrison, *Drink and the Victorians: The Temperance Question in England, 1815–1872* (Keele: Keele University Press, 1994) and Phil Withington (2011), 'Intoxicants and Society in Early Modern England', *The Historical Journal*, 54 (3), pp. 631–57.

141 Gutske, *Women Drinking Out*, p. 83.

142 Ibid., p. 132; for London as a centre of wine bars and the appeal of 'watching the assignations' they attracted, see Michael Elliott, *Heartbeat London: The Anatomy of a Supercity* (London: Firethorn, 1986), p. 147. They were for people who wanted to engage 'a lot more in talking than drinking' but for all the emphasis on non-threatening conviviality, wine bars introduced a new classed dimension to having drinks, requiring the ability to negotiate sometimes long lists of French vintages, plus an appetite for cheese from Paris and smoked goose, ibid., p. 133 and Barbara

Rogers, *Men Only: An Investigation Into Men's Organizations* (London: Pandora, 1988), pp. 10–11.

143 *Bistros, Inns and Wine Bars in Britain* (Basingstoke: Automobile Association, 1985), pp. 8–9.

144 *Singles*, 1 (May 1977), p. 6.

145 Sinclair, *Manhunt*, p. 65. Sinclair gives the cost in dollars presumably because she used to buy the wine during a period, discussed earlier, in which she lived in California.

146 Paul Reizen, *Date Expectations: One Man's Voyage Through the Lonely Hearts* (London: Bantam, 2005), p. 18.

147 Ibid., pp. 14–24.

148 Ibid., p.18.

149 Ibid., p. 85.

150 Email correspondence with Pen Fudge, 2015.

151 *Singles*, 6 (November 1977), p. 8.

152 Ibid., 47 (April 1981), p. 25.

153 Ibid., 42 (November 1980), p. 5.

154 Ibid., 45 (February 1980), p. 5.

155 Bailey, *From Front Porch*, p. 58.

156 Elaine described mediated dating as something 'you kept to yourself', Interview, 2016.

157 Interview with Marsha, 4 June 2015, London.

158 Bailey, *From Front Porch*, p. 58; see also Langhamer, *The English In Love*, p. 195.

159 Interview, 16 December 2015.

160 Jane Lewis, *The End of Marriage? Individualism and Intimate Relations* (Cambridge: CUP, 2002), p. 16.

161 Interview with Mary, 2015.

162 Although she is particularly concerned with the exchange value of emotional labour, Arlie Hochschild still provides the key framework for thinking about the gendered ways in which women do emotional heavy lifting on and off the job: 'as traditionally more accomplished managers of feeling in private life, women more than men have put emotional labor on the market, and they know more about its personal costs'. *The Managed Heart: Commercialization of Human Feeling* (Berkeley: University of California Press, 1983), p. 11. See too the discussion of women's 'unseen labour' that is 'crucial to getting things done' in all spheres, ibid., esp. p. 167. Here, Mary is extracting emotional labour demanded and honed in her job as a social worker, and applying it to a private setting. For recent historical work on the interplay between gender, the workplace, personal skills and different types of emotional labour, see Claire Langhamer (2017), 'Feelings, Women and Work in the Long 1950s', *Women's History Review*, 26 (1), pp. 77–92.

163	Interview with Mary, 2015.

164	Ibid.

165	Ibid.

166	Arguably, gender has never been stable. See Joan Scott's recent meditation on the constitutive instability of gender as a historical concept, *The Fantasy of Feminist History* (Durham, NC: Duke University Press, 2011).

167	Interview with Mary, 2015.

168	Interview with Rose, 10 December 2016, London.

169	Interview with Elaine, 2016.

170	Sinclair, *Manhunt*, p. 142.

171	Personal email correspondence, 2015.

172	MOP, DR, B2917, Summer 2001.

173	Sinclair, *Manhunt*, p. 40.

174	Interview with Mary, 2015.

175	Ibid.

Conclusion

1	Victoria Mapplebeck, 'Bridget Jones: now all over TV: Helen Fielding's book has a lot to answer for … soon you won't be able to switch on without seeing a thirtysomething confessing all in a soap doc', *The Guardian*, 23 March 1998, p. C10; Ellen Fein and Sherrie Schneider, *All the Rules: Time-Tested Secrets for Capturing the Heart of Mr Right* (New York: Grand Central Publishing, 1995).

2	Joe Moran, 'Decoding the Decade', *The Guardian*, 14 November 2009, p. 30. See discussion of the decadal 'shorthand' among popular and academic alike in Lawrence Black (2012), 'An Enlightening Decade? New Histories of 1970s' Britain', *International Labor and Working-Class History*, 82, pp. 174–86: 175.

3	Hera Cook, *The Long Sexual Revolution*; Callum Brown (2011), 'Sex, Religion, and the Single Woman: The Importance of a "Short" Sexual Revolution to the English Religious Crisis of the 1960s', *Twentieth Century British History*, 22 (2), pp. 189–215.

4	Ben Mechen (2015), *Everyday Sex in 1970s Britain*, PhD thesis, UCL.

5	Sandy Nye, the former wife and business partner of Dateline's founder John Patterson, was clear that both she and Patterson were fans of Thatcher for the business climate her premiership created: 'We loved her. We loved her … She was for the young business, people willing to put their back into it'. Interview, 18 February 2016, Kent.

6	In addition to *Singles* and *Man Seeks Woman*, the 1990s also saw frank investigations of women's sexuality such as *The Truth About Women* (ITV, 1998), as well as in dramas such as *Real Women* (BBC, 1998) and *This Life* (BBC, 1997).

Earlier, comedic treatments of mediated dating on TV include quiz show *Blind Date*, launched in 1985 and a *Carry On* film dedicated to computer dating fraud, *Carry On Loving* (1970).

7   Penrose Halson, *Happily Ever After: How To Meet Your Match* (London: Pan, 1999), p. 108.

8   *Love Island* takes place in a villa in Majorca, but ITV announced in July 2019 that in light of the programme's ratings it would add a winter edition to take place in a villa in South Africa. 'Love Island Goes to Two Series a Year in 2010', BBC News, 24 July 2019.

9   I interviewed Sinclair in her London flat in 2018. She was married to her fifth husband and seemed very content with her romantic life. She did not meet her present husband through a third-party matchmaker: they were introduced through a friend.

10 Bernie Hogan, Nai Li and William Dutton (2011), 'A Global Shift in the Social Relationships of Networked Individuals: Meeting and Dating Online Comes of Age', Oxford Internet Institute, University of Oxford; Eli Finkel et al. (2012), 'Online Dating: A Critical Analysis From the Perspective of Psychological Science', *Psychological Science in the Public Interest*, 13 (1), pp. 3–66.

11 Linda Sonntag, *Finding the Love Of Your Life Using Dating Agencies and Small Ads* (London: Piccadilly, 1993), p. 20. For discussion of 'the one', see note 45, p. 150.

12 Eva Illouz, *Why Love Hurts: A Sociological Explanation* (Cambridge: Polity, 2013), p. 59.

13 Eva Illouz, *Cold Intimacies: The Making of Emotional Capitalism* (Cambridge: Polity, 1997); Beth Bailey, *From Front Porch to Back Seat: Courtship in 20th Century America* (Baltimore: Johns Hopkins University Press, 1988); Rebecca Heino et al. (2010), 'Relationshopping: Investigating the Market Metaphor in Online Dating', *Journal of Social and Personal Relationships*, 27 (4), pp. 427–47.

14 Sonntag, *Finding the Love of Your Life*, p. 52.

15 Charlotte Greenhalgh, *Ageing in 20th Century Britain* (Berkeley: University of California Press, 2018).

16 Pearl Jephcott, *Rising Twenty. Notes on Some Ordinary Girls* (London: Faber & Faber, 1942); Andrew Davies, *Leisure, Gender and Poverty: Working-Class Culture in Salford and Manchester, 1900–1939* (Buckingham: Open University Press, 1992), pp. 102–8; Simon Szreter and Kate Fisher, *Sex Before the Sexual Revolution: Intimate Life in England 1918–1963* (Cambridge: CUP, 2010).

17 Josue Ortega and Philipp Hergovich (2018), 'The Strength of Absent Ties: Social Integration Via Online Dating', *Physics and Society*, Papers 1709.10478, arXiv.org.

18 John Godwin, *The Mating Trade* (Garden City: Doubleday, 1973).

Bibliography

Unpublished primary sources

Mass Observation Archive, University of Sussex, Directive Replies, Summer 2001 (Courting and Dating)

Online sources

ABIA website, www.abia.org.uk/advice/the-ABIA-code-of-practice

'About Brian Snellgrove', ezinearticles.com/expert/Brian_Snellgrove/1427473

Bloomberg: Bloomberg.com
'Lonely Billionaires Roam Globe for Luxury Love Therapy', 24 January 2011. www.bloomberg.com/news/articles/2011–01-19/lonely-billionaires-roam-globe-seek-luxury-love-therapy-a-craig-copetas.

Campaign: campaignlive.co.uk
'Magazines ABCs: Top 100 at a Glance', 12 February 2015. www.campaignlive.co.uk/article/magazines-abcs-top-100-glance/1333599

Dallas Business Journal: www.bizjournals.com/dallas
'Customers Sue Match.com', 4 January 2011. www.bizjournals.com/dallas/news/2011/01/04/matchcom-customers-sue-their-matchmaker.html.

Financial Times: ft.com
'Online Dating? Swipe Left', 12 February 2016. www.ft.com/content/b1a82ed2–8e34–11e5–8be4–3506bf20cc2b

Hansard Online: hansard.parliament.uk
Parliamentary Debates (Hansard) House of Lords Official Reports (London: HMSO).

The New York Times: Nytimes.com
'A Trans-Atlantic Bridal Broker', 10 March 1981. www.nytimes.com/1981/03/10/style/a-trans-atlantic-bridal-broker.html

The Washington Post: Washingtonpost.com
'Singles: Merry Olde Matches', 15 May 1981. www.washingtonpost.com/archive/
lifestyle/1981/05/15/singles-merry-olde-matches/9a47421c-2d14–4138-a067–
11c09ebb0b90/.

Vanity Fair: Vanityfair.com
'Tinder and the Dawn of the Dating Apocalypse', September 2015. www.vanityfair.com/
culture/2015/08/tinder-hook-up-culture-end-of-dating.

Published sources

Newspapers and journals

City Limits
Company
Cosmopolitan
The Daily Mail
The Daily Mirror
The Economist
The Financial Times
The Guardian
The Independent
The Jewish Chronicle
The London Weekly Advertiser
Look Magazine (US)
Man & Woman
Man & Woman: The Marshall Cavendish Encyclopaedia of Adult Relationships (London:
Marshall Cavendish, 1970–1972).
Review of Reviews
Singles
The Telegraph
The Times
Time Out
Which?
Woman's Own

Reports

'Divorces in England and Wales, 2010', Office of National Statistics, www.ons.gov.uk/
    ons/dcp171778_246403.pdf.
Dunnell, Karen, *Family Formation*. HMSO, 1976.

Dyson, A.E. and Cox, Brian, *The Black Papers on Education*. London: 1971.

Erens, Bob et al., *National Survey of Sexual Attitudes and Lifestyles II: Reference Tables and Summary Report*. National Centre for Social Research: April 2003.

'Families and Households' (2014), Office of National Statistics, www.ons.gov.uk/peoplepopulationandcommunity/birthsdeathsandmarriages/families/bulletins/familiesandhouseholds/2015–01–28.

Jansson, Krista, *British Crime Survey – Measuring Crime For 25 Years*. London: HMSO, 2007.

National Survey of Sexual Attitudes and Lifestyles II. Reference Tables and Summary Report, National Centre for Social Research: April 2003.

Royal Commission on the Press. Parliamentary Debates (Hansard) House of Commons Official Reports. London: HMSO, 1949.

Single Person Households: Single Living, Diverse Lifestyles, Mintel International. London, 1992.

'Values and the Changing Family: A Final Report from the Working Party on Values'. London: Study Commission on the Family, 1982.

Wellings, Kaye et al., *Sexual Behaviour in Britain: The National Survey of Sexual Attitudes and Lifestyles*. London: Penguin, 1994.

Memoirs

Albertine, Viv, *Clothes Clothes Clothes Music Music Music Boys Boys Boys*. London: Faber & Faber, 2014.

Fisher, Hedi, *Matchmaker, Matchmaker*. London: Book-Line, 1993.

Parkin, Molly, *Moll: The Making of Molly Parkin: An Autobiography*. London: Gollancz, 1993.

Proops, Marje, *Dear Marje*. London: Coronet, 1977.

Reizen, Paul *Date Expectations: One Man's Voyage Through the Lonely Hearts*. London: Bantam, 2005.

Sinclair, Colette *Manhunt*. London: Sidgwick & Jackson, 1989.

Other contemporary sources

The Permissive Society: The Guardian Inquiry. London: Panther Modern Society, 1969.

Adams, Margaret, *Single Blessedness: Observations on the Single State in Married Society*. London: Heinemann, 1976.

Barr, Ann and York, Peter, *The Official Sloane Ranger Handbook: The First Guide To What Really Matters In Life*. London: Ebury, 1984.

Booth, William, *In Darkest England and the Way Out*. London International Headquarters of the Salvation Army, 1890.

Cockburn, John, *Lonely Hearts: Love Among the Small Ads*. London: Guild, 1988.

Comfort, Alex, *Sex In Society*. Harmondsworth: Penguin, 1964.

Comfort, Alex, *The Joy of Sex*. London: Quartet, 1974.

Durkheim, Emile, *On Suicide*. London: Penguin Classics, 1996 [1897].

Encyclopaedia of Love & Sex: A Comprehensive Guide to the Physiology of Sex, the Art of Loving, and the Psychology of Love. London: Marshall Cavendish, 1972.

Fein, Elle and Schneider, Sherrie, *All the Rules: Time-Tested Secrets for Capturing the Heart of Mr. Right*. New York: Grand Central Publishing, 1995.

Fielding, Helen, *Bridget Jones' Diary*. London: Picador, 1996.

Ford, Anna, *Men: A Documentary*. London: Corgi, 1986.

Fyfield, Frances, *Blind Date*. London: Bantam, 1988.

Godwin, John, *The Mating Trade*. Garden City: Doubleday, 1973.

Gordon, Suzanne, *Lonely in America*. New York: Simon & Schuster, 1976.

Gorer, Geoffrey, *Sex and Marriage in England Today: A Study of the Views and Experience of the Under-45's*. London: Panther, 1973.

Halson, Penrose, *Happily Ever After: How To Meet Your Match*. London: Pan, 1999.

Harvey, John, *Lonely Hearts*. London: Mandarin, 1989.

Hatfield, Elaine and Walster, William, *A New Look at Love: A Revealing Report on the Most Elusive Of All Emotions*. London: Addison-Wesley, 1978.

Heath, Stephen, *The Sexual Fix*. London: Macmillan, 1982.

Hills, Marjorie, *Live Alone and Like It: A Guide For the Extra Woman*. London: Virago, 2005 [1937].

Johnson, Anne et al., *Sexual Attitudes & Lifestyles*. Oxford: Blackwell Scientific Publications, 1994.

Kelly, Vivien, *Take One Young Man*. London: Arrow, 1999.

Kurtz, Irma, *Loneliness*. Oxford: Blackwell, 1983.

Murstein, Bernard, 'A taxonomy of love', unpublished manuscript. Connecticut College, 1977.

North, Maurice, *The Secular Priests*. London: Allen and Unwin, 1972.

Putnam, Robert, *Bowling Alone: The Collapse and Revival of American Community*. New York: Simon and Schuster, 2000.

Raban, Jonathan, *Soft City*. London: Fontana, 1975.

Rogers, Barbara, *Men Only: An Investigation Into Men's Organizations*. London, Pandora, 1988.

Rolheiser, Ronald, *The Loneliness Factor: Its Religious and Spiritual Meaning*. Denville, NJ: Dimension Books, 1979.

Rubin, Zick (1970) 'Measurement of Romantic Love', *Journal of Personality and Social Psychology*, 16 (2), pp. 265–73.

Schofield, Michael, *The Sexual Behaviour of Young People*. London: Longmans, 1965.

Shalit, Wendy, *Return to Modesty: Discovering the Lost Virtue*. New York: Free Press, 1999.

Simmel, Georg, *The Philosophy Of Money*. London: Routledge, 2004 [1900].

Sonntag, Linda, *Finding the Love Of Your Life Using Dating Agencies and Small Ads*. London: Piccadilly, 1993.

Stead, W.T., 'In the City of Dreadful Solitude: A Plea for a Matrimonial Bureau', *Review of Reviews*. February 1897, pp. 154–6.

Stern, Robert and Barnes, Michael (eds), *The Psychology of Love*. New Haven: Yale University Press, 1988.

Stopes, Marie, *Married Love: A New Contribution to the Solution of Sex Difficulties*. London: Putnam, 1933.

Tanner, Ira, *Loneliness: The Fear of Love*. New York: Harper and Row, 1973.

The Permissive Society: The Guardian Inquiry. London: Panther Modern Society, 1969.

Thorn, Tracey, *Bedsit Disco Queen: How I Grew Up and Tried to Be a Pop Star*. London: Virago, 2003.

Thornton, Penny, *Romancing the Stars: Astrology of Love and Romance*. London: Aquarian Press, 1988.

Weinberg, George, *Self Creation*. London: Raven Books, 1978.

Whitehorn, Katherine, *Cooking In A Bedsitter*. London: Penguin, 1974.

Woodside, Moya (1946), 'Courtship and Mating in an Urban Community', *Eugenics Review*, 38, pp. 29–30.

Young, Michael and Wilmott, Peter, *The Symmetrical Family*. London: Kegan Paul, 1973.

Young, Baroness, House of Lords, Debates, 29 February 1996, c. 1638.

Zussman, Leon, *Getting Together*. New York: William Morrow, 1978.

Audio/visual sources

Blind Date. London Weekly Television, from 1985, BFI/335656.

Carry On Loving (1970), www.youtube.com/watch?v=nZmuxl9949c.

Cole, Martin, 'Growing Up', *The Joy of Sex Education*. BFI: 2009, Wellcome Library, 4265D.

Cook, Matt, 'AIDS and Mass Observation', Mass Observation podcasts, 97, www.massobs.org.uk/podcasts/97-matt-cook-aids-and-mass-observation.

First Dates. Channel 4, 2013.

Lonely Hearts. Thames, 1977, BFI/ 219871.

Man Seeks Woman. BBC, 1995, BFI/453374.

Marriage Bureau 1939, British Pathe, www.britishpathe.com/video/marriage-bureau-1.

Mr and Mrs. Border Television, from 1961, BFI/8210.

Real Women. BBC, 1998, BFI/487103.

Sex and the City. HBO, 1998–2004.

Singles. Carlton, 1993, BFI/781348.

The Love Tapes. New Decade Films, 1979, BFI/222095.

The Truth About Women. ITV, 1998, BFI/787718.
This Life. BBC, 1997, YouTube.
Would Like to Meet. BBC, 2001, BFI/633004.

Conferences/ seminars:

'Consuming/Culture: Women and Girls in Print and Pixels', Oxford Brookes University, 5–6 June 2015.
Mangion, Carmen, 'The "Modern Girl" and Catholic Religious Life, 1940–1970', Institute of Historical Research, Modern Religious History Seminar, 18 November 2015.

Ephemera

'Barratt Homes, Building a legend' (c. 2012), marketing pamphlet (in author's possession through private correspondence)

Unpublished theses

Mechen, Ben (2015), *Everyday Sex in 1970s Britain*, UCL.
Strimpel, Zoe (2013),'Meat Market or Brave New World? How Women Go Shopping For Dates Online', MPhil thesis, University of Cambridge.

Oral histories

(All names changed apart from Pen Fudge's – years indicate period of mediated dating).
Rose – Heather Jenner agency, London (early 1970s)
Elaine – Dateline and *Time Out* (1970s)
Hilary – agency and *City Limits* (1983)
Marsha – *Private Eye* and *Time Out* (1978–1980)
Mary – Avenues agency, Essex (mid-nineties)
Michael – Hedi Fisher agency, London (1990)
Millie – Hedi Fisher agency, London (1990)
Pen Fudge – lonely hearts ads and agencies, unspecified (1985–1990)

Interviews with industry figures

Irene Campbell, lonely hearts manager, *Time Out*, 1970s

Jane Rackham, lonely hearts manager, *Time Out*, 1970s

Julia (named changed on request), matchmaker at 'exclusive' US-owned London agency, 1990s

Mary Balfour, owner of Drawing Down the Moon agency, 1986–2016

Peter Knights, ad manager at *Time Out*, 1970s

Robin Dunbar, Professor of Anthropology, Oxford

Sandy Nye, widow and former business partner of John Patterson, Dateline's founder

Simon Garfield, editor of *Time Out*, 1988–1989

Suzy Marwood, lonely hearts manager, *Time Out*, late 1970s

Tony Elliott, founder and owner of *Time Out*, 1968–present

Secondary sources

Adorno, Theodor, *The Jargon of Authenticity*. London: Routledge and Kegan Paul, 1973.

Adorno, Theodor, *The Stars Down To Earth And Other Essays on the Irrational In Culture*. London: Routledge, 1994.

Aitchison, Cara (1999) 'New Cultural Geographies: The Spatiality of Leisure, Gender and Sexuality', *Leisure Studies*, 18 (1), pp. 19–39.

Albury, Kath et al. (2017) 'Data Cultures of Mobile Dating and Hook-up Apps: Emerging Issues for Critical Social Science Research', *Big Data and Society*, 4 (2), pp. 1–11.

Aldgate, Anthony, *Censorship and the Permissive Society: British Cinema and Theatre, 1955–1965*. Oxford: Clarendon Press, 1995.

Anderson, Michael (1985) 'The Emergence of the Modern Life Cycle In Britain', *Social History*, 10 (1), pp. 69–87.

Atkinson, Ti-Grace, 'Radical Feminism and Love' (1972), in Susan Ostrov Weisser (ed.), *Women and Romance: A Reader*. New York: NYU Press, 2001.

Bailey, Beth, *From Front Porch to Back Seat: Courtship in 20th Century America*. Baltimore: Johns Hopkins University Press, 1988.

Bainbridge, Cyril and Stockdill, Roy, *The News of the World Story: 150 Years of the World's Bestselling Newspaper*. London: Harper Collins, 1993.

Bakewell, Joan, *The Centre of the Bed*. Bath: BBC Audio Books, 2004.

Bathmaker, Ann-Marie, 'The Expansion of Higher Education: A Consideration of Control, Funding and Quality', in Steve Bartlett and Diana Burton (eds), *Education Studies: Essential Issues*. London: Sage, 2003, pp. 169–89.

Bauman, Zygmunt, *Modernity and Ambivalence*. Cambridge: Polity, 1991.

Bauman, Zygmunt, *Liquid Love: On the Frailty of Human Bonds*. Cambridge: Polity, 2003.

Bauman, Zygmunt, 'Sociology and Postmodernity', in Patrick Joyce (ed.), *Class*. Oxford, OUP, 1995, pp. 74–83.

Beck, Ulrich and Beck-Gernsheim, Elisabeth, *The Normal Chaos of Love*. Cambridge: Polity, 1995.

Becker, Gary (1973) 'A Theory of Marriage: Part I', *The Journal of Political Economy*, 81 (4), pp. 813–46.

Beckett, Andy, *Promised You A Miracle: Why 1980–82 Made Modern Britain*. London: Penguin, 2015.

Beers, Laura, 'Thatcher and the Women's Vote', in Robert Saunders and Ben Jackson (eds), *Making Thatcher's Britain*. Cambridge: CUP, 2012, pp. 113–32.

Bell, David and Valentine, Gill (eds), *Mapping Desire: Geographies of Sexualities*. London: Routledge, 1995.

Bellah, Robert et al., *Habits of the Heart: Middle America Observed*. Berkeley: University of California Press, 1985.

Benson, John, *The Rise of Consumer Society in Britain, 1880–1980*. London: Longman, 1994.

Bingham, Adrian, *Family Newspapers? Sex, Private Life, and the British Popular Press 1918–1978*. Oxford: OUP, 2009.

Bingham, Adrian (2012) 'Newspaper Problem Pages and British Sexual Culture Since 1918', *Media History*, 18 (1), pp. 51–63.

Bingham, Adrian, 'Media Products As Historical Artefacts', in Martin Conboy and John Steel (eds), *Routledge Companion to British Media History*. London: Routledge, 2014, pp. 19–29.

Bistros, Inns and Wine Bars in Britain. Basingstoke: Automobile Association, 1985.

Black, Lawrence (2012) 'An Enlightening Decade? New Histories of 1970s' Britain', *International Labor and Working-Class History*, 82, pp. 174–86.

Black, Lawrence and Pemberton, Hugh, 'Introduction: the Benighted Decade? Reassessing the 1970s', in Lawrence Black, Hugh Pemberton and Pat Thane (eds), *Reassessing 1970s Britain*. Manchester: MUP, 2013.

Bloch, Marc, *The Historian's Craft*. Manchester: MUP, 1992 [1949].

Boden, Margaret, 'Purpose, Personality, Adventure: A Computational Adventure', in Geoff Bunn (ed.), *Psychology in Britain: Historical Essays and Personal Reflections*. Oxford: Blackwell, 2001, pp. 353–63.

Boden, Sharon, *Consumerism, Romance, and the Wedding Experience*. Basingstoke: Palgrave Macmillan, 2003.

Bonner, Paul and Aston, Lesley, *Independent Television in Britain, ITV and IBA 1981–92: The Old Relationship Changes*. Basingstoke: Palgrave, 1998.

Bornat, Joanna (1994) 'Is Oral History Auto/Biography?', *Auto-Biography*, 3.1/3.2, pp. 17–30.

Bourdieu, Pierre, *Distinction: A Social Critique of the Judgement of Taste*. London: Routledge, 2010.

Bourke, Joanna, *Working Class Cultures in Britain, 1890–1960*. London: Routledge, 1994.

Bourke, Joanna, *Dismembering the Male: Men's Bodies, Britain and the Great War*. Chicago: University of Chicago Press, 1996.

Bowlby, Rachel, *Carried Away: The Invention of Modern Shopping*. London: Faber, 2000.

Brines, Julie (1993) 'The Exchange Value of Housework', *Rationality and Society*, 5 (3), pp. 302–40.

Brooke, Stephen (2014) 'Living in "New Times": Historicizing 1980s Britain', *History Compass*, 12 (1), pp. 20–32.

Brooke, Stephen, '"A Certain Amount of Mush": Love, Romance, Celluloid and Wax in the Mid-Twentieth Century', in Alana Harris and Timothy Willem Jones (eds), *Love and Romance in Britain, 1918–1970*. London: Palgrave, 2015, pp. 81–100.

Brown, Callum, *The Death of Christian Britain: Understanding Secularisation 1800– 2000*. London: Routledge, 2000.

Brown, Callum (2011) 'Sex, Religion, and the Single Woman: The Importance of a "Short" Sexual Revolution to the English Religious Crisis of the 1960s', *Twentieth Century British History*, 22 (2), pp. 189–215.

Brunt, Rosalind, '"An Immense Verbosity": Permissive Sexual Advice in the 1970s', in Rosalind Brunt and Caroline Rowan (eds), *Feminism, Culture and Politics*. London: Lawrence and Wishart, 1982, pp. 143–70.

Bunzl, Matt, *Symptoms of Modernity: Jews and Queers in Late-Twentieth Century Vienna*. Berkeley: University of California Press, 2004.

Burgoyne, Jacqueline, 'Rethinking the Family Life Cycle: Sexual Divisions, Work and Domestic Life in the Post-war Period', in Alan Bryman et al. (eds), *Rethinking the Life Cycle*. Basingstoke: Macmillan, 1987, pp. 72–87.

Burnett, John, *England Eats Out: A Social History of Eating Out in England From 1830 to The Present*. Harlow: Pearson/Longman, 2004.

Butcher, James, Perry, Julia and Hahn, Jungwon (2004) 'Computers in Clinical Assessment: Historical Developments, Present Status, and Future Challenges', *Journal of Clinical Psychology*, 60 (3), pp. 331–45.

Campbell, Beatrix, *The Iron Ladies: Why Do Women Vote Tory?*. London: Virago, 1987.

Campbell, Colin, *The Romantic Ethic and the Spirit of Modern Consumerism*. Oxford: Basil Blackwell, 1987.

Campion, Nicholas, 'Horoscopes and Popular Culture', in Bob Franklin (ed.), *Pulling Newspapers Apart: Analysing Print Journalism*. London: Routledge, 2008, pp. 253–63.

Chauncey, Geoffrey, 'Privacy Could Only Be Had in Public: Gay Uses of the Streets', in Joel Saunders (ed.), *Stud: Architectures of Masculinity*. New York: Princeton Architectural Press, 1996, pp. 224–67.

Chettiar, Terri (2016) '"More than a Contract": The Emergence of a State-Supported Marriage Welfare Service and the Politics of Emotional Life in Post-1945 Britain', *Journal of British Studies*, 55 (3), pp. 566–91.

Cocks, Harry (2013) 'The Cost of Marriage and the Matrimonial Agency in Late Victorian Britain', *Social History*, 38 (1), pp. 6–88

Cocks, Harry (2004) 'Peril in the Personals: The Dangers and Pleasures of Classified Advertising in Early Twentieth-Century Britain', *Media History*, 10 (1), pp. 3–16.

Cocks, Harry, *Nameless Offences: Homosexual Desire in the 19th Century*. London: IB Tauris, 2003.

Cocks, Harry, *Classified: The Secret History of the Personal Column*. London: Random House, 2009.

Cohen, Deborah, Birmingham Modern British Studies Working Paper No. 1, 9 October 2014. https://mbsbham.wordpress.com/2014/10/29/deborah-cohen-response-to-working-paper-no-1/

Cohen, Deborah, *Family Secrets: Shame and Privacy in Modern Britain*. Oxford: OUP, 2013.

Cohen, Stanley (ed.), *The Manufacture of News: Social Problems, Deviance and the Mass Media*. London: Constable, 1993.

Coleman, David and Salt, John, *The British Population: Patterns, Trends and Processes*. London: Clarendon, 1991.

Collins, Marcus (1999) 'The Pornography of Permissiveness: Men's Sexuality and Women's Emancipation in Mid Twentieth-Century Britain', *History Workshop Journal*, (47), pp. 99–120.

Collins, Marcus, *Modern Love: An Intimate History of Men and Women in Twentieth Century Britain*. London: Atlantic, 2001.

Collins, Marcus, 'Introduction', in Marcus Collins (ed.), *The Permissive Society and its Enemies: Sixties British Culture*. London: Rivers Oram, 2007, pp. 1–40.

Cook, Hera, *The Long Sexual Revolution: English Women, Sex, and Contraception, 1800–1975*. Oxford: Oxford University Press, 2004.

Cook, Hera, 'Complaining About Therapy Culture', in Jonathan Reinarz and Rebecca Winter (eds), *Complaints, Controversies and Grievances in Medicine: Historical and Social Science Perspectives*. London: Routledge, 2012, pp. 56–75.

Cook, Hera (2014), 'From Controlling Emotion to Expressing Feelings in Mid-Twentieth-Century England', *Social History*, 47 (3), pp. 627–46.

Cook, Matt, *London and the Culture of Homosexuality, 1885–1914*. Cambridge: Cambridge University Press, 2003.

Cook, Matt, *Queer Domesticities: Homosexuality and Home Life in Twentieth-Century London*. London: Palgrave, 2014.

Cook, Matt and Evans, Jennifer (eds), *Queer Cities, Queer Cultures: Europe Since 1945*. London and New York: Bloomsbury, 2014.

Coontz, Stephanie, *Marriage, A History: From Obedience to Intimacy, Or How Love Conquered Marriage*. New York: Viking, 2005.

Daunton, Martin and Rieger, Bernhard (eds), *Meanings of Modernity: Britain from the Late-Victorian Era to World War II*. Oxford: Berg, 2001.

Davies, Andrew, *Leisure, Gender and Poverty: Working-Class Culture in Salford and Manchester, 1900–1939*. Buckingham: Open University Press, 1992.

Davis, Simon (1990) 'Men as Success Objects and Women as Sex Objects: A Study of Personal Advertisements', *Sex Roles*, 23, pp. 43–50.

de Beauvoir, Simone, *The Second Sex*. London: Everyman, 1993.

Deaux, Kay and Hanna, Randel (1984) 'Courtship in the Personal Column: The Influence of Gender and Sexual Orientation', *Sex Roles*, 11, pp. 363–75.

Degim, Alev, Johnson, James and Fu, Tao (eds), *Online Courtship – Interpersonal Interactions Across Borders*. Amsterdam: Institute of Network Cultures, 2016.

Delap, Lucy (2010), review of Bingham, *Family Newspapers?, Journal of British Studies*, 49 (1), pp. 224–6: 224.

Delap, Lucy (2018), 'I didn't know where to look: Feminism, Masculinities and Emotional Politics in Late Twentieth-Century Britain', *Cultural and Social History*, 15 (4), pp. 571–93.

Doan, Laura, 'A Peculiarly Obscure Subject', in Brian Lewis (ed.), *British Queer History, New Approaches and Perspectives*. Manchester: MUP, 2013, pp. 87–109.

Douglas, Carol Ann, *Love and Politics: Radical Feminist and Lesbian Theories*. San Francisco: ISM Press, 1990.

Douglas, Susan, *Where the Girls Are: Growing Up Female with the Mass Media*. New York: Random House, 1994.

Dreyfus, Hubert, *What Computers Can't Do: The Limits of Artificial Intelligence*. New York: Harper Row, 1972.

Dror, Yehezkel (1959) 'Law and Social Change', *Tulane Law Review*, 33 (4), pp. 787–802.

Drucker, Donna J. (2013) 'Keying Desire: Alfred Kinsey's Use of Punched-Card Machines for Sex Research', *Journal of the History of Sexuality*, 22 (1), pp. 105–25.

Drucker, Donna, *The Classification of Sex: Alfred Kinsey and the Organization of Knowledge*. Pittsburgh: University of Pittsburgh Press, 2014.

Durham, Martin, *Sex and Politics: The Family and Morality in the Thatcher Years*. Basingstoke: Macmillan, 1991.

Dyhouse, Carol, *Glamour: Women, History and Feminism*. London: Zed, 2010.

Dyhouse, Carol, *Heartthrobs: A History of Women and Desire*. Oxford: OUP, 2017.

Elliott, Michael, *Heartbeat London: The Anatomy of a Supercity*. London: Firethorn, 1986.

Fabian, Ann, *The Unvarnished Truth; Personal Narratives in Nineteenth Century America*. Berkeley: University of California Press, 2001.

Faludi, Susan, *Backlash: The Undeclared War Against Women*. London: Vintage, 1993.

Ferri, Elsa and Smith, Kate, *Parenting in the 1990s*. London: Family Policy Studies Centre, 1996.

Finch, Janet and Mason, Jennifer, *Negotiating Family Responsibilities*. London: Tavistock/ Routledge, 1993.

Finkel, Eli et al. (2012) 'Online Dating: A Critical Analysis From the Perspective of Psychological Science', *Psychological Science in the Public Interest*, 13 (1), pp. 3–66.

Firestone, Shulamith, *The Dialectic of Sex: The Case for Feminist Revolution*. New York: Farrar, Straus & Giroux, 2001.

Fisher, Kate, *Birth Control: Sex and Marriage in Britain, 1918–1960*. Oxford: OUP, 2006.

Francis, Martin, *The Flyer: British Culture and the Royal Air Force, 1939–1945*. Oxford: OUP, 2008.

Francis, Matthew (2012), '"A Crusade to Enfranchise the Many": Thatcherism and the "Property-owning Democracy"', *Twentieth Century British History*, 23 (2), pp. 275–97.

Friedman, Ted, *Electric Dreams: Computers in American Culture*. New York: NYU Press, 2005.

Froide, Amy, *Never Married: Singlewomen in Early Modern England*. Oxford: OUP, 2005.

Frost, Ginger, *Promises Broken: Courtship, Class and Gender in Victorian England*. Charlottesville: University of Virginia Press, 2015.

Furedi, Frank, *Therapy Culture: Cultivating Vulnerability in an Uncertain Age*. London: Routledge, 2003.

Geiringer, David, *The Pope and the Pill: Sex, Catholicism and Women in Post-War England*. Manchester: MUP, 2019.

Geppert, Alexander (ed.) *Imagining Outer Space: European Astroculture in the Twentieth Century*. London: Palgrave, 2012.

Giddens, Anthony, *The Transformation of Intimacy: Sexuality, Love and Eroticism in Modern Societies*. Cambridge: Polity, 1992.

Giles, Judy (1992) '"Playing Hard to Get": Working-Class Women, Sexuality and Respectability in Britain, 1918–40', *Women's History Review*, 1 (2), pp. 239–55.

Giles, Judy, '"You Meet 'Em and That's It": Working Class Women's Refusal of Romance Between the Wars in Britain', in Lynne Pearce and Jackie Stacey (eds), *Romance Revisited*. London: Lawrence & Wishart, 1995, pp. 279–92.

Giles, Judy, *The Parlour and the Suburb: Domestic Identities, Class, Femininity and Modernity*. London: Bloomsbury, 2004.

Gillis, John, *For Better, For Worse: British Marriages, 1600 to the Present*. Oxford: OUP, 1985.

Glennie, Paul, 'Consumption Within Historical Studies', in Daniel Miller (ed.), *Acknowledging Consumption: A Review of New Studies*. London: Routledge, 1995, pp. 163–203.

Green, Adam, *Sexual Fields: Toward A Sociology of Collective Sexual Life*. Chicago: University of Chicago Press, 2013.

Greer, Germaine, *The Female Eunuch*. London: Harper Perennial, 2006.

Gunter, Barrie, 'The Study of Online Relationships and Dating', in William Dutton (ed.), *The Oxford Handbook of Internet Studies*. Oxford: OUP, 2013, pp. 173–94.

Gutzke, David, *Women Drinking Out in Britain Since The Early Twentieth Century*. Manchester: MUP, 2016.

Hakim, Catherine, *Honey Money: The Power of Erotic Capital*. London: Allen Lane, 2011.

Hall, Lesley (1985) '"Somehow Very Distasteful": Doctors, Men and Sexual Problems between the Wars', *Journal of Contemporary History*, 20 (4), pp. 553–74.

Hall, Lesley, *Sex, Gender and Social Change Since 1880*. London: Palgrave, 2000.

Hall, Stuart, *The Hard Road to Renewal: Thatcherism and the Crisis of the Left*. London: Verso, 1988.

Halsey, Alan and Webb, Josephine (eds), *Twentieth-Century British Social Trends*. Basingstoke: Macmillan, 2000.

Halsey, Albert et al., *Origins and Destinations: Family, Class and Education in Modern Britain*. Oxford: Clarendon Press, 1980.

Harris, Alana, *Faith in the Family: A Lived Religious History of English Catholicism, 1945–82*. Manchester: MUP, 2013.

Harris, Alana and Willem Jones, Timothy (eds), *Love and Romance in Britain, 1918–1970*. London: Palgrave, 2015.

Harrison, Brian, *Drink and the Victorians: The Temperance Question in England, 1815–1872*. Keele: Keele University Press, 1994.

Harrison, Brian, *Finding a Role: The United Kingdom 1970–1990*. Oxford: OUP, 2010.

Hatch, J. Amos and Wisniewsky, Richard (eds), *Life History and Narrative*. Falmer: Falmer Press, 1995.

Heelas, Paul, *The New Age Movement: The Celebration of the Self and the Sacralization of Modernity*. Oxford: Blackwell, 1996.

Heineman, Elizabeth D. (2006) 'The Economic Miracle in the Bedroom: Big Business and Sexual Consumption in Reconstruction West Germany', *Journal of Modern History*, 78, pp. 846–77.

Heino, Rebecca et al. (2010) 'Relationshopping: Investigating the Market Metaphor in Online Dating', *Journal of Social and Personal Relationships*, 27 (4), pp. 427–47.

Herzog, Dagmar (2009) 'Syncopated Sex: Transforming European Sexual Cultures', *The American Historical Review*, 114 (5), pp. 1287–308.

Hicks, Marie (2016), 'Computer Love: Replicating Social Order Through Early Computer Dating Systems', *Ada: A Journal of Gender and New Media Technology*, 10. adanewmedia.org/2016/10/issue10-hicks.

Higgins, Patrick, *The Heterosexual Dictatorship: Male Homosexuality in Postwar Britain*. London: Fourth Estate, 1996.

Hilton, Matthew, *Consumerism in Twentieth-Century Britain: The Search For a Historical Movement*. Cambridge: CUP, 2003.

Hochschild, Arlie, *The Managed Heart: Commercialization of Human Feeling*. Berkeley: University of California Press, 1983.

Hochschild, Arlie, *The Second Shift: Working Parents and the Revolution at Home*. London: Piatkus, 1990.

Hochschild, Arlie, *The Commercialization of Intimate Life: Notes from Home and Work*. Berkeley: University of California Press, 2003.

Hogan, Bernie, Li, Nai and Dutton, William (2011) 'A Global Shift in the Social Relationships of Networked Individuals: Meeting and Dating Online Comes of Age', Oxford Internet Institute, University of Oxford. www.oii.ox.ac.uk/archive/downloads/publications/Me-MySpouse_GlobalReport.pdf

Holden, Katherine, *The Shadow of Marriage: Singleness in England, 1914–60*. Manchester: MUP, 2007.

Horn, Adrian, *Juke Box Britain: Americanisation and Youth Culture, 1945–60*. Manchester: MUP, 2009.

Hornsey, Richard, *The Spiv and The Architect: Unruly Life in Postwar London*. Minneapolis: University of Minnesota, 2010.

Horrocks, Roger, *Masculinity in Crisis*. Basingstoke: Macmillan, 1994.

Horrocks, Roger, *Male Myths and Icons*. New York: St Martin's Press, 1995.

Houlbrook, Matt, *Queer London: Perils and Pleasures in the Sexual Metropolis, 1918–57*. Chicago: University of Chicago Press, 2005.

Houlbrook, Matt (2013) 'Fashioning an Ex-Crook Self: Citizenship and Criminality in the Work of Netley Lucas', *Twentieth Century British History*, 24 (1), pp. 1–30.

Houlbrook, Matt, *Prince of Tricksters: The Incredible True Story of Netley Lucas, Gentleman Crook*. Chicago: University of Chicago Press, 2016.

Hubbard, Phil, *Sex and the City: Geographies of Prostitution in the Urban West*. Aldershot: Ashgate: 1999.

Illouz, Eva, *Cold Intimacies: The Making of Emotional Capitalism*. Cambridge: Polity, 1997.

Illouz, Eva, *Consuming the Romantic Utopia: Love and the Cultural Contradictions of Capitalism*. Berkeley: University of California Press, 1997.

Illouz, Eva, 'The Lost Innocence of Love: Romance as a Post-Modern Condition', in Mike Featherstone (ed.), *Love and Eroticism*. London: Sage, 1999, pp. 161–87.

Illouz, Eva, *Saving the Modern Soul: Therapy, Emotions, and the Culture of Self-Help*. Berkeley: University of California Press, 2008.

Illouz, Eva, *Why Love Hurts: A Sociological Explanation*. Cambridge: Polity, 2013.

Ingraham, Chrys, *White Weddings: Romancing Heterosexuality in Popular Culture*. London: Routledge, 1999.

Jackson, Ben, 'The Think Tank Archipelago: Thatcherism and Neoliberalism', in Ben Jackson and Robert Saunders (eds), *Making Thatcher's Britain*. Cambridge: CUP, 2012, pp. 43–61.

Jackson, Stevi and Scott, Sue (2004) 'Sexual Antinomies in Late Modernity', *Sexualities*, 7 (2), pp. 233–48.

Johnson, Anne et al., *Sexual Attitudes & Lifestyles*. Oxford: Blackwell Scientific Publications, 1994.

Jones, Ben and Searle, Rebecca (2013) 'Humphrey Jennings, the Left and the Experience of Modernity in Mid Twentieth-Century Britain', *History Workshop Journal*, 75 (1), pp. 190–212.

Jones, Harriet, Östberg, Kjell and Randeraaad, Nico (eds), *Contemporary History on Trial*. Manchester: MUP, 2007.

Joyce, Patrick (ed.), *Class*. Oxford: OUP, 1995.

Kern, Stephen, *The Culture of Love: Victorians to Moderns*. Cambridge, MA: Harvard University Press, 1992.

Kuhn, Annette, *An Everyday Magic: Cinema and Cultural Memory*. London: IB Tauris, 2002.

Lakoff, George and Johnson, Mark, *Metaphors We Live By*. Chicago: University of Chicago Press, 1980.

Langhamer, Claire (2006) 'Adultery in Post-War England', *History Workshop Journal*, 62 (1), pp. 86–115.

Langhamer, Claire (2007) 'Love and Courtship in Mid-Twentieth-Century England', *The Historical Journal*, 50 (1), pp. 173–96.

Langhamer, Claire (2012), 'Love, Selfhood and Authenticity in Post-war Britain', *Cultural and Social History*, 9 (2), pp. 277–97.

Langhamer, Claire, *The English in Love*. Oxford: OUP, 2013.

Langhamer, Claire (2017) 'Feelings, Women and Work in the Long 1950s', *Women's History Review*, 26 (1), pp. 77–92.

Langhamer, Claire (2018), 'Who the Hell are "Ordinary People"? Ordinariness as a Category of Historical Analysis', *Transactions of the Royal Historical Society*, 28, pp. 175–95.

Lawrence, Jon, 'Paternalism, Class, and the Path to Modernity', in Simon Gunn and James Vernon (eds), *The Peculiarities of Liberal Modernity in Imperial Britain*. Berkeley: University of California Press, 2011, pp. 174–65.

Leadbetter, Charles, 'The Politics of Prosperity', Fabian tract no. 523. London: Fabian Society, 1987.

Leavis, Queenie, *Fiction and the Reading Public*. London: Chatto & Windus, 1932.

Levy, Ariel, *Female Chauvinist Pigs: Women and the Rise of Raunch Culture*. London: Simon & Schuster, 2005.

Lewis, Brian (ed.), *British Queer History, New Approaches and Perspectives*. Manchester: MUP, 2013.

Lewis, Jane and Kiernan, Kathleen (1996) 'The Boundaries Between Marriage, Nonmarriage, and Parenthood: Changes in Behavior and Policy in Postwar Britain', *Journal of Family History*, 21 (3), pp. 372–87.

Light, Alison, *Forever England: Femininity, Literature and Conservatism Between the Wars*. London: Routledge, 2013.

Lovenduski, Joni (1996) 'Sex, Gender and British Politics', *Parliamentary Affairs*, 49 (1), pp. 1–16.

Lury, Celia, 'A Public Romance: "the Charles and Di Story"', in Lynne Pearce and Jackie Stacey (eds), *Romance Revisited*. London: Lawrence & Wishart, 1995, pp. 225–38.

Lystra, Karen, *Searching the Heart: Women, Men and Romantic Love in Nineteenth Century America* (Oxford: OUP, 1989).

Macfarlane, Alan, *Marriage and Love in England 1300–1840: Modes of Reproduction 1300–1840*. Oxford: Basil Blackwell, 1986.

Maitland, Sara, *Very Heaven: Looking Back at the 1960's*. London: Virago, 1988.

Mandler, Peter (2004) 'The Problem With Cultural History', *Cultural and Social History*, 1 (1), pp. 94–117.

Mandler, Peter, 'The Responsibility of the Historian', in Harriet Jones, Kjell Östberg and Nico Randeraaad (eds), *Contemporary History on Trial*. Manchester: MUP, 2007, pp. 12–27.

Marwick, Arthur, *The Sixties: Cultural Revolution in Britain, France, Italy and the United States, 1958–1974*. Oxford: Oxford University Press, 1998.

McAleer, Joseph, *Passion's Fortune: The Story of Mills and Boon*. Oxford: OUP, 1999.

McDaniel, Patricia, *Shrinking Violets and Caspar Milquetoasts: Shyness, Power, and Intimacy in the United States, 1950–1995*. New York: NYU Press, 2003.

McGillivray, David, *Doing Rude Things: The History of the British Sex Film, 1957–81*. London: Sun Tavern Fields, 1992.

McKibbin, Ross (2014), Review of Selina Todd, 'The People: The Rise and Fall of the Working Class 1910–2010' *Twentieth Century British History*, 25 (4), pp. 651–54.

McLellan, Josie, *Love in the Time Of Communism: Intimacy and Sexuality in the GDR*. Cambridge: CUP, 2011.

McRobbie, Angela, *Feminism and Youth Culture: From 'Jackie' to 'Just Seventeen'*. Basingstoke: Macmillan Education, 1991.

McRobbie, Angela, *The Aftermath of Feminism: Gender, Culture and Social Change*. London: Sage, 2009.

Millar, Robert, *The New Classes*. London: Longmans, 1966.

Miller, Alison (2013) 'Am I Normal? American Vernacular Psychology and the Tomboy Body, 1900–1940', *Representations*, 122 (1), pp. 23–50.

Modleski, Tania, *Loving with a Vengeance: Mass-Produced Fantasies For Women*. London: Routledge, 2007.

Moores, Chris (2014) 'Opposition to the Greenham Women's Peace Camps in 1980s Britain: RAGE Against the "Obscene"', *History Workshop Journal*, 78 (1), pp. 204–27.

Moran, Joe (2004) 'Housing, Memory and Everyday Life in Contemporary Britain', *Cultural Studies*, 18 (4), pp. 607–27.

Moran, Joe (2007) 'Early Cultures of Gentrification, 1955–1980', *Journal of Urban History*, 34 (1), pp. 101–21.

Moran, Joe, 'Decoding the Decade', *The Guardian*, 14 November 2009, p. 30.

Morley, David, *Home Territories: Media, Mobility, and Identity*. New York: Routledge, 2000.

Mort, Frank, *Cultures of Consumption: Commerce, Masculinities and Social Space*. London: Routledge, 1996.

Mort, Frank, *Capital Affairs: London and the Making of the Permissive Society*. London: Yale University Press, 2010.

Mowatt, Simon and Cox, Howard, *Revolutions from Grub Street: A History of Magazine Publishing in Britain*. Oxford: OUP, 2014.

Mullen, Bob, *The Mating Trade*. London: Routledge & Kegan Paul, 1984.

Murphy, Michael (2000) 'The Evolution of Cohabitation in Britain, 1960–95', *Population Studies*, 54 (1), pp. 43–56.

Murphy Paul, Annie, *The Cult of Personality: How Personality Tests Are Leading Us to Miseducate Our Children, Mismanage Our Companies, and Misunderstand Ourselves*. New York: Free Press, 2005.

Nava, Mica, *Changing Cultures: Feminism, Youth and Consumerism*. London: Sage, 1992.

Noakes, Lucy, '"Sexing the Archive": Gender in Contemporary History', in Brian Brivati, Julia Buxton and Anthony Seldon (eds), *The Contemporary History Handbook*. Manchester: MUP, 1996, pp. 74–83.

North, Maurice, *The Secular Priests*. London: Allen and Unwin, 1972.

Nott, James, *Going to the Palais: A Social And Cultural History of Dancing and Dance Halls in Britain, 1918–60*. Oxford: Oxford University Press, 2015.

O'Hara, Diana, *Courtship and Constraint: Rethinking the Making of Marriage in Tudor England*. Manchester: MUP, 2002.

Oakley, Ann, *The Sociology of Housework*. London: Robertson, 1974.

Offer, Avner, *The Challenge of Affluence: Self-Control and Wellbeing in the United States and Great Britain since 1950*. Oxford: OUP, 2006.

Oram, Alison, *Her Husband Was A Woman! Women's Gender-Crossing In Modern British Popular Culture*. London: Routledge, 2007.

Ortega, Josue and Hergovich, Philipp (2018) 'The Strength of Absent Ties: Social Integration Via Online Dating', *Physics and Society*, Papers 1709.10478, arXiv.org

Osgerby, Bill, *Youth in Britain Since 1945*. Oxford: Blackwell, 1998.

Ostrov Weisser, Susan (ed.), *Women and Romance: A Reader*. New York: NYU Press, 2001.

Parkin, Molly, *Moll: The Making of Molly Parkin: An Autobiography*. London: Gollancz, 1993.

Pawowski, Boguslaw and Dunbar, Robin (1998) 'Withholding Age as Putative Deception in Mate Search Tactics', *Evolution and Human Behavior*, 20 (1), pp. 53–69.

Pearce, Lynne and Stacey, Jackie (eds), *Romance Revisited*. London: Lawrence & Wishart, 1995.

Peppis, Paul, *Sciences of Modernism: Ethnography, Sexology, and Psychology*. Cambridge: CUP, 2013.

Phillips, Angela, 'Advice Columnists', in Bob Franklin (ed.), *Pulling Newspapers Apart: Analysing Print Journalism*. London: Routledge, 2008, pp. 102–12.

Plamper, Jan, *The History of Emotions: An Introduction*. Oxford: OUP, 2015.

Pollen, Annebella (2013) 'Research Methodology in Mass Observation Past and Present: "Scientifically, About as Valuable as a Chimpanzee's Tea Party at the Zoo"?', *History Workshop Journal*, 75 (1), pp. 213–35.

Prasad, Monica, *The Politics of Free Markets: The Rise of Neoliberal Economic Policies in Britain, France, Germany, and the United States*. Chicago: University of Chicago Press, 2006.

Putnam, Robert, *Bowling Alone: The Collapse and Revival of American Community*. New York: Simon and Schuster, 2000.

Rappaport, Erika, *Shopping for Pleasure: Women in the Making of London's West End*. Princeton: Princeton University Press, 2001.

Real, Terence, *I Don't Want To Talk About It: Overcoming the Secret Legacy of Male Depression*. Upper Saddle River, NJ: Prentice Hall, 1998.

Reddy, William, *The Making of Romantic Love: Longing and Sexuality in Europe, South Asia, and Japan, 900–1200 CE*. Chicago: The University of Chicago Press, 2012.

Regan, Milton, *Family Law and the Pursuit of Intimacy*. New York: NYU Press, 1993.

Richards, Jeffrey, *The Age of the Dream Palace: Cinema and Society in 1930s Britain*. London: IB Tauris, 2010.

Robinson, Lucy, *Gay Men and the Left in Post-War Britain: How The Personal Got Political*. Manchester: MUP, 2007.

Rokach, Amy (2004) 'Loneliness Then and Now: Reflection on Social and Emotional Alienation in Everyday Life', *Current Psychology*, 23 (1), pp. 24–40.

Roper, Michael, 'Oral History', in *Contemporary History Handbook*. Manchester: MUP, 1996, pp. 345–65.

Roper, Mike (2005) 'Slipping Out of View: Subjectivity and Emotion in Gender History', *History Workshop Journal*, 59 (1), pp. 57–73.

Roper, Mike (2007) 'Between the Psyche and the Social: Masculinity, Subjectivity and the First World War Veteran', *Men's Studies Press*, 15 (3), pp. 251–70.

Rose, Jonathan, *The Intellectual Life of the Working Classes*. New Haven: Yale University Press, 2001.

Rose, Nikolas, *The Psychological Complex: Psychology, Politics and Society in England, 1869–1939*. London: Routledge and Kegan Paul, 1985.

Rose, Nikolas, *Inventing Our Selves: Psychology, Power, and Personhood*. Cambridge: CUP, 1996.

Rose, Nikolas, *Governing the Soul: The Shaping of the Private Self*. London: Routledge, 1999.

Rowan, John, *Ordinary Ecstasy: Humanistic Psychology in Action*. London: Routledge, 1988.

Rubery, Matthew, *The Novelty of Newspapers: Victorian Fiction After the Invention of the News*. Oxford: OUP, 2009.

Sarsby, Jacqueline, *Missuses and Mouldrunners: An Oral History of Women Pottery Workers at Work and at Home*. Milton Keynes: Open University Press, 1988.

Savage, Mike, 'Status, Lifestyle and Taste', in Frank Trentmann (ed.), *The Oxford Handbook of the History of Consumption*. Oxford: OUP, 2012, pp. 551–68.

Schaffer, Gavin, *The Vision of a Nation: Making Multiculturalism on British Television, 1960–1980*. Basingstoke: Palgrave MacMillan, 2014.

Scott, Joan Wallach (1986) 'Gender: A Useful Category of Historical Analysis', *The American Historical Review*, 921 (5), pp. 1053–75.

Scott, Joan Wallach (1991) 'The Evidence of Experience', *Critical Inquiry*, 17 (4), pp. 773–97.

Scott, Joan, *The Fantasy of Feminist History*. Durham, NC: Duke University Press, 2011.

Segal, Lynne, *Slow Motion: Changing Masculinities, Changing Men*. London: Palgrave, 1997.

Segal, Lynne, *Making Trouble: Life and Politics*. London: Serpent's Tail, 2007.

Sheridan, Dorothy (1994) 'Using the Mass-Observation Archive As A Source For Women's Studies', *Women's History Review*, 3 (1), pp. 101–13.

Sheridan, Dorothy (1996) 'Damned Anecdotes and Dangerous Confabulations: Mass-Observation as Life History', Mass Observation Occasional Paper No. 7, University of Sussex Library.

Shields, Rob, 'Dirty Weekends and the Carnival of Sex', in *Places on the Margin: Alternative Geographies of Modernity*. London: Routledge, 1992, pp. 105–17.

Shumway, David, *Modern Love: Romance, Intimacy and the Marriage Crisis*. New York: NYU Press, 2003.

Skolnick, Arlene, *Embattled Paradise: The American Family in an Age of Uncertainty*. New York: Basic Books, 1991.

Skolnick, Arlene and Skolnick, Jerome, *Family in Transition*. New York: Pearson, 1980.

Sommerfield, Stafford, *Banner Headlines*. Shoreham-By-Sea: Scan Books, 1979.

Stanley, Liz, *Sex Surveyed, 1949–1994: From Mass-Observation's 'Little Kinsey' to the National Survey and the Hite Reports*. London: Taylor and Francis, 1995.

Stedman Jones, Daniel, *Masters of the Universe: Hayek, Friedman, and the Birth of Neoliberal Politics*. Princeton: Princeton University Press, 2012.

Steedman, Carolyn, *Landscape For a Good Woman: A Story of Two Women*. London: Virago, 1986.

Stone, Lawrence, *The Family, Sex and Marriage in England 1500–1800*. Harmondsworth: Penguin, 1972.

Strimpel, Zoe, *The Man Diet: One Woman's Quest to End Bad Romance*. London: Harper Collins, 2013.

Strimpel, Zoe (2017) 'Computer Dating in the 1970s: Dateline and the Making of the Modern British Single', *Contemporary British History*, 31 (3), pp. 319–42.

Strimpel, Zoe (2017) 'In Solitary Pursuit: *Singles* Magazine and the Search for Love, 1977–1983', *Cultural and Social History*, 14 (5), pp. 691–715.

Summerfield, Penny (2004) 'Culture and Composure: Creating Narratives of the Gendered Self in Oral History Interviews', *Cultural and Social History*, 1 (1), pp. 65–93.

Surra, Catherine and Gray, Christine, 'From Courtship to Universal Properties: Research on Dating and Mate Selection, 1950 to 2003', in Anita L. Vangelisti and Daniel Perlman (eds), *The Cambridge Handbook of Personal Relationships*. Cambridge: CUP, 2006, pp. 113–31.

Sutcliffe-Braithwaite, Florence (2012) 'Neoliberalism and Morality in the Making of Thatcherite Social Policy', *The Historical Journal*, 55 (2), pp. 497–520.

Sutcliffe-Braithwaite, Florence and Lawrence, Jon, 'Margaret Thatcher and the Decline of Class Politics', in Ben Jackson and Robert Saunders (eds), *Making Thatcher's Britain*. Cambridge: CUP, 2012, pp. 132–48.

Szreter, Simon and Fisher, Kate, *Sex Before the Sexual Revolution: Intimate Life in England 1918–1963*. Cambridge: CUP, 2010.

Taylor, Barbara and Alexander, Sally (eds), *History and Psyche: Culture, Psychoanalysis, and the Past*. New York: Palgrave Macmillan, 2012.

Thane, Pat and Evans, Tanya, *Sinners? Scroungers? Saints? Unmarried Motherhood in Twentieth-Century England*. Oxford: OUP, 2012.

Thomson, Mathew, *Psychological Subjects: Identity, Culture, and Health in Twentieth-Century Britain*. Oxford: OUP, 2006.

Tosh, John, *A Man's Place: Masculinity and the Middle-Class Home in Victorian England*. New Haven: Yale University Press, 1999.

Townsend, Peter, *The Family Life of Old People*. Harmondsworth: Penguin, 1963.

Tucker, Andrew, *Queer Visibilities: Space, Identity, and Interaction in Cape Town*. Oxford: Wiley Blackwell, 2009.

Turkle, Sherry, *The Second Self: Computers and the Human Spirit*. London: Granada, 1984.

Turner, Fred, *From Counterculture to Cyberculture: Stewart Brand, the Whole Earth Network, And the Rise of Digital Utopianism*. Chicago: University of Chicago Press, 2006.

Van de Kaa, Dirk (1987) 'Europe's Second Demographic Transition', *Population Bulletin*, 42 (1), pp. 1–59.

Walkowitz, Judith, *City of Dreadful Delight: Narratives of Sexual Danger in Late-Victorian London*. Chicago: University of Chicago Press, 1992.

Walter, Natasha, *Living Dolls: The Return of Sexism*. London: Virago, 2010.

Waynforth, David and Dunbar, Robin (1995), 'Conditional Mate Choice Strategies in Humans: Evidence from "Lonely Hearts" Advertisements', *Behaviour*, 132 (9/10), pp. 755–79.

Weeks, Jeffrey, *The World We Have Won: The Remaking of Erotic and Intimate Life*. London: Routledge, 2007, pp. 87–107.

Weeks, Jeffrey, *Sex, Politics and Society: The Regulation of Sexuality Since 1800*. Harlow: Longman, 2012.

Weighel, Moira, *Labor of Love: The Invention of Dating*. New York: Farrar, Straus and Giroux, 2016.

Weizenbaum, Joseph, *Computer Power and Human Reason: From Judgement to Calculation*. Harmondsworth: Penguin, 1979.

Wellings, Kaye et al., *Sexual Behaviour in Britain: The National Survey of Sexual Attitudes and Lifestyles*. London: Penguin, 1994.

Whannel, Gary, 'The Lads and the Gladiators: Traditional Masculinities in a Postmodern Televisual Landscape', in Edward Buscombe (ed.), *British Television: A Reader*. Oxford: OUP, 2000, pp. 290–303.

Wheen, Francis, *Strange Days Indeed: The Golden Age of Paranoia*. London: Fourth Estate, 2009.

White, Jerry, *London in The Twentieth Century: A City and Its People*. London: Vintage, 2008.

Whitty, Monica and Joinson, Adam, *Truth, Lies and Trust On the Internet*. London: Routledge, 2009.

Willem Jones, Timothy (2013) 'Postsecular Sex? Secularisation and Religious Change in the History of Sexuality in Britain', *History Compass*, 11 (11), pp. 918–30.

Williams, Raymond, *The Long Revolution*. Harmondsworth: Penguin, 1965.

Willis, Frank and Carlson, Roger (1993) 'Singles Ads: Gender, Social Class, and Time', *Sex Roles*, 29 (5), pp. 387–404.

Winship, Janice, *Inside Women's Magazines*. London: Pandora, 1987.

Withington, Phil (2011) 'Intoxicants and Society in Early Modern England', *The Historical Journal*, 54 (3), pp. 631–57.

Wolf, Naomi, *The Beauty Myth*. New York: Chatto and Windus, 1990.

Worsley, Peter, *The New Introducing Sociology*. London: Pelican, 1987.

Yates, Anna Gough, *Understanding Women's Magazines: Publishing, Markets and Readerships*. London: Routledge, 2002.

York, Peter, *Style Wars*. London: Sidgwick & Jackson, 1983.

Young, Michael and Willmott, Peter, *The Symmetrical Family*. London: Kegan Paul, 1973.

Zweiniger-Bargielowska, Ina (ed.), *Women in 20th Century Britain: Social, Cultural and Political Change*. London: Routledge, 2001.

Zytgo, Doug et al. (2014), 'Impression Management Struggles in Online Dating', Proceedings of the 18th International Conference on Supporting Group Work, Sanibel Island, Florida, pp. 53–62. pdfs.semanticscholar.org/5cd4/59be3637acb24b3d fa518ae1e58aa83e7d48.pdf

Index